Volume Fifteen

The Encyclopedia of

Photography

THE COMPLETE PHOTOGRAPHER:
The Comprehensive Guide and Reference for All Photographers

WILLARD D. MORGAN
General Editor

GREYSTONE PRESS/NEW YORK

Title Page Picture Credits:

Copal Company Limited

HANS BURST/*Zeiss Ikon Photo*

LOU BERNSTEIN

GEORGE L. HONEYCUTT/*Charlotte Observer and News*

The editors wish to express their appreciation for permission to use the color photographs in this volume to the following photographers and organizations:

RICHARD V. LUSBY / *Leica Photo*
RICHARD GROSS / *Capitol Records*
HORN / GRINER / *Created for Elizabeth Arden by Trahey / Cadwell*
LEE FRIEDLANDER / *Atlantic Records*
HY PESKIN / *Sports Illustrated*
KEN VEEDER / *Capitol Records*

Cover and Book Designed by Harold Franklin

MANUFACTURED IN THE UNITED STATES OF AMERICA

Table of Contents | *Volume Fifteen*

Figure 1 and 2. *Straight negative (left) and positive (right). See chart for the relation between these basic images and the other illustrations.*

PHOTOGRAPHIC CONTROL PROCESSES

ANDREAS FEININGER
Photographer, Author of "Total Picture Control," "The Face of New York," and other books on photography.

[Quite distinct from earlier control processes such as bromoil transfer and control mediums such as the soft-focus lens and the texture screen are the photographic processes described in this article. In these processes, the image is changed in the emulsion by mechanical and photographic means. Here, a wellknown photographer tells about the techniques of bas-relief, reticulation, and solarization.]

All illustrations by Andreas Feininger.

• *Also see: Bas-Relief Photography, Reticulation, Solarization.*

COMPARED WITH OTHER ARTISTS, the creative photographer is handicapped to no small degree by a certain stiffness and narrowness inherent in the photographic technique itself. Other artists can form and shape their subjects in any way they see fit; they can alter outlines and proportions to suit their individual intentions, add things or leave things out, simplify or exaggerate in order to emphasize certain important points. But the photographer is usually confined to an almost geometrically correct projection of his subject with all its superfluous and distracting details in background and foreground, in texture and form, in tone value and gradation. While of great importance for documentary, industrial, or scientific photography, the ability of a photographer to record even the smallest and most significant detail becomes decidedly undesirable when the artistic translation of a certain subject is attempted.

Well aware of this particular handicap, many photographers have tried in different ways to supplant their mechanical technique with more flexible methods, treatments that allow the introduction of at least a certain amount of individuality in the picture. Best known of these means of introducing a more artistic point of view into a photograph are the bromoil-transfer process, soft-focus lenses, and the use of special screens through which to print the picture. The common base is the desire for artistic simplification, for the suppression of superfluous and distract-

Scheme of illustrations. Given a simple negative image and its positive, the possibilities of photographic control are almost limitless. Arrows show the derivations of the illustrations which accompany this article.

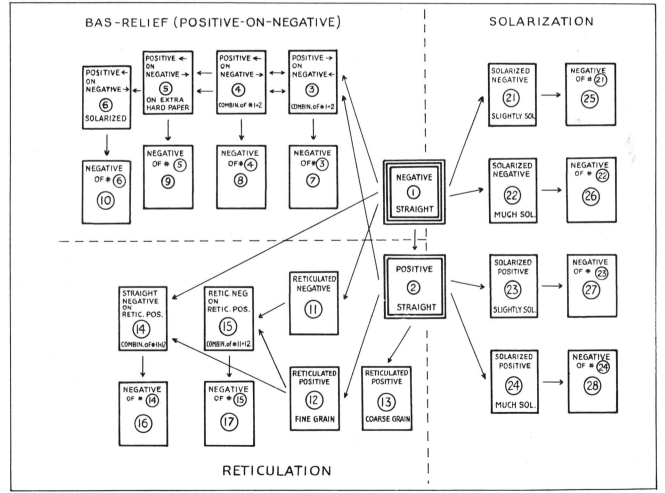

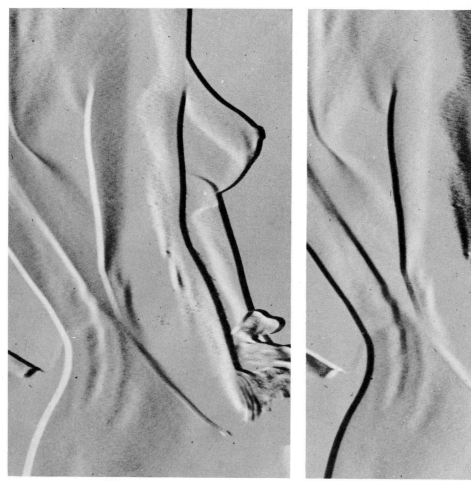

Figures 3, 4, 7, and 8. *Picture No. 4 (see chart) is at top left and shows the simple bas-relief effect, with positive moved to the left in relation to the negative. Top right is No. 3, where the positive has been moved to the right. Below are negative images, No. 8 to the left and No. 7 to the right.*

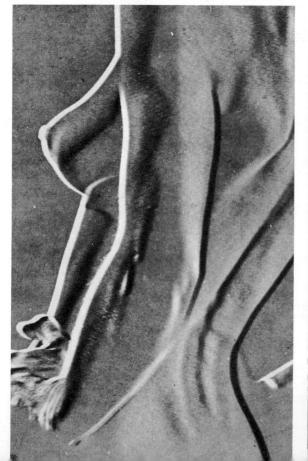
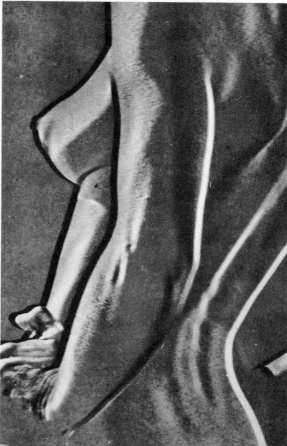

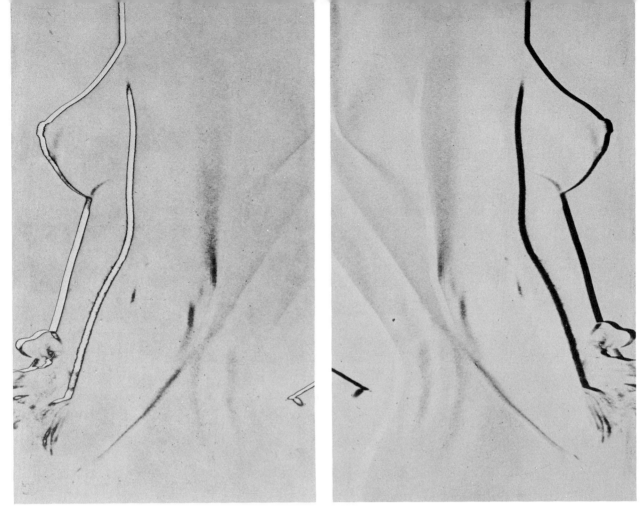

Figures 5, 6, 9, and 10. *Referring again to the chart, these images are identified as (top left, No. 6) a solarized bas-relief and (top right, No. 5) a bas-relief on extra-hard paper. Below are negative images, No. 10 to the left and No. 9 to the right.*

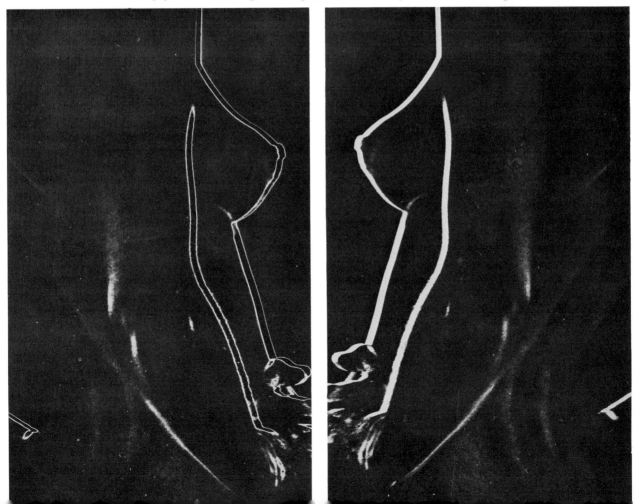

ing detail, and for greater freedom with regard to the process of rendering.

However, in spite of certain achievements, all these treatments fall far short of the perfect solution. The bromoil transfer, by introducing a purely manual element into the process, robs a photograph of most of its typically "photographic" quality, producing a not-too-ideal hybrid between a photo and a litho. Soft-focus lenses, while giving excellent results if used in the proper way (for cases where light and lighting are the subject of the picture and mood is more important than a definite object), are rather limited in their scope. And screens of various kinds introduce alien elements in no way related to photography (textures of etchings, weavings, oil paintings) and will never, in spite of their simplifying effect, be able to improve the artistic value of any photograph.

GRAPHICAL-CONTROL METHODS

To overcome these difficulties, a number of avant-garde photographers have perfected some entire-

Figures 11-13. *No. 11* (top) *is a simple reticulated negative; No. 12* (below left) *is a reticulated positive showing fine-grain pattern; No. 13* (below right) *is a reticulated positive showing a coarse grain pattern.*

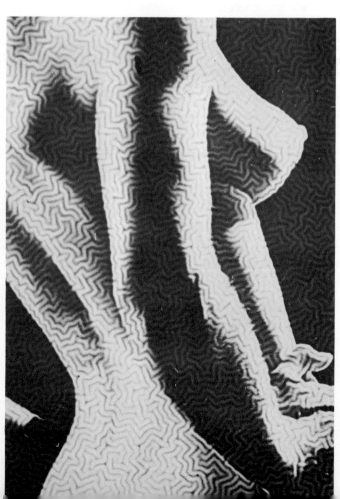

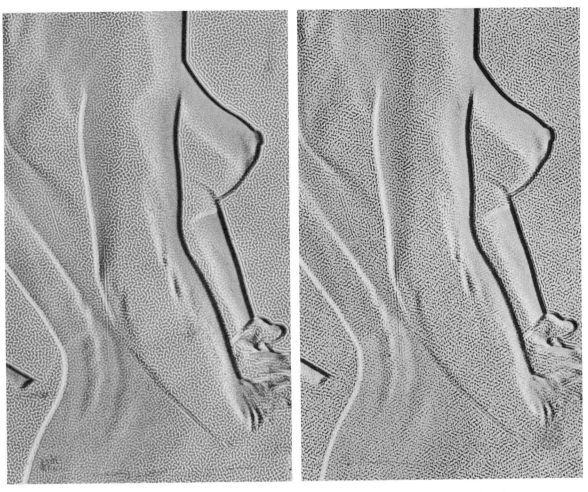

Figures 14-17. Top left *shows a straight negative on a reticulated positive—printed in bas-relief—and at* top right *is a reticulated negative on a reticulated positive.* Below *these are their negative images.*

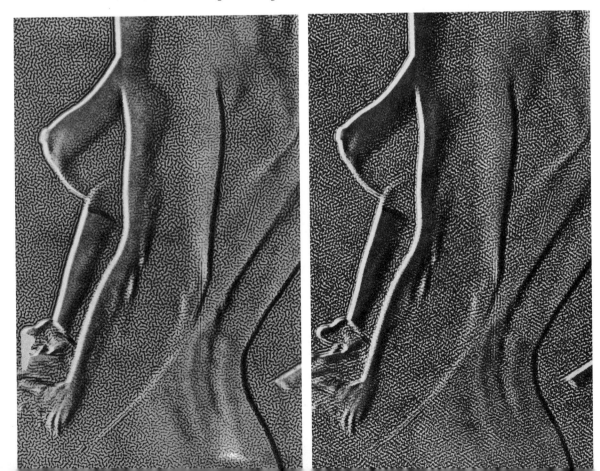

ly new photographic techniques, now known as the bas-relief process, solarization, and reticulation. Their advantage over all other similar treatments is simplification combined with perfect preservation of all characteristics which are typically photographic. The results emphasizes the graphic features of a subject: outline (silhouette), contrasts between light and dark, ornamental design (pattern). These treatments can be controlled to the same degree as any other photographic process, and can be used in combinations of two and sometimes even three together, offering a practically unlimited choice for the creation of specific effects.

In order to show the scope of the "graphical technique," I have prepared several series of pictures, each derived from one and the same negative, demonstrating the more important steps of the various processes and their combinations (Figures 1-31). Of course, some of these steps could not be considered ideal forms for the rendering of this particular subject, and their appearance here serves only to

make this survey as complete as possible. How these various steps are related to each other, and how they are derived from one and the same negative, is demonstrated in the chart.

While quite a few "ordinary" photogaphs might successfully be converted into "graphical" pictures, better results will usually be obtained when the special laws involved in these techniques are considered during the planning of the shot. They are fundamentally identical with the rules that govern the creation of any other artistic photograph: simplicity of form and design, concentration on one essential motif, suppression of superfluous and distracting detail, first-class technical execution with regard to sharpness of contours, and sufficient contrasts between light and dark. Depending on the special features to be emphasized, proper care has to be taken in regard to composition and grade of contrasts, placements of lights and shadows, and so on. The better the advance planning the stronger and more effective will be the

expression of the finished print.

THE BAS-RELIEF PROCESS

Characteristics. The bas-relief process serves to emphasize lines, outlines, and forms. While in an ordinary photograph a silhouette can be accentuated only by means of contrasts which pronounce merely the borderline of a form, this graphical treatment permits actual separation of the outline and form from each other, emphasizing the one to the benefit of the other. Photographs to be treated along these lines should consist of simple forms, sharply defined and separated by strong contrasts. Unsharp and contrastless negatives are bound to prove disappointing.

Technique. Make a contact print of your negative on film, and develop it to approximately the same contrast as that of the negative. Put this positive transparency (diapositive) and the original negative together, emulsion facing emulsion, move them slightly out of register, and print or enlarge them together.

Depending on the grade of the offset, wider or narrower lines will result along the edges of the forms, white or black according to the direction into which the films were moved out of register (notice arrows within rectangles 3 and 4 of the

Figures 18-20. *These show three stages in the reticulation of an emulsion. At the left is the result of too much hardening, with reticulation incomplete; at the center is the result of too little hardening, with the emulsion beginning to flow off. At the right is good reticulation, with the grain following the outlines of the design organically.*

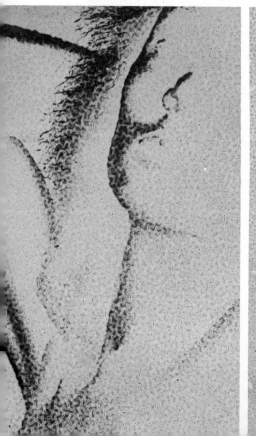
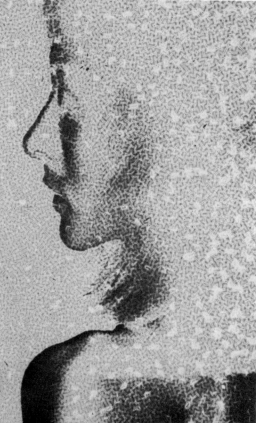
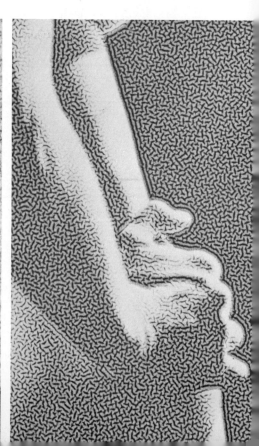

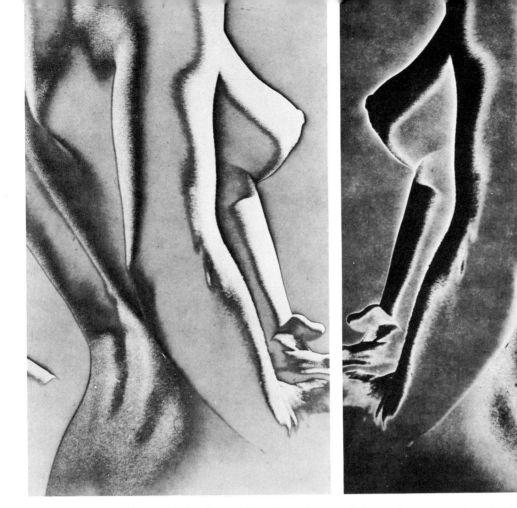

Figures 21, 22, 25 and 26. *Top right is a slightly solarized negative with its print at the left (25). Below is the same combination with full solarization of the negative (22) at the left, and its print (26) at the right.*

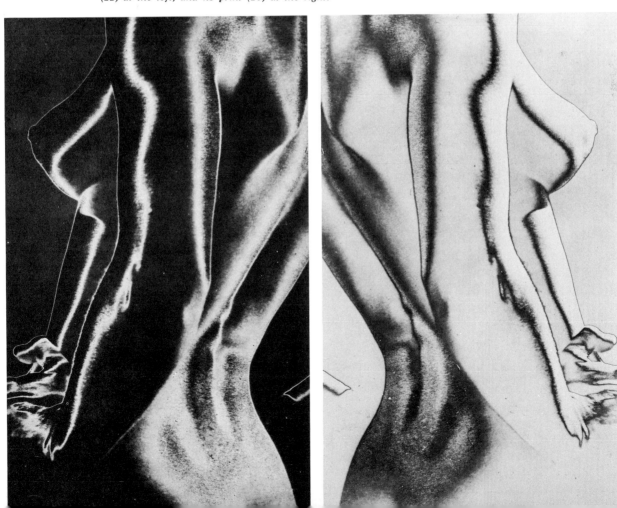

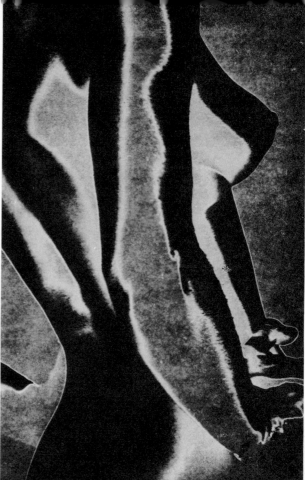

Figures 23, 24, 27 and 28. *These are the last figures represented on the chart. At the left are a slightly solarized (above) and highly solarized (below) positive, and at the right are the negative images of these.*

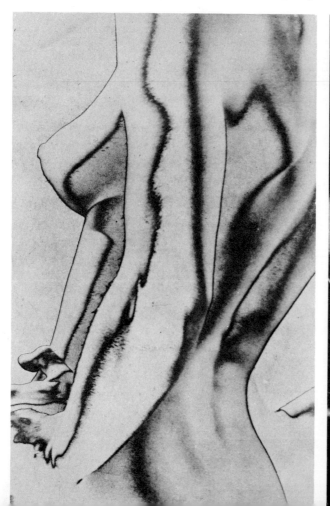

chart). If printed on extra-hard paper, pure black-and-white designs can be obtained.

Reversal into the negative form doubles the number of possibilities. Negative prints can most easily be obtained by making contacts directly from the bas-relief print with the help of a printing frame.

RETICULATION

Characteristics. Reticulation emphasizes planes and forms, supresses distracting details of texture as well as pattern, and unifies the composition in any desired degree

depending on the size of the grain. While printing through a screen impresses an alien pattern in a thoroughly mechanical way, the grain obtained through reticulation follows the forms of the design organically. Sharpness and detail are

Figure 29. *Solarized nude. Made the same way as image No. 22. Notice that the solarization negative has given the image an all-over mysterious darkness, with delicately traced contours and accentuated highlights.*

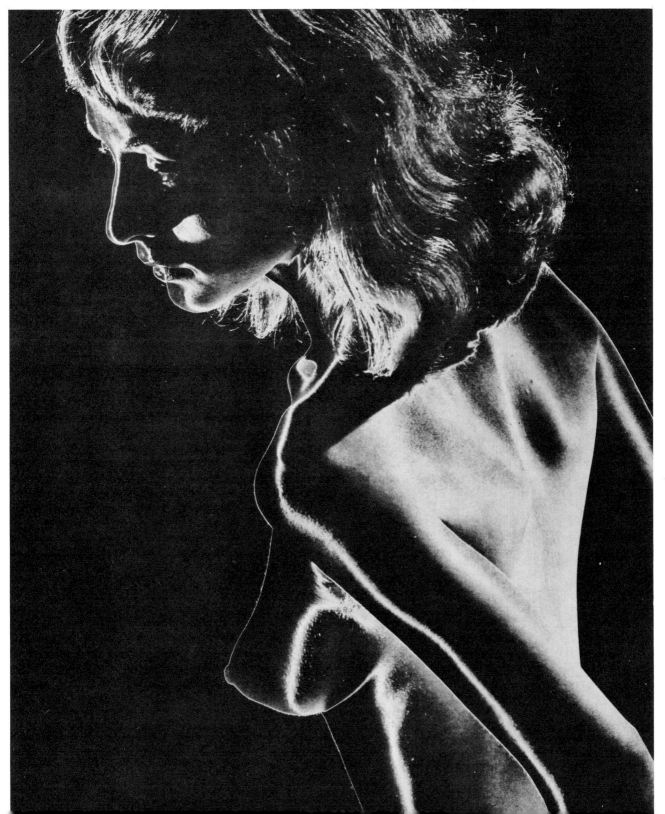

eliminated by the process. The fewer the dominating forms of the subject, the better will it fit the general requirements of reticulation.

Technique. As this process sometimes ends in disaster, only duplicate negatives (or positive transparencies) should be reticulated, in order to avoid the possible loss of an original.

Films to be reticulated should be only slightly hardened. If fixed too long in a recently prepared hardening fixing bath, incomplete reticulation or none at all will result; if hardened too little, the emulsion will flow off the film base before reticulation starts. Only tests can determine the proper strength of the hardening fixing bath.

For reticulating, immerse the film immediately after the fixing in warm water of approximately 85 or 90 F, floating it horizontally on clips made from cork. According to the type of emulsion and the degree of hardening, reticulation starts in about ½ to 1-½ minutes, and the size of the grain grows slightly with the length of the time of treatment. Beyond a certain size of grain, however, the emulsion starts to crack and to float off along the edges of the film.

To terminate reticulation, remove the film slowly (without tilting) from the warm water and place it carefully in a tray filled with very cold water or a strong solution of hardening fixer, where the emulsion will harden almost immediately. Then rinse and dry the film as usual.

If a very fine grain is desired, reticulate a large-size film; if necessary, make an enlargement of film especially for this purpose. If a very large grain is wanted, reticulate a small-size film; if need be, make a reduction on film and enlarge it.

Figure 30. *Solarized-reticulated image. Made with a reticulated negative on a reticulated positive, the latter having been solarized to set the figure off from the background. The composition has been confined to emphasis of one essential, the silhouette, and the rest can be filled in by the imagination.*

SOLARIZATION

Characteristics. Solarization emphasizes the outlines as well as the planes, reduces contrasts, and blends negative and positive features into one and the same photograph. This process gives, at the same time, the most natural and the most original results of all three treatments—pictures that show a graphical quality comparable to that of very fine etchings without losing their thoroughly photographical character. Solarization can be applied to almost any kind of photographs, provided the negative is sharp and contrasty; otherwise the typical seams along the borderlines between light and dark cannot form themselves.

Technique. Simply stated, solarization results when a partially developed negative or paper print is exposed once again to a small amount of white light, after which the development is carried on for a certain length of time. The result is a "negative" (even if a regular positive print on paper is solarized), either on film or on paper which, when held against the light, will show the typical light seams along the edges of all dark forms.

The times of the second exposures and the second development depend on the power of the light source, its distance from the film or paper negative, and the type of negative or positive material used; no fixed times can be given. Tests must be made for every special case. Only duplicate negatives or paper prints should be treated, as very slight changes in the times of the second exposure or second development will lead to vastly different results.

COMBINATIONS

One of the main advantages of the graphical treatments is that their number of variations can be increased almost indefinitely by combining two or three of the processes. Reversing a photograph into the negative form (easiest through contact printing from either film or paper print) doubles the possibilities for creative expression. Further variety can be obtained by making proper use of papers of different gradations both for negative and positive prints, from soft to extra hard, from gray-in-gray to pure black-and-white. By this choice of paper, the extent of tonal gradation and therefore the amount of detail is controlled.

Although, theoretically, each one of the three processes can be combined with one or both of the others, some of these combinations are rather ugly. Practical experience has resulted in the following general rules: bas-relief pictures can very well be solarized (provided, their contrasts are strong enough), but should not be reticulated. Reticulations can be used in connection with bas-relief as well as with solarization. Solarization is always at its best when used by itself. Any form of graphical treatment or any combination of different graphical treatments can be solarized as a last step or can be reversed into the negative form.

CONCLUSION

Graphical photography is a special form of photography, following

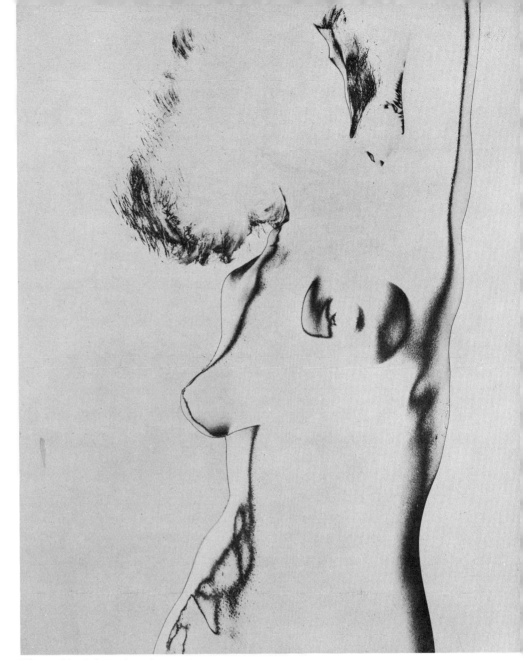

Figure 31. *Solarized nude. Made the same way as image No. 26, the merest suggestion of form leaves free play to the imagination.*

its own rules and dealing with its own problems. Its goal is not the achievement of highest possible "likeness" of the depicted subject, but the creation of an abstract work of art, featuring composition instead of documentation; pattern, lines, and forms instead of objects; black-and-white effects instead of light and shadow. Graphical photographs have to be pleasing, beautiful, or dramatic, and sometimes even shocking. And it matters little how far the objects used for this purpose are recognizable in the finished product. They appeal to emotion rather than the reason, are symbolic instead of rational as ordinary photographs might be. The graphical photographer, using the human form for a theme, uses this form to achieve a certain purpose, to create a certain impression for the sake of composition, lines, and forms. The only way to judge such a photograph is to observe the impressions it makes on you. If you find it boring, dull, and uninteresting, then it is probably bad. But if it stirs your imagination, if you like it even without being able to explain why you do so, if you can't forget it easily—then there must be something worthwhile in it.

PHOTOGRAPHIC INSTRUMENTATION

RAE HARGRAVE
Journal of the SMPTE, New York

[Photoinstrumentation is concerned with the cooperative efforts of science and photography to record the unseen phenomena of nature. This article reviews the various applications of photoinstrumentation and discusses equipment and techniques used.]
• *Also see: Recording Photography, Space Photography.*

"THE TERM PHOTOGRAPHIC INSTRUMENTATION is... defined as: the use of the photosensitive medium for the detection, recording, and/or measurement of scientific and engineering phenomena. Photographic instrumentation thus includes the apparatus, the techniques, the processes and the applications in scientific endeavors." ("Progress in Photographic Instrumentation in 1950," Kenneth Shaftan, *Journal of the SMPTE,* November 1951; also in *High-Speed Photography,* volume 4.)

Photoinstrumentation is so closely associated with the art and science of high-speed photography that it might seem to entail the use of this technique. However, other types of photography can, if used for scientific purposes, fall within the definition of photoinstrumentation—the operative word of the definition being *use.*

Before going on to the 1960's and exploring the icy reaches of outer space and the glass and metal environment of the laboratory, it

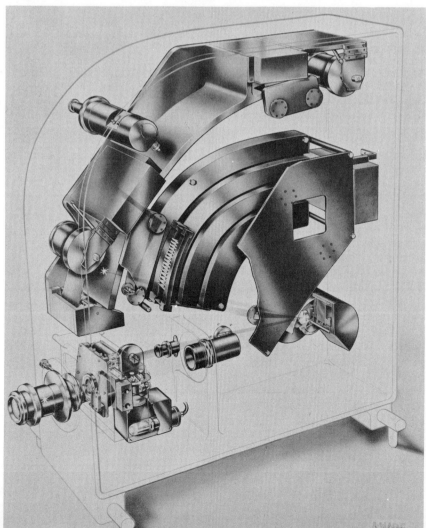

Top: *Twelve-channel Kerr-cell camera as used for conventional explosive studies.* (Photo: George H. Lunn, Atomic Weapons Research Establishment, England)

Bottom: *Rotating-mirror framing camera designed by AWRE, England. Suitable mirrors have been rotated up to 500,000 rpm, with a frame size of about 8 mm square. Usually the number of pictures in a sequence is between 30 and 200, this being sufficient to record such events as the controlled thermonuclear reactor studies and the early phases of explosions.* (Photo: George H. Lunn)

Left: *Beckman & Whitley Model 350 Continuous-Writing Framing Camera. Picture capacity is 224 frames of standard 16 mm frame size on a 34-inch length of 35 mm perforated film. Pictures are recorded in two rows.*

Right: *Beckman & Whitley Model 189A Synchronized Framing Camera. Records 25 high-resolution 35 mm frames at rates from 48,000 to 4,080,000 frames per second. For use in research laboratories for obtaining critical information in the study of such ultra-high-speed phenomena as lasers, plasmas, nucleation, detonations, shock, and vibration.*

might be interesting to note that photography was used for scientific purposes at least as soon as it was used for portraiture and entertainment. For example, in 1840, shortly after the development of the daguerreotype process, Dr. John W. Draper photographed the moon—

a noteworthy "first." And at Harvard College Observatory, attempts to photograph the stars were finally successful one night in 1850 when a clear photograph of the star, Vega, was obtained. Long before the development of motion photography, Muybridge and Eakins photo-

graphed exactly how men and animals accomplished the feat of getting from one place to another by taking series of photographs.

MODERN TECHNIQUES

The high-speed camera of today extends perception beyond the reach of the five senses. From 500 feet

DMB 10 space camera is carried into space aboard the boosters, takes its pictures and then is ejected in a specially designed, recoverable capsule for its long free fall and parachute landing. 400-foot 166 mm film capacity with speeds from 4 to 400 frames per second. (Photo: D.B. Milliken Company, California)

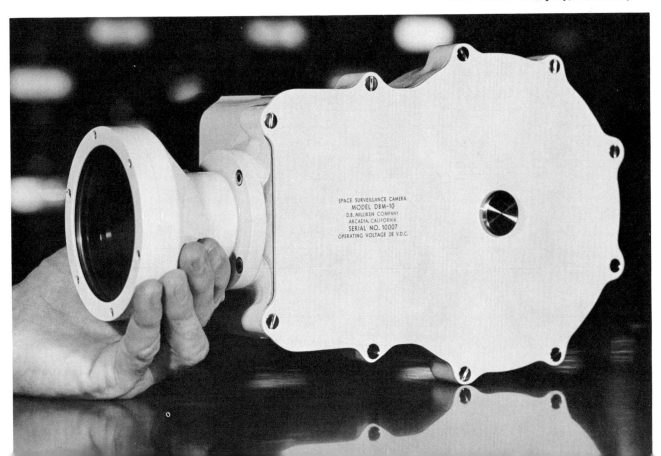

Above: Model 206B Lightweight 70 mm Space Camera (cover removed) made by Flight Research, Inc., Richmond, Virginia, with 125-foot film capacity. Takes full-frame pictures 2½ × 2½ inches in size at the rate of 40 frames per second. After the film is exposed it enters an armored magazine which is automatically sealed and pressurized at the end of the run.

Below: Beckman & Whitley Model 200 simultaneous streak and framing camera. Recording rate of the framing module is 500,000 frames per second and the streak module records at 6.9 mm per microsecond.

under the sea to 500 miles above the earth, in temperatures ranging from near absolute zero to 1000 F, specially developed equipment is continually gathering data of immeasurable value to science and industry.

Measuring, recording, observing, and evaluating by means of modern equipment, a man can watch unharmed the play of flames and the behavior of gases from the center of the hottest fiery furnace built. He can "catch the wind in a net," a net of photographic film as he photographs the behavior of air currents rushing faster than the speed of sound—winds that would mash him as flat as a pancake if he were in their path.

A record of what happens to wheels, springs, engine, bones, muscles, and skulls in an automobile smashup can be recorded by means of photoinstrumentation and the record studied so that death by auto will become less common.

High-voltage Sparks.

High-voltage sparks make air currents visible in wind-tunnel experiments. If high-voltage sparks are made to occur between two electrodes in a rapid air current, then the plasma ionized by the

spark path is carried away by the air current. Sparks fired in rapid succession follow the pre-ionized path, which consequently lights up intermittently. In this way the air current's velocity and spatial displacement can be made visible and photographically recorded.

Since the time intervals between the high-voltage sparks are all preset, the displacements of traces show the air-curent conditions prevailing at the time of sparkover. (Frank Früngel, Walter Thorwart, and H. G. Patzke, "High-Speed Photography using a High Frequency Spark Source and a Kerr Cell in Combination," *Journal of the SMPTE,* March 1962; also in *Proceedings of the Fifth International Congress on High-Speed Photography)* and since the color of the spark path varies with different gases—e.g., air, blue-white; argon, white; neon, red—the movement and mixture of the different gases can be followed in space and time, either by taking color photographs or by visual observation.

Ballistics.

Study of the behavior of explosions, projectiles, rockets, nuclear reactors, and the like, would be severely limited, if not impossible,

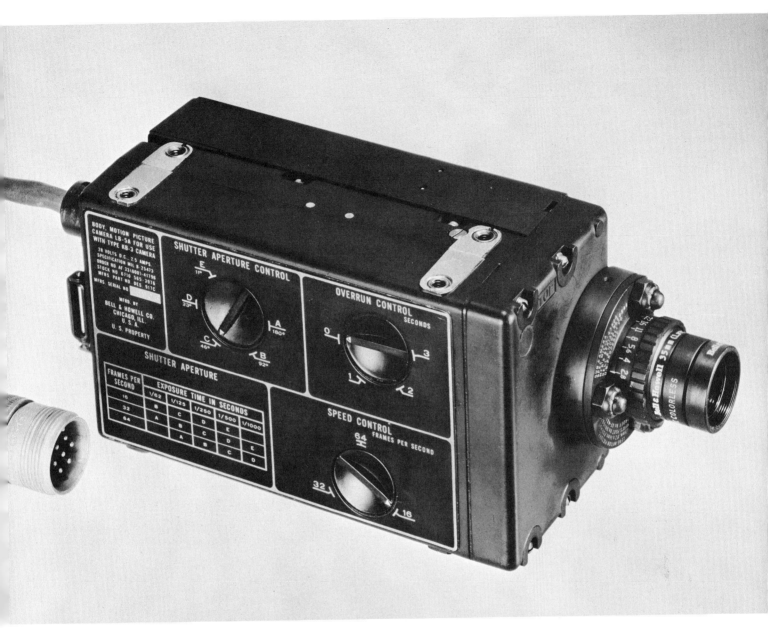

On the camera body, the following labels appear:

BODY, MOTION PICTURE
CAMERA LB-5A FOR USE
WITH TYPE KB-3 CAMERA

28 VOLTS D.C. 2.5 AMPS.
SPECIFICATION MIL B 25473
ORDER NO AF 33(600)-41798
STOCK NO 6710 565-2978
MFRS. PART NO DES 517C
MFRS. SERIAL NO

MFRD. BY
BELL & HOWELL CO.
CHICAGO, ILL.
U.S.A.
U. S. PROPERTY

SHUTTER APERTURE CONTROL

E 11°
D 23°
C 46°
A 180°
B 92°

OVERRUN CONTROL SECONDS

0
1
2
3

SHUTTER APERTURE

FRAMES PER SECOND	EXPOSURE TIME IN SECONDS					
	1/62	1/125	1/250	1/500	1/1000	
16	B		C	D	E	
32	A		B	C	D	E
64		A	B	C	D	E

SPEED CONTROL FRAMES PER SECOND

64
32
16

KB-3A 16 mm Gun Camera has been used in the continued improvement of fire control systems and methods, filming the separation from an on-board missile flight, or a recording job in the laboratory. Made by Traid Corp., Encino, California.

without the tools of photoinstrumentation. An example of photoinstrumentation equipment used in ballistics is a time-resolving spectograph built by Beckman & Whitley, Inc., for the Poulter Laboratories of Stanford Research Institute for obtaining hitherto unobtainable information about processes taking place in the few millionths of a second during a detonation.

Life Sciences.

Although photoinstrumentation is usually thought of in connection with the physical sciences, it is also useful in the life sciences. Recording the speed of a rattlesnake's bite and the intricacies of its poison-releasing mechanism; showing the kinetics of a frog's leap as it sails through the air in a graceful arc, landing right on target, and photographing also, in slow motion, the struggles of the unfortunate target, a grasshopper, are all within the province of photoinstrumentation, as are other areas of research in biology, medicine, organic chemistry.

EQUIPMENT

In scientific research, the most minute deviation can result in failure and perhaps disaster. So equipment for photoinstrumentation must be built with the utmost precision and carefully engineered to fit the exact purposes for which it is in-

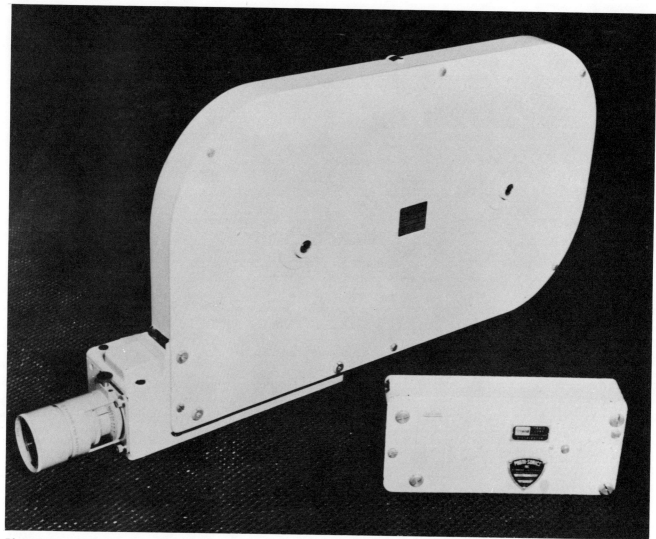

Photo-Sonics I B 16 mm high-speed camera with 1200-foot magazine. 100-foot magazine below.

tended. A growing number of firms, many of them located on the West Coast, are engaging in the manufacture of photoinstrumentation equipment.

Types of motion-picture camera systems used for photoinstrumentation include: rotating-mirror systems, image-dissection systems, Kerr-cell shutter systems, image-tube systems, drum cameras, streak cameras, and framing cameras or a combination streak and framing camera. Variations of these main types are manufactured for special purposes, for space flights, data recording, oscilloscopes, and so on.
Kerr-cell Shutter.

Many cameras used in photoinstrumentation are based on the Kerr-cell shutter. Briefly, a Kerr cell is a small glass vessel which contains a liquid, such as nitrobenzene, between two flat electrodes. When an electric potential is impressed between the electrodes, the liquid becomes doubly refracting, with the optic axis parallel to the electric lines of force. In a Kerr-cell shutter, a polarizer is placed in front of the cell to polarize the incoming light at an angle of 45 degrees to the electric field. An analyzer is placed in back of the Kerr cell and is rotated by 90 degrees from the front polarizer so that no light is transmitted in the absence of an electric field.

The shutter duration is determined by the length of the electrical pulse on the Kerr-cell electrodes. The width of the pulse is, in turn, determined by the characteristics of a pulse-forming network. These pulse-forming networks are available in pulse widths from five nanoseconds (one nanosecond is one-billionth of a second) to several microseconds. Various types of high-speed cameras are based on the Kerr cell. In a rotating-mirror system, the film is stationary; the event is imaged onto the surface of a plane mirror which is rotating at tremendous speeds and then reimaged onto the film. There are many variations of this basic principle. For example, one type of rotating-mirror camera uses concave mirrors. A description of this type may be found in: S.J. Jacobs, J.D. McLanahan and P.F. Donovan, "A Rotating-Mirror Framing Camera with Multiple Focal-Plane Shutters," *Proceedings of the Fifth International Congress of High-Speed Photography.*

The streak (or smear) camera is so called because a narrow segment of the event to be recorded is selected. The light variations with time within the segment are imaged onto the film by various means, such as the rotating drum. Streak or smear cameras are used for such purposes as analyses of the behavior of sparks, ballistics studies, and numerous types of industrial research, such as the behavior of porous materials. This type of photographic recording is often used in combination with other types of high-speed photography.

RECENT DEVELOPMENTS

With photoinstrumentation an indispensable tool in almost every field of scientific research, more and

more precise instruments are continuing to be made.

Typical of the high-grade special-purpose cameras now available are simultaneous streak and framing cameras, and synchronized framing cameras. Among the manufacturers in this field is Beckman & Whitley, of San Carlos, California. Another firm, Photo-Sonics, Inc., of Burbank, California, has recently announced a 70 mm recording camera and a 70 mm pulse camera, and the Photographic Instrumentation Development Company of Tarzana, California has recently brought out a 70 mm oscilloscope recording camera.

The D. B. Milliken Company of Arcadia, California, may be cited as representative of the rapidly

growing number of firms specializing in the design and development of cameras for space photography to give eyewitness accounts of exactly what happens both inside and outside the space craft at the moment of launching and throughout the flight, including the re-entry into the earth's atmosphere. Another "sign of the times" is a 70 mm camera built to withstand extreme altitudes, recently announced by Flight Research, Inc., of Richmond, Virginia. Photoinstrumentation on the moon and beyond is one of the

This rotating-mirror framing camera with multiple focal-plane shutters will write six tracks of image on two 70 mm film strips to give a total of about 216 frames. (Photo: U.S. Naval Ordnance Laboratory, White Oak, Maryland)

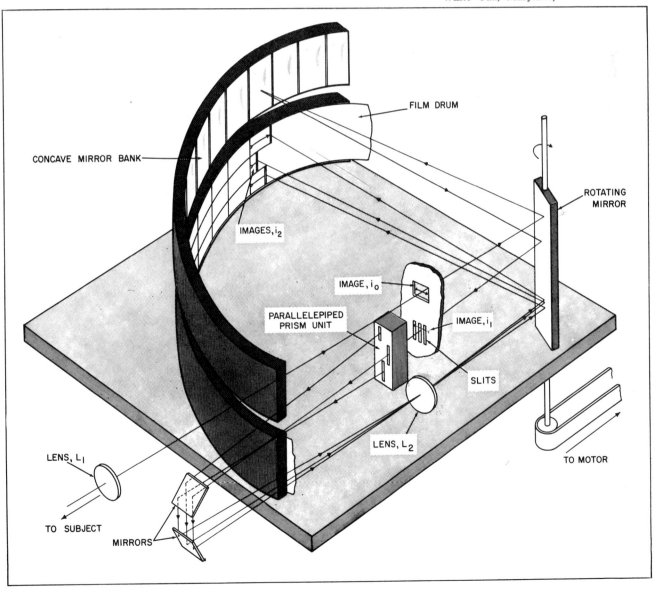

more intriguing aspects of this tool of science.

More mundane but no less useful studies have been and are being made in almost every conceivable area of industrial research. For example, the paper-making industry used high-speed photography to discover why apparently identical fibres behaved differently in the same situation.

Photoinstrumentation has also been used to reduce "around-the-home" accidents in such situations as mowing the lawn. For example, a pebble, a small metal object, a piece of wire, a broken teacup can all become lethal flying objects when struck by the blade of a lawnmower. Studies of exactly what happens when a lawnmower blade encounters such an object have led to the redesign of the blades to provide for the greatest possible safety.

Head-on collision at 50 mph is photographed from various angles by the high-speed motion-picture camera. (Photo: Derwyn M. Severy, Institute of Transportation and Traffic Engineering, University of California)

SPECIAL PROBLEMS

In the study of such high-speed events as the flight of a bullet, the fragmentation that occurs when an explosion takes place, or the collision of two speeding vehicles, one of the main problems encountered is that of lighting. The researcher who uses photoinstrumentation must thoroughly understand not only what types of lighting are suitable for various events, but how to use special speed light sources, such as explosive flash lights.

It must not be forgotten that one of the important uses of photo-instrumentation is that of making an accurate record of events occurring in environments that would be instantly destructive to the human body—for example, studies of shock waves, or photographs made inside blast furnaces, or from the nose cone of a rocket. For events such as these, cameras remotely controlled or robot cameras with built-in automatic controls are among the commonplace wonders of science.

PHOTOGRAPHIC PRINTING PAPERS

Paper Manufacturing Division, Eastman Kodak Company
[This article deals with the structural and photographic characteristics of photographic paper. A knowledge of this subject will enable the serious photographer to appreciate his working material and to understand the handling of photographic papers. Such knowledge is necessary in producing enlargements of the finest quality.]
• *Also see: Beginner's Guide to Developing and Printing; Emulsion Manufacture; Enlarging Photographs.*

SILVER-HALIDE GRAINS (CRYSTALS OF chloride, bromide, and iodide salts of silver) are the key to the photographic process. They record the light falling upon them and when processed produce a metallic-silver image of proper structure to give the final print. The physical and chemical nature of the silver-halide

grains and the binder which carries them are modified by additional reagents to produce the desired print quality, but all must be carefully controlled. The grains may be pure silver chloride or pure silver bromide, but mixtures of chloride and bromide are much more common, often with a little iodide as well.

The binder in which the emulsion grains are dispersed plays as important a part in the photographic system as the silver halide itself. It must keep the grains well separated during their precipitation in order to prevent clumping and consequent background for a granular image. As the emulsion is carried through various operations, leading finally to coating and drying, the binder supports the grains to prevent settling out and provides a uniform coating.

GELATIN

The binder must permit processing solutions to penetrate it rapidly and yet be both flexible and tough to withstand the strong processing solutions and the necessary handling of photographic papers. These characteristics must be retained for a reasonable length of time before processing and for many years after processing. Synthetic vehicles are used for special purposes, but only gelatin has all these properties and is also available in large quantities of fairly uniform quality at a reasonable cost.

Gelatin is not a well-defined chemical compound, but is a residue from the protein group of natural products, such as animal hides and bones. Only the finest gelatin, carefully extracted from hides and

When a subject has great contrast, like this one with its black shadows and brilliant white sun glare, the choice of paper is particularly important. A full black silhouette would have been achieved if contrast paper had been used. As it is, normal paper served to give the black-lighted effect, while still preserving a bit of detail and softness in the shadowed foreground. (Photo: Charles Phelps Cusing)

bones, can be used for photographic emulsions.

Chemical purity must be obtained without violent treatments that would destroy necessary physical properties such as good strength and high viscosity. This is accomplished by cold alkali treatments, often extending over several months, followed by extraction of the gelatin with water. The conditions under which these steps are performed and origin and condition of the raw hides and bones determine the pho-

When the baryta layer has been applied it is dried in a long drying alley and wound into rolls as shown here.

tographic and physical properties of the final gelatin.

When dissolved in warm water, gelatin forms a clear colloidal solution capable of supporting the emulsion grains and keeping them from sticking together. Upon chilling, the solution forms a solid gel which is strong enough to allow shredding of the emulsion and washing in cold water to remove unwanted by-products of the emulsion-making reactions. The emulsion can be stored in this gelled form until needed and then liquefied with gentle heating. During emulsion coating on the paper support, the gel-forming property permits setting of the emulsion to prevent its flowing during drying.

When the dried gelatin layer containing the emulsion grains is immersed in processing solution, it swells enough to allow easy entrance of processing chemicals and discharge of by-products. Swelling would be excessive in these solutions, however, if the gelatin were not chemically hardened before coating.

Apart from its role as a vehicle, gelatin plays a vital part in the photochemical reactions of latent-image formation, the process whereby the light falling on the emulsion is registered. Halogen is liberated during the exposure to light and must be trapped to prevent excessive loss in sensitivity. Gelatin is an efficient acceptor of the liberated halogen.

Impurities are found in all gelatins which greatly affect the delicate reactions. Both sensitizing and inhibiting substances are present, and the balance between their effects helps determine the speed, contrast, and other characteristics of the final coating. The impurities can be largely removed by suitable treatment of the gelatin, and this is sometimes done to allow the use of specially chosen reagents to give the desired speed and contrast. More often, the emulsion maker takes advantage of the impurities and uses their effects to provide combinations of characteristics available in no other way.

EMULSION CHARACTERISTICS

Speed.

Enlarging-paper emulsions vary widely in speed. For commercial use where rapid print production is paramount, the highest speed is sought. In portraiture where control of exposure in small areas during exposure of the whole print and local control of development are common, lower speeds are preferable. Some high grade portrait papers are so low as to serve for contact printing as well as for enlarging.

The principal control of speed in emulsion making is maintained through control of emulsion-grain size—large grains are fast, small ones slow. If the grains are precipitated in a solution in which they are appreciably soluble, for instance in an excess of bromide, small grains tend to dissolve and contribute to the growth of large ones. This process is called Ostwald ripening. By control of temperature, solution concentrations, and reaction times, grains of widely varying sizes can be made.

The proportions of chloride and iodide also have a marked effect on speed. While it is generally true that the higher bromide and iodide contents are found in the faster emulsions, considerations other than speed often lead the emulsion maker to compromise.

For grains of desirable size to be fast enough for enlarging, their sensitivity must be enhanced by chemical sensitization. This term is applied to a number of processes which modify the surface of a grain to make latent-image formation easier and so to raise speed. To take one example, digesting an emulsion with small quantities of sulfur-containing compounds leads to the formation of minute specks of silver sulfide which increase the emulsion's sensivity to light.

Another useful device for increasing emulsion speed is optical sensitization, a process in which grains are dyed to make them respond to the colors of light to which they are not ordinarily sensitive. The emulsion grain being pale yellow if a bromide, and nearly colorless if a chloride, absorbs only blue light which represents very little of the energy practical light sources emit. The grain cannot react to energy it does not absorb, so making it absorb light of other colors, usually blue-green or green, increases the energy available to it and thus increases the speed of the emulsion.

The emulsion maker usually avoids sensitizing to red light, leaving that part of the spectrum available for safelighting the darkroom. Whether a particular emulsion is safe under a certain safelight depends not only upon its speed, but upon the nature of its optical sensitization as well.

When the baryta-coated paper is dried, some papers receive further treatment by winding through a supercalender. Here, alternate steel and cotton rolls help to smooth and even the baryta surface.

Contrast.

The contrast, or gradient, of an emulsion is determined by the uniformity of speed among its individual grains. In a given emulsion, the speed of a grain is determined by its size and therefore in practice grain-size distribution controls contrast. As a rule, the more quickly the grains are formed, the smaller and more uniform they are in size. But by careful control of ripening and the other emulsion-making re-

actions, fairly large, fast grains of uniform size can be made. A fast enlarging paper of the highest contrast takes all the emulsion maker's skill.

Most commercial papers and some portrait papers are offered in a series of four to six different contrasts, allowing the printing of almost any negative that might be encountered. The emulsions used in such a series must be accurately matched for all characteristics other

than contrast.

Some portrait papers are made in only one contrast. This is practical where the photographer, by control of lighting and processing, can secure the appropriate contrast in all his negatives.

Image Tone.

Enlarging papers can be obtained in a range of image color, or image tone, from blue-black to brown. Tone depends upon the physical structure of the 'developed silver image. Large grain size, a well-hardened gelating layer, the presence of toning agents, and rapid development all lead to a cold bluish tone, while the opposite conditions produce warm browns. A moderate range of tones can be produced by using developer formulas of different strength.

Image tones more extreme than those available from the emulsion itself can be produced by treating the developed print in toning baths containing, for example, selenium or gold salts. The emulsion maker must take care that his product works properly in these baths.

Surfaces.

A dried gelatin layer is normally quite glossy. Small variations in gloss accompany differences in the rate of drying. To make a semi-matte or matte surface, various inert, granular materials are added to the emulsion. If it is to interfere least with good blacks, the matting agent must be transparent in the gelatin layer and act only through its effect on the surface.

Oil coloring and retouching requires surface roughness different from that needed to reduce gloss. Other agents, usually of larger particle size, can be added to make a surface which will accept these media well. Use of appropriate matting agents and coating on stock embossed with various patterns produces a wide variety of enlarging-paper surfaces and textures.

Compromise.

It is evident emulsion making is fraught with compromise. Consider the problem of producing a high-speed, contrasty, warm-toned enlarging paper with good resistance to damage in processing. To be fast the grains must be large, but to be

Printing papers with a glossy finish are·used to preserve sharp detail and retain deep blacks. This is of particular importance in scientific and other recording photography.

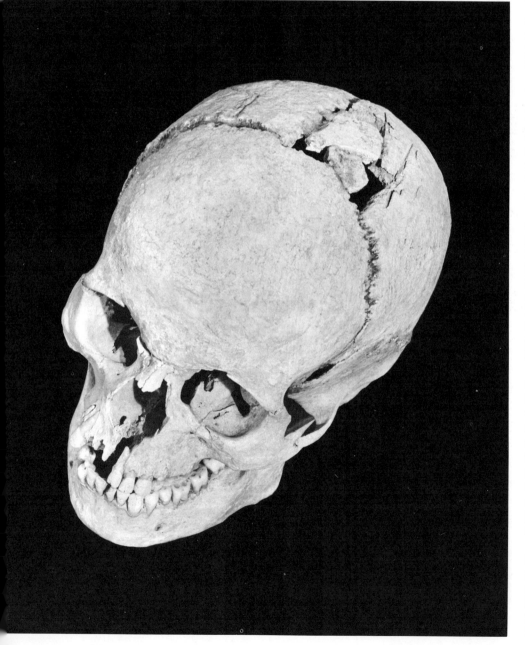

This is a photograph of middle tones; there are few real blacks or whites in the picture. Care must be taken in selecting the printing paper in order to produce a pleasing balance of tones. (Photo: Arthur Rothstein)

warm-toned they must be small. High contrast requires rapid precipitation, which normally leads to small, slow grains. Good hardness to resist processing damage makes image tone colder. Compromise is essential.

PAPER STOCK

One of the prime requisites for photographic paper stock is permanence, that is, resistance to change under continued exposure to heat and light. This requirement can be met with a mat of pure cellulose fibres (ancient Egyptian papyrus documents are still in existence today) blended with chemicals which are also heat and light resistant.

Resistance to contamination is also important for all photographic papers. Great care is taken to see that all active compounds (particularly sulfur-containing ones) or heavy metals (iron, copper) are either removed or destroyed. In this modern-day testing of nuclear explosive force, radioactive contamination has resulted in special air and water filtration both for the pulp manufacturer and the paper maker.

Almost any plant that can be separated into fibres can be used for the manufacture of at least some types of paper. For many years the fibres of flax and cotton were the standard raw materials for papers used for permanent records, whether written or photographic.

At first, a permanent paper could not be made from wood pulp (the greatest source of cellulose) because no means were available for removing the impurities which destroyed strength and permanence. About forty years ago the Eastman Kodak Company, in cooperation with a pulp manufacturer, developed a modern method of making large quantities of pure cellulose fibres from which photographic paper of the highest quality, embodying permanence and inertness, could be made. By 1931, virtually all photographic paper bases were made of wood cellulose. For many years the Eastman Kodak Company was the only manufacturer of photographic paper in the United States. There are now several in this country, but Kodak remains the largest producer of this type of paper in the world.

Although virtually all photographic-paper stock is made from

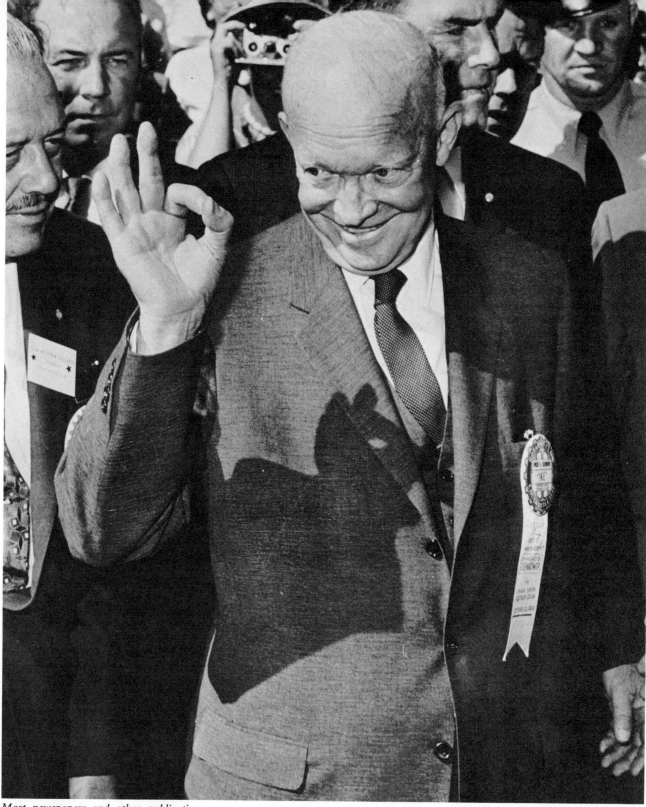

Most newspapers and other publications prefer that photographs be printed on a glossy paper and ferrotyped to preserve detail. (Photo: Roy Jarvis / The San Diego Union)

wood cellulose, there are still some papers which are made from cotton (rag) fibres, to meet certain government specifications or where the ultimate in strength is required.

Papers have been made from most synthetic fibres such as nylon or orlon, but are very costly and are limited to specialty uses.

PAPER MAKING

To trace in detail the saga of a spruce tree in Oregon to a photographic-paper coating machine in New York would require a volume. The picture can only be sketched here. Felled logs are floated down rivers and through lakes to the pulp mills where de-barkers remove the unsuitable outer layers from the logs. The logs are disintegrated into small chips which are placed in cookers. The lignin which holds the individual cellulose fibres together in the chip is removed by the cooking, as are the other impurities such as the natural resins and pitches. These would cause oxidation and weaken the paper. The now brown fibres are bleached virtually pure white in almost the same manner as the housewife bleaches her clothes.

The paper maker will require several types of pulp, varying from short hardwood fibers for uniformity to the sulfite-cooked softwoods for smooth surface and the long, bleached kraft fibres for strengths Varying amounts of these fibres, depending upon the requirements of the particular paper that is being made, are blended into a large tank, called a "hydrapulper," where the sheets of wood pulp are chewed up in hundreds of gallons of water within just a few minutes. Small amounts of dye are added to make the paper whiter, or to make it any other desired color.

Other chemicals are now added to the slurry of the pulp in the water. These materials, which are called sizing agents, must necessarily be incorporated in photographic paper to facilitate handling in the subsequent coating and processing operations. These chemicals include starch to improve dry strength, a synthetic resin to improve wet strength, and a soap or rosin to impart resistance to water.

Since most fibres are too long to make a satisfactory paper, they must now be cut to the desired length in a machine called a "jordan," which is a large cone inside of which are many cutting blades whirling at high speed. The pulp slurry is then introduced into the "wet end" of a paper-making machine. At this point, the mixture is about 99 percent water (actually it requires about 18 gallons of water to make one pound of paper).

This watery mixture is fed onto an endless moving belt made of very fine mesh-wire screen. By a shifting sideways motion, the mixture is spread evenly over the moving belt. As the pulp mixture starts its way along the paper machine, the water drains out through the moving belt. Soon the paper is "formed" enough to be removed from the wire belt and to be carried on felt blankets through wringers. Sometimes these blankets, which remove more water from the paper, have special textures, for example, "tweed," which impress into the wet paper the same mark or texture.

The paper continues to move in one never-ending web, traveling over hot drums and through sets of hot rollers which dry and press it. Frequently one of these rollers has a mark on its surface which will imprint the paper to give the desired texture. Marking rolls and marking felts are usually not used in conjunction with each other, however.

At the end of the paper machine, the paper passes under pressure, between several highly polished, very smooth rolls, which impart the final surface to the paper. The paper is then rolled into large rolls which are tested by quality-control specialists who determine if it meets the rigid requirements of a photographic paper base.

Special effects can be obtained by using different grades of paper. Here, the abstract quality is emphasized with a high-contrast paper. Nikon F and 50mm Auto-Nikor f/1.4 lens with Plus-X film. (Photo: Ross Lowell)

SURFACE AND TINT

The surface and tint are only partially established during the paper-making operation, and it is the function of the baryta coat to provide final control over these characteristics.

The basic ingredients in a baryta-coating solution are usually barium sulfate as pigment, gelatin plus appropriate hardener as binder, and dye. The layer must be photographically inert, and extreme caution

Deep blacks and good detail, combined with over-all lustre can be obtained with an "F"-type paper and a matte-dried finish. (Photo: Brisanelli)

Because strobe light is considerably softer than other types of illumination, it is sometimes necessary to use a more contrasty paper. This was especially true in this photo where a high-contrast paper was used to bring out the texture in the kitten's fur. Leica M2 and lens head of 90mm Elmarit f/2.8 on Visoflex. Plus-X film exposed 1/50 of a second and at f/4. (Photo: Michael L. Edelson)

is exercised to eliminate any source of external contamination. After coating, the paper can be finished in any one of several ways. If a glossy surface is desired, it will be processed through a supercalender. An embossing technique can produce a surface with a very specialized mark. It is also possible to retain a particular surface pattern built in during the paper-making operation; in this event, no special finishing after coating is required. It is obvious that the paper making and baryta coating must represent a highly coordinated effort.

COATING

Emulsion coating consists of two operations: application and drying. The emulsion layer must be applied to the support very accurately to produce constant photographic performance and to present an unvarying load to the dryer. Of course, there must be no defects or irregularities which would blemish the print.

A classic application method is skim coating, in which the support passes under a roller just touching the surface of a pool of liquid emulsion. The amount of emulsion applied depends upon its viscosity and the speed at which the support is moving, being greater at high viscosity and high speed. Many devices have been developed to allow coating thin layers even at very high speeds. These are not peculiar to emulsion coating, but are used in the paper industry for the application of many kinds of surface coatings.

Surface tension and other surface phenomena are important in obtaining a smooth coating. Materials called "coating agents" are always added to the emulsion to provide optimum characteristics.

The first stage in drying is to immobilize the liquid emulsion layer by chill setting so it will not run on the paper. Then, as drying proceeds, the temperatures can be gradually increased while still avoiding remelting. The particular schedule of drying—temperatures, humidities, air velocities, and so forth—must be closely maintained to control curl, brittleness, sheen, and the effectiveness of the gelatin hardeners.

A low-contrast paper is helpful in accenting the soft feminine quality of a young girl. (Photo: Michael L. Edelson)

FINAL OPERATIONS

Before the photographic paper is converted into sizes for customer usage, it is thoroughly tested for its photographic characteristics such as speed, contrast, and image tone. It is also subjected to inspection to determine the physical characteristics of the coating.

Cutting photographic paper is a procedure that requires an efficient layout of cuts to be made with a giant knife or guillotine, though the product is also slit and furnished in roll form for the customer. Large rectangular pieces are cut from the master roll, and several dozens are piled upon the platform of the guillotine. Cuts are taken through the pile, each one yielding a pile of sheets of a given size. Sheets of different sizes are usually made with successive cuts so that it is possible to utilize all of the original sheets without waste.

Finally, the sheets of paper are counted. They are then wrapped and boxed to protect the photographic paper from light, moisture, and contamination during delivery to the user. From the coating operation to the packaging operation, all activities are carried on under lighting conditions that are "safe" for the product—usually a dim red. The next light to strike the enlarging paper will be in the exposing on the easel of the enlarger.

TONE REPRODUCTION

What does a good photographic print accomplish? If we neglect the aspect of color we can say that it gives the observer the same impression of a scene, person, or object that the original gave the photographer. Since seeing the original is possible only by virtue of the varying intensities of the light reflected from its component areas, then a photograph would seem to require the same reflection variations.

This is often impossible because the maximum useful range of reflecting power, from black shadow to clear highlight (print-brightness range) in a lustre or glassy print is about 1-50, whereas many scenes present a range much greater than

Multicontrast papers are now becoming very popular since it is possible to print hard and soft enlargements, or even areas, on the same print by changing the filters. In this Baltimore street scene, the steps were printed with a soft filter to preserve detail, while the balance of the photo was done with a more contrasty filter to emphasize the slum atmosphere. Leica M2 with 50mm Summicron f/2 lens and yellow filter. Plus-X film exposed 1/125 of a second and at f/5.6. (Photo: Michael L. Edelson)

this. That such scenes can be photographed successfully is due to the fortunate subjective accommodation that the eye can make when it views a print.

The theory of tone reproduction is a complex one; even today there are many aspects still to be ana-lyzed. The following discussion is intended to give a brief outline of the general considerations.

Brightness Range.

There are three main problems involving scene-brightness ranges as represented on the photographic print. The first entails choosing an original with a brightness range that can be encompassed by the paper. This is easy to do in still-life subjects and in portraiture, for here the amount of light reflected by the darkest and the brightest parts of the subject can be controlled by the photographer in illuminating the subject. (Specular reflections such as catch lights in the eyes can be disregarded.) The shaded flesh under the chin in a portrait can be lighted so that it is about a quarter as bright as the cheek: then in the

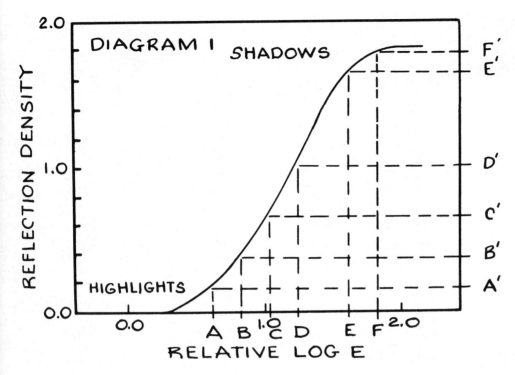

Figure 1. *Sensitometric curve. This typical sensitometric or characteristic curve is fully discussed in the text.*

lighted. Such scenes, when printed on a paper of suitable contrast, can be photographically represented without the necessity of considerable brightness compromises in shadow and highlight detail.

The third situation presents strong contrast as well as a long brightness range. It can be exemplified by a beach scene. The sun shines almost into the camera and makes brilliant highlights on the water and bright patches on the sand. The sand is of a light tone; the skin of a girl standing in the water is a middle tone; the water is moderately dark. The girl is wearing a dark bathing suit and casts a very dark shadow on the water. This scene has a brightness range that is not possible to portray photographically without making compromises. Some sacrifice in brightness rendition at the extreme ends of the range is necessary whereas the middle tones, that in this case embrace the object of interest, should be printed to a suitable contrast and density for yielding pleasing representation.

In the above scene, it might be necessary to give the bathing suit less exposure than the rest of the scene in order to show roundness and detail. The bright patches on the sand might have to be given more exposure so that the texture of the beach is not lost.

print this shadow can be printed four times darker than the cheek. A good print can result without appreciably changing the reflection characteristics in transferring them from subject to image as long as the tonal range lies within the scope of the materials used.

The second problem involves a subject in which the tone range is just within that which the paper can accommodate, and yet the range embodies no sharp contrast, so that a great deal of black or white is not desirable on the print. Such subjects are usually termed flat-

CONTRAST

A more tangible property of enlarging papers is contrast. Contrast involves two factors: density range and exposure scale.

Density Range.

Density range is the range of reflection densities which the paper will produce, from clear unexposed areas to the deepest black. Since the print is viewed by reflected light, the density in the highlights is prac-

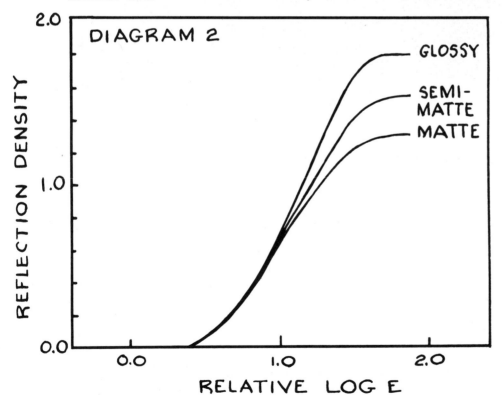

Figure 2. *Here the effect of paper surfaces upon the shape of the sensitometric curve is shown. Notice that the glossy curve is steeper and longer, indicating a greater tonal gradation. With 2.0 as an arbitrary and theoretical top in black density, the 1.8 of glossy is excellent.*

tically that of the clear paper, while the density of the deepest possible shadows (full black) is limited by the light reflected from the surface of the developed silver particles and the gelatin.

The density range varies with the surface texture of the paper, and to a lesser extent with the emulsion type. The maximum density of glossy papers is about 1.80 in an arbitrary range of 0 to 2. For semi-matte, fine grain, and lustre surfaces, the value is about 1.50. The matte-surface papers have maximum density values between 1.30 and 1.20.

Density range affects the visual contrast of a print. For example, if the same negative is printed on both glossy and matte papers, chosen to have the same exposure scale, the glossy print will appear more contrasty. Thus, the higher the density range of photographic paper the more contrasty the appearance of the print.

Exposure Scale.

Exposure scale must not be confused with the speed of the paper or the exposure time required. It relates to the range of light intensities required to produce a print having the full range of useful tones from white to black. For example, in the case of a "soft" paper of low contrast, if a light intensity of one produces a just noticeable effect, then a light intensity 50 times as great might be required to produce a full black.

The values from which the limits of the exposure scale can be determined are most usefully based on gradient measurements on the characteristic curves. The gradient of a curve is a measure which indicates the slope (or contrast of the material) at a given point on the curve. The exposure scale thus defined is often stated by indicating the exposure interval between one point on the low or highlight end of the curve and another point on the shoulder or shadow end of the curve. A method of determining log exposure-scale values for the sensitometric curves of the papers

is defined in the *American Standard for Sensitometry and Grading of Photographic Papers*, PH 2.2 - 1953.

This range approaches in most cases the range of light intensities transmitted by the significant parts of the appropriate negative. Exposure scale, in comparison to density range, is essentially the same for different surfaces of the same contrast grade of a given paper.

The essential difference between contrast grades of the same paper is one of exposure scale—the higher the contrast of the paper, the lower the exposure scale. Logarithmic values of paper exposure scales are comparable to the density range in negatives and are often used in certain enlarging exposure and contrast meters of calculators.

SENSITOMETRIC CURVES

The physical and chemical forces that produce the photographic image seem to have one very human aspect. When they start building image density on a print, they need to get "warmed up" to the work; results are slow in accruing at first. Then they "hit their stride" and work efficiently until a point is reached in which they slow down.

The exposing light, does a small initial part of the job; then developing agents are set to work to build up the image. The more persuasion (in the form of exposure) that the light can apply, the more useful the work obtained from the developer. This goes on until a point is reached where the exposure has been sufficient to yield a black. Greater exposures, which yield more silver on the print result only in small additional visual effects like a second coat of paint on a fence. As more and more silver is deposited, practically no darkening occurs, just as four or five coats of black paint would not result in a much blacker fence.

The most convenient way to show these effects is by means of a sensitometric curve. The sensitometric curve tells in one graphic line characteristics about a paper that would require hundreds of words to describe fully. The fundamental concepts are dealt with below.

The first requirement for obtaining a sensitometric curve is a test strip made on the paper to be examined. This is done in a sensitometer, which gives the paper a series of exposures that varies logarithmically along the strip over an exposure range somewhat greater than that encountered in practice when printing from negatives. Re-

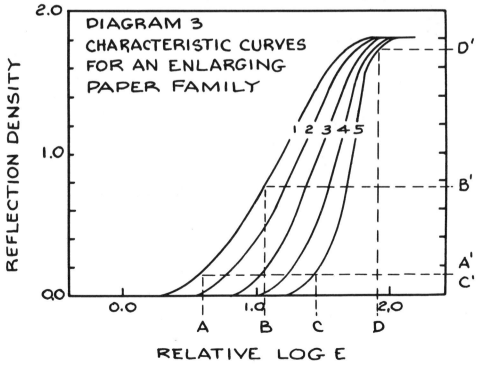

Figure 3. *These curves represent an enlarging paper family of five different contrasts.*

flection densities or degrees of blackness are measured along the strip, and the results are plotted on a graph. This yields the sensitometric curve shown in Figure 1.

If the paper were such that equal logarithmic changes in exposure produced equal changes in print density, then the sensitometric curve shown would be a straight line. This is not the case and the curved response is the result. It will be seen that the print density difference (A' to B') between exposures A and B is less than the difference (C' to D') between exposures C and D. The difference E' to F' is also less than C' to D'. This differential response, taken throughout the exposure range, results in the rendering shown by the sensitometric curve.

A certain definite amount of exposure is required to produce the first noticeable gray. Then, as the exposure increases (shown logarithmically increasing horizontally to the right), the density increases (shown increasing vertically upwards). The growth of density from exposure is slow at first; it then accelerates, finally slowing up as a maximum useful density is approached. At the latter point further increase in exposure results in only a slight growth in density that is not useful in practice. This is indicated by the leveling off of the curve.

So much for the response aspects of the sensitometric curve. There are other things that the curve tells. Figure 2 shows the curves for papers of different surface characteristics though with the same emulsion. It will be seen that the glossy paper produces a maximum black density of 1.8 which means that black reflects $1/_{63}$ of the brightness of the white. The matte paper, on the other hand, has a maximum density of less than 1.3 and thus reflects about $1/_{20}$ of the white brightness. Thus it is evident that a scene with strong contrast is most faithfully reproduced on a glossy surface and that subjects with a short brightness scale (such as a high-key portrait) can be printed effectively on a matte paper.

Sensitometric curves for five grades of an enlarging paper are shown in Figure 3. It will be noticed that the slopes of the curves are not the same, 5 being steeper than one. The comparison of 1 and 5 shows that equal exposure ranges —A to B, C to D—yield unequal density ranges—A' to B', C' to D'. Thus, a good print from a portrait negative with a modeling density range that happens to be from A to B might be found to possess shadows four times darker than the highlights (a reflection density difference of 0.6). The print was, of course, made on contrast grade 1, for that contrast grade shows a density change of 0.6 for the exposure change AB. The use of grade 5 would yield a density difference of 1.3 (20 to 1), resulting from AB. This would look to harsh or contrasty.

The maximum useful black that a paper can yield also has some bearing upon the contrast grade chosen. For example, a brilliant snow scene with strong contrast would look best on a lustrous, silk-textured paper with a long tone range. However, should it be necessary to use a matte or semimatte surface, it is likely that (at the expense of highlight and shadow detail) a grade of higher contrast than that chosen for the glossy print would have to be used to obtain the results desired.

The sensitometric curve reveals other characteristics of a paper such as speed and gradient. However, the former is easily determined in practice or from manufacturer's data. The mathematical theory behind rating the contrasts of papers involves the average gradient of the curve and the density range of the paper.

□

PHOTOGRAPHIC SOCIETY OF AMERICA (PSA)

The Photographic Society of America is the world's largest photographic organization with an international membership of more than 9500 amateur photographers and 1500 affiliated camera clubs. The purpose of the society is to provide the means for cooperative action in promoting the arts and sciences of photography and for furthering public education therein.

Anyone interested in these aims is eligible for membership and can participate in the activities of any of PSA's seven Divisions. These Divisions are: Color (color slides), Motion Picture, Nature (slides and prints), Photojournalism, Pictorial (monochrome and color prints), Stereo, and Techniques.

In addition the Society publishes the *PSA Journal,* a monthly magazine distributed to all members, and each Division publishes its own periodical dealing with its field of special interest.

PSA and its Divisions make available some 80 services to individual members and 45 services to affiliated clubs. These services include tape-recorded instructional lectures accompanied by color slides, exhibitions of slides and prints, slide- and print-exchange circuits (study groups) for groups of members, picture evaluation and commentary by experts, and competitions with classes for beginners and advanced workers. Travel aides assist members in finding subjects and making pictures wherever they travel in most countries around the world. All functions of PSA are based on voluntary activities of its members.

PSA conducts an annual international convention and several regional conventions at different cities each year. These events offer outstanding programs of lectures and demonstrations on different fields of photography. They are open to interested photographers, whether PSA members or not, and an attendance of 2000 or more is not unusual at an international convention in a major city of the United States.

Outstanding contributions to photography are recognized by the Society through its Associateship (APSA) and Fellowship (FPSA) awards to members, and its Honorary Membership (Hon.PSA) and Honorary Fellowship (Hon.FPSA) awarded to members or non-members. It also awards an annual Progress Medal and other medals, citations, trophies, and scholarships. Headquarters are located at 2005 Walnut Street, Philadelphia 3, Pa.

PHOTOGRAPHY AND THE ARCHEOLOGIST

Part I

RIGMOR JACOBSEN
Formerly Photographer, Oriental Institute, Chicago

[Photography has become such an important part of every archeological expedition that all the modern techniques should be understood by the archeological photographer. Given here is specific information for particular problems of excavation photography, studio work, darkroom processing, as well as the requirements of the photographer.]
• *Also see: Anthropology and the Camera, Tropical Photography.*

WHEN ARCHEOLOGY WAS YOUNG, excavators used to measure the suc-cess or failure of a season in terms of impressive objects carried home and displayed in the museum for which they worked. Nowadays the archeologist realizes that his task is of far wider scope, that the purpose of his work is to furnish a complete and exact picture of ancient civilization, and that such a picture can only be obtained by detailed observation and careful recording of the context and condition of every single find. Thus not only what he finds, but also how he finds it is important. Often the layer in which an object is discovered will determine the age of the object, or the original place of a fallen statue may be deduced from the way it lies in the ground. The general character of a building or a room can sometimes give a clue to purpose and function of objects found in them. And it often happens that a mere impression in the ground will tell about the size and shape of an instrument made of

The modern city of Ankara, Turkey overlooks the ruins of ancient Ancyra, capital of ancient Galatia. In the foreground are the Roman baths. (Photo: Dominique Lajoux, Courtesy of UNESCO)

perishable material that has decayed in the course of time.

Obviously all such facts must be completely and exactly recorded. They are essential to the proper understanding of what is found. Moreover, the record made at the spot at the time of discovery, will often be the only record which can ever be made. It must be complete, detailed, and trustworthy.

Photography, of course, is ideally suited to the making of such records. No sketch is so exact, no description so graphic that it will not find a valuable supplement in a clear and dependable record made with the camera. For that reason every object of any importance and almost every square meter of ground in level after level is photographed,

and sometimes several times, as it is exposed by the excavator.

Considering the importance of photographic recording and the considerable amount of time and skill such recording involves, it is not surprising that more and more expeditions appoint a full-time photographer to their staffs.

PHOTOGRAPHER'S REQUIREMENTS

Many and varied demands will be made on the excavation photographer. It goes without saying that his technical ability must insure uniformly high standards of perfection, for the records which he makes are scientific documents that can never be replaced.

Besides ordinary technical ability, he should also have a degree of adaptability. Important as are the records he produces, he may have to make them under highly primitive conditions and with limited equipment. Sooner or later he is

Left: *Colossus of Abu Simbel, Egypt. Calotype made by Maxime Ducamp in 1850. For over a century photography has been an important recording medium for the archeologist.* (Photo: George Eastman House collection)

Below: *Relief from Apadan stairway discovered by the Oriental Institute's Iranian expedition at Persepolis.*

confronted with situations for which he is not prepared, situations in which his success depends upon ability to improvise workable substitutes for the equipment he lacks. To understand and carry out intelligently the excavators' wishes and specific directions before making a picture, it is essential that the photographer understand the fundamentals of archeology and have at least a general knowledge of the culture with which he is working. An apparently simple thing such as recording what he has photographed, the layer to which it belongs, and the exact point in the excavated area from which the picture has been taken involves knowledge of the grid-system which the excavation uses, of the immediate progress of the work, and of archeological terminology in general.

In the field, and especially in the studio, the photographer will be called upon to handle archeological objects. These objects are often of great value and may be extremely fragile. It is therefore necessary for the photographer to be well-acquainted with the care of antiquities, how to handle and clean them safely to avoid the inadvertent destruction of priceless objects and of evidence

that can never be recovered.

On top of all this, the photographer should acquire at least a working knowledge of the native language spoken in the country in which the excavation takes place, for all during his work he will have to direct workmen, pose them in excavation pictures, indicate where he wants his heavy equipment placed, train a native to help with studio and darkroom work, and so on.

EQUIPMENT

The excavation photographer divides his time between field work, studio work, and darkroom work. Equipment for all three is, of course, necessary and that includes cameras, filters, tripods, sunshades, flash and floodlight arrangements, and the usual darkroom equipment. For work in the field, a view camera, supplemented with a miniature, is most convenient. The miniature will take care of the frequent cases in which the object is in such a position that a camera stand set-up is impossible. A typical expedition will have a studio camera (8×10 with swings and tilts), a 5×7 view camera, a miniature, and perhaps a smaller camera to be used by

members of the excavation whenever a situation calls for photo work that is not important enough to warrant sending for large cameras.

PROCEDURE

Before the photographer makes his exposure the object to be photographed should be cleaned as much as possible without moving it from its original position. The area around it should be smoothed to present an orderly and even background on which the subject stands out clearly. If precise scale is important, a foot-rule or meter-stick should be placed as close to the object as possible. Otherwise some implement such as a knife or brush, can be left in the picture to suggest in a natural and inconspicuous manner the approximate size of the object.

Lighting is usually a serious problem. Important finds may be made at any time of day and must be photographed at once to obtain a record of their original position before they are taken out of the ground. Since the photographer cannot choose his own time he must make the best of the existing light conditions. In most cases satisfactory results can be obtained by judicious use of shading, using mats or sheets held by workmen, and reflection from white sheets or mirrors.

Slightly different problems face the photographer when his subject is of architectural character, for example, a single room of special importance such as a throne room, a sanctuary, or an ancient kitchen with its furnishings still in place.

In arranging the picture it will usually be advantageous to focus interest on one or more important points by including workmen in the scene. This also heightens the impression of depth, gives scale, and generally livens a picture that otherwise may look bleak and lifeless. In posing the men it is best to give them a familiar task to perform, such as brushing lightly with a small brush or cleaning with a knife. In special cases it may be of value to pose the men for their activities to illustrate the original function of the room and its features. In an ancient kitchen a man might be placed carrying firewood toward the oven, another posed with a pitcher near the well. It is obvious that such reconstruction should only be undertaken under supervision of the field director and at his wish.

Subjects of this nature usually present fewer lighting problems than objects in their natural original position. An excavated room or other architectural detail can usually be left until the time of day when the light is most favorable. In the desert the contrast between light and shad-

Detail of the God of the Nile on the Façade of the Great Temple, Abu Simbel, Egypt. The strong sidelighting accentuates the important detail in this relief sculpture made over 3000 years ago. (Photo: Laurenza, coutesy of UNESCO)

ow is violent. This fact can sometimes be used to advantage, but as a rule it means loss of essential details. If the photographer is not favored with one of the rare cloudy days, he will have to be up just before sunrise or wait till just after sunset when light is fairly even to make his exposure. At those times, however, the intensity of the light changes rapidly; the photographer must work fast and keep his exposure meter handy.

HIGH CAMERA ANGLE

For more extensive views of architecture, the chief need is a high point from which to make the exposure. Too often such a point is lacking and the photographer must think of some artificial means to get the desired view. The easiest way to get elevation is by a movable scaffold, usually shaped as a large wooden tripod. This tripod is built to combine lightness with maximum strength. It should be wide enough at the base to reach comfortably from wall to wall of an average ancient room, yet light enough so that three men can set it up at any point of the excavation. At the top of the tripod is a movable head on which the camera is fastened, and further down the side a board on which the photographer can stand while he is taking the picture.

A tripod of this type will usually suffice for all ordinary needs as regards elevation. It will not, however, give anything approaching a bird's-eye view of the complete excavated area.

From an airplane the maze of details which an excavation constitutes from the ground miraculously becomes a clear picture of streets, squares, and houses. At times it is even possible to see the complete plan of houses that have not yet

Above: *As the excavations progress photographs are made to keep original records for later reference. This burial mound was opened in the Chaco Canyon, New Mexico.* (Photo: American Museum of Natural History)

Below: *Close-up details are important in archeological objects found in the diggings. This black frog figure with turquoise inlay came from Pueblo Bonito in New Mexico.* (Photo: American Museum of Natural History)

Probably cliff-dwelling Indians made these petroglyphs in the Rocky Mountains near Vernal, Utah. (Photo: N.J. Parino, courtesy of Cities Service Company)

been excavated because difference in color will make the walls stand out. Aerial photos help the archeologist by giving him a preview of the plan which his architect will later draw up, by showing him promising buildings not yet attacked, and by giving the general lines of the ancient town with which he works.

The well-financed expedition will usually have a private plane for this work; even more useful is a helicopter which can hover over a given area while pictures are being taken. Many smaller expeditions, unfortunately, cannot afford a private plane, or the cost of carrying the load of fuel and supplies it requires.

STUDIO WORK

The amount of work in the field is largely dictated by the immediate needs of the excavation. A single lucky day may produce a cache of hundreds of objects to be photographed; at other times weeks may go by with hardly any new objects with which to deal.

One such lull comes after the preliminary dig pictures have been taken at the opening of the campaign and before the excavation gets going in full swing. This lull may last anywhere from a few days to a few weeks and should be used by the photographer for experimenting with his film and developer. In the Near East, for example, the light is highly deceptive and must be studied closely before satisfactory results can be obtained.

Another matter that will need the photographer's attention is getting the studio ready to receive the objects when they begin to come in. The photographer should design and supervise the making of unobtrusive stands suitable for photographing the large numbers of pots which come by the hundreds in most excavations. Such stands are usually made of wood and painted white. For small objects a low table with glass top over white background is a necessity. Objects placed on this glass plate will not cast disturbing shadows.

The most important fixture of the studio is the studio camera itself and almost as important as a good camera, is a sturdy and practical stand for it. Since most of the excavated objects have to be photographed directly from above, it is therefore essential that the camera stand have an adjustable top and be capable of moving in a vertical direction. Lighting arrangements will depend on the circumstances. If electric light is available one or two strong studio lamps will prove of great advantage; otherwise flash-lamps or one or two portable, battery-operated strobes will suffice.

The objects that will pass through the studio will be many and varied. Less important objects can often be grouped and photographed as a unit, while important objects may call for many exposures from different angles and under different lighting.

Photographing groups and photographing individual objects naturally present different problems. In arranging a group of small objects such as pendants or amulets, the difference in color usually constitutes the chief difficulty. This difficulty can, however, be fairly easily overcome by placing the objects of lighter color together and then during part of the exposure holding a piece of dull-black cardboard between them and the lens of the camera.

Mosaic panel in a small peristyle court at Ptolemais, Libya, Tolmeita. (Photo: Courtesy Oriental Institute, University of Chicago)

In photographing objects of special importance, the basic consideration to keep in mind is that excavation photography is, first of all, a means of recording. The photographer must therefore aim for sharp and detailed rendering of his subject. But that does not always end his responsibilities. The object may be a piece of art in its own right. As such it has a certain esthetic value. In addition to standard views, the photographer will have to study the object carefully and decide on lighting and angles which will bring out most clearly and vigorously the esthetic merits of the piece. This more artistic lighting will depend, of course, on the size, shape, texture, and use of the piece.

SEALS, CLAY TABLETS, AND INSCRIPTIONS

In all excavations there will be certain types of objects that call for special treatment. Two such types, seals and clay tablets, common in excavations in the Near East, will be mentioned here.

Several thousand years ago the inhabitants of Mesopotamia used to seal documents with stamp seals or with small engraved cylinders of shell or stone. These seals were pressed into or rolled over the wet

Detail of a small gypsum vessel found with a cache of votive objects in the Temple of Inanna, Iraq, Nippur. (Photo: Oriental Institute, University of Chicago)

clay of the tablets on which they wrote their contracts, leases, and other documents. At times these seals have the name of the owner engraved on them; more often, however, they merely show decorative designs with flowers, animals, and human beings as chief elements. It can readily be understood that seals are important witnesses to ancient culture and must be carefully recorded.

Relatively easy to deal with are the stamp seals. They merely have to be pressed down on a slab of plasticine to give a satisfactory impression. More difficult are the cylinder seals. To obtain a really sharp impression showing every detail, the seal must first be thoroughly cleaned and then be rolled over a perfectly smooth slab of plasti-

cine that has been rubbed with talcum powder to prevent the plasticine from adhering to the seal. After a satisfactory impression has been made, superfluous plasticine should be cut away. It is well to leave a narrow strip along top and bottom to set the impression off.

The richest source of information about ancient civilization is naturally the inscription. In Mesopotamia most writing was done on small rectangular clay tablets. The signs were impressed in the clay when it was still wet by means of a wedge-shaped stylus. The photographer's task is to get the shadows in all the wedge-shaped impressions which make up the signs to stand out against the highlights.

The tablets are often dark brown, even black, and the thousands of

years which have passed over them have often left their mark in disturbing discolorations. It is therefore worthwhile to mention a method used in the Oriental Institute of the University of Chicago to overcome this difficulty. Vapors of heated ammonium chloride are blown onto the tablet from a glass tube. This gives the tablet a thin, perfectly even white coating which can easily be brushed off when the tablet has been photographed.

DARKROOM PROBLEMS

The problems which confront the photographer in the darkroom are chiefly lack of electric light, scarcity and impurity of the water at his

Famous ruins of the old Inca fortress town called Machupicchu, Peru. (United Nations Photo)

disposal, and difficulties in keeping the developer at the right temperature.

To manage without electric light is not as difficult as it may seem at first. Darkroom lamps in which an old-fashioned oil lamp takes the place of the electric bulb can still be found on occasion, and if the photographer objects to the oil lamp, a strong flashlight can be substituted for it. For printing, daylight can be used. The simplest way is to have a window with dark curtains behind which the photographer simply slips a frame containing the film and paper. Another method is by burning magnesium ribbon. A strip of magnesium ribbon held on a skewer is lighted at some distance from the frame containing film and paper. The photographer can regulate the amount of light by varying the size of the strips and their distance from the frame. This process has the advantage over ordinary contact printing in that thin areas of a negative can be shaded during part of the exposure.

Another source of difficulty is the water. At the excavation at Tell Asmar all our water had to be brought from a muddy irrigation canal 12 miles away. However carefully filtered, this water always contained large quantities of the very fine clay which forms Mesopotamia's soil. This clay was deposited on both negatives and prints and had to be removed by means of a piece of chamois leather which had first been soaked in water and afterwards squeezed dry.

At places where water is scarce it is obviously important not to waste it. However, it would be bad economy not to clear the prints of all the hypo. Under such circumstances the photographer should make frequent use of the easy potassium-permanganate test. Water from one of the prints is allowed to drip into a weak (pink) solution of potassium permanganate. If the color changes, hypo is still present and the washing has to be continued.

During hot weather it may be extremely difficult to keep the temperature of the developer suffi-

Forecourt of the great Temple of Amon, Karnak, Egypt. This structure, which is nearly one quarter of a mile long, was nearly 2000 years in the course of building, starting about 2000 B.C. This shows the importance of photographing the general view for reference. (Photo: Oriental Institute, University of Chicago)

ciently low. The photographer can use only the cool morning hours for developing and must take his water from the earthenware water-coolers used for drinking water in all warm climates. Even so the temperature of his developer will often be above that recommended for his film in which case he will have to cut down on the time of developing.

Also the other extreme, cold weather, may cause trouble. Contrary to common belief the temperature often drops to freezing and below in the Near East and since most houses are unheated and poorly insulated, the temperature in the darkroom becomes correspondingly low. It is therefore necessary to begin tray developing by heating the tray so that it will not cool off the developer. If the day is very cold, it is advisable to place the tray containing the developer inside a larger tray containing water a few degrees warmer than the temperature desired for the developer.

INFRARED PHOTOGRAPHY

No account of archeological photography would be complete without at least a mention of infrared photography. We are still far from the point where it can be said that this type of photography has been thoroughly tried out in archeological work. The few experiments which

have been made are, however, most promising. Infrared photographs of ancient Egyptian wall paintings have shown details invisible to the eye; writing given up as lost has become readable. In coming years this new field in archeological photography will undoubtedly be further developed. Clearly archeology cannot afford to ignore the exceptional possibilities which it offers.

THE SMALL CAMERA

The 35 mm and the 2¼ × 2¼ cameras have fundamentally changed the archeologist's conception of field photography. In addition to the few carefully prepared publication photographs that are usually taken, the small cameras are responsible for taking numerous pictures throughout the digging day, pictures of architectural details, graves, men at work, and objects which continuous excavating quickly removes.

In the field, the valuable attributes of small camera photography are found to be fundamentally three: economy, compact size, and speed in use.

Economy is the first and most natural reason for the change from the admitted extreme of an 8 × 10 view camera to the 35 mm instrument. Negative costs and other darkroom expenses are, of course, reduced.

Buhen, Sudan. Earlier excavations of the western fortifications of the fortress showing bastions, arrow slits, ramparts, and the inner ditch. (Photo: Keating, Courtesy of UNESCO)

The advantage of compact size begins with the ability to ship a complete developing-and-printing outfit in one relatively small box with the paper, films, and chemicals for an entire season in another. Space saving continues into camp where the work area needed for bulky tanks and quantities of chemicals gives way to a convenient minimum. Even a changing bag is sufficient to load film and process negatives. And finally this space economy ends with the inch-thick book-like file wherein thousands of easily accessible negatives repose.

Speed in use is perhaps an odd-sounding advantage in archeological research, but it has a triple significance. First, it helps immeasurably during that short period each day after sunset and before dark when even lighting and lack of action

provides the ideal set-up for many necessary pictures. Even with a tripod the ease of handling a small camera at least triples the number of exposures possible in this limited available time—work previously done with a large and cumbersome view camera.

The second value of speed in use is the action picture. Workmen in the Near East are most curious and interested. Though they may not be able to take a photograph, they are susceptible to the technique of the photographer and will stop any labor to stare into a lens. The small camera has made possible many a picture before this rapt and photo-killing interest was aroused.

Finally, the small camera permits the dig photos to be made by a staff member working personally with the essential subject matter.

In the change to the 35 mm negative, print quality has suffered little if any. It is true that the 8 × 10 negative and contact print

contain more detail than the 35 mm negative, but the newer fine-grain films have redressed the balance to a considerable extent. In addition, the lenses of the smaller camera are usually superior to all but the very best used on larger cameras. When published, it is difficult to distinguish a picture taken with a large camera from one made with the miniature, especially when the degrading effect of the halftone screen is taken into account.

One of the greatest advantages of the 35 mm camera is the greatly reduced loss of color film. Using the color negative films, it is possible to make color transparencies, color slides, color prints, and black-and-white prints, all from the same negative. Where maximum detail is desired in the black-and-white print, it is probably better still to use a fine-grain black-and-white film, but for many purposes the black-and-white print from a color negative is altogether satisfactory.

PHOTOGRAPHY AND THE ARCHEOLOGIST

Part II: PHOTOGRAPHIC EQUIPMENT AND TECHNIQUES IN ARCHEOLOGICAL PHOTOGRAPHY

CHARLES F. NIMS
Photographer and Archeologist, Egyptian Headquarters, The Oriental Institute of the University of Chicago, Luxor, Egypt

[The proper choice of equipment for archeological photography and the practical techniques for work under field conditions are thoroughly discussed in this section. Advice is also given on development procedures away from home base.]

THE TASK OF THE ARCHEOLOGIST is to discover, record, and interpret the remains of human effort in earlier times, and to communicate his results. In this, photography has become an indispensable aid.

A large expedition, or one where photographic recording is the chief aim, often has a professional photographer and sometimes a photographic laboratory. Smaller expeditions may select the photographer at random; photography will only be one of several duties. In the field he usually operates with a minimum of equipment and in primitive conditions unforeseen by most writers of photographic handbooks.

Though the major part of my work has been in Egypt, where the Epigraphic Survey of the University of Chicago's Oriental Institute is recording the graphic representations in temples and tombs, it has also included photography on expeditions about the southeastern end of the Mediterranean. In Luxor we have adequate equipment and a good darkroom, but in other places work has been carried on with few

such conveniences available. Some of the lessons learned through experience, often by trial and error, may be of help to those who find themselves in similar circumstances.

The photographer who has had little experience in the more technical aspects of photography should have at hand a book which makes clear the basic principles of the photographic process. These principles include the nature of the camera as a scientific instrument, the properties of films and printing papers, their exposure and development, and the basic accessories needed for adequate results. As far as possible this article will assume such knowledge.

EQUIPMENT

Almost every kind of camera can and has been used in archeology. My personal experience has been with a 35 mm camera, a twin-lens reflex, and press and view cameras from $2\frac{1}{4} \times 3\frac{1}{4}$ to 8×10. No one camera can serve every purpose, and each photographer has his favorites. The demands of archeological photography make it advisable to have a camera which uses interchangeable lenses, with which photographs of the scale of 1:1 can be

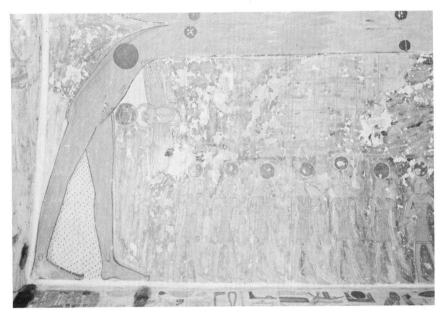

Top: Photograph taken without a filter of a mural in a temple at Luxor, Egypt. Bottom: The same mural as shown above, but taken with a G (yellow) filter. (Photo: Charles Nims / The Epigraphic Survey, The Oriental Institute, University of Chicago)

taken. It should have both range-finder and groundglass focusing, and vertical and lateral movements of the lens board. The larger the film size the less evident will be slight scratches and dust marks, as the diameter of the necessary en-largement will be decreased.

These requirements fairly well limit the choice to press cameras, of which the usual sizes now marketed are 2¼ × 3¼ and 4 × 5. The smaller can use 120 roll film with full format. The larger will take a Polaroid-film holder, and this feature makes it a better choice. If the camera is never to be hand-held, then a view camera will serve.

The 35 mm camera is in such general use that several members of the expedition may have their own. The single-lens reflex, or camera with reflex attachment, can be use-

Sharp detail is important in making record pictures. (Photo: Charles Nims / The Oriental Institute, University of Chicago)

View of the Monastery of St. Catherine, Mt. Sinai, Egypt. One of the best remaining examples of late-Roman 6th-century military architecture. Photographed with the Sinar view camera. (Photo: Fred Anderegg / Kelsey Museum, The University of Michigan)

ful in the photography of small objects. One maker has recently introduced a 35 mm lens which can be moved off center in any direction up to 11 mm. Experience may show that this lens will make the single-lens reflex camera almost as useful in archeology as the press camera. Whatever camera is employed, a wide-angle lens is a necessity, for very often pictures must be taken in a cramped space.

If a new camera is obtained, the instruction booklet accompanying it should be read carefully. All movable parts should be tested. If any are stiff, they must not be forced; the camera should be returned to the dealer for further instruction. With a press camera, check the focus on the groundglass and with the rangefinder to make sure they both show the same results.

Where the expedition already has photographic equipment, the photographer must take the same precautions in learning its operation.

He must also make certain that it is in good working order. Dust from the field or long storage on a shelf will tend to make the shutter slow or inoperative. It is wise to have all old equipment examined by a competent repair man and put in full working order. All too often cameras taken to the field have failed because such precautions were not observed.

On excavation, dust is always present and the camera should always be protected. It should be kept in the case and never laid on the ground. Nor should it be left to the windward of the digging, either on the tripod or in the case. It should be dusted regularly, using a soft brush for the lens and a stiffer one for other parts. Never rub the lens with a cloth. If brushing is not sufficient use lens cleaner and lens tissue according to instructions. In a dry climate, electrostatic attraction makes it difficult to eliminate dust from the lens.

Anti-static brushes are available. Some workers have had good success by using instead a large feather, alternately brushing it across a silk cloth.

Check the camera each day for loose screws; a set of jeweler's screwdrivers will be useful in tightening them. Never take apart any section of the camera unless you have had training in camera repair.

SPECIAL ACCESSORIES

There are several small accessories which will prove useful. A small bubble-level will indicate when the camera is straight horizontally and vertically. A picture where the horizon is on a slant, or with vertical lines converging, is very annoying.

A four-power magnifying glass will help in getting a sharp focus on the groundglass, especially when the photographer wears glasses. It is wise to check the composition of the picture on the groundglass wherever possible. Where there is vertical or lateral movement of the lens, this is a necessity. The rangefinder does not operate on extreme close-up pictures, nor when the drop bed of the press camera is used.

The back of the camera may sometimes have to be too close to a wall or other object to see the groundglass from behind. Here a small hand mirror will be of assistance. It is also useful when setting the aperture and shutter speed, when the camera is in such a position that one cannot get in front of it easily, as when on a high tripod, or at the edge of a cliff or excavation.

Though press cameras have hoods to keep the direct light of the groundglass back, a black cloth is often needed and it must be used with a view camera. It should be large enough to cover the camera and the head and shoulders of the photographer.

TRIPODS

The tripod should be sturdy enough to hold the camera steady in a brisk wind. A reversible elevator post helps to get the camera in the exact position needed, particularly in object photography. The head should be capable of being tilted to a position 90 degrees from the horizontal. The reversible center post will be useful when photographing with the camera in a low position or when doing overhead photography. Here the photographer must usually lie on his back to view the proper focus and composition. There is one tripod of this sort which can be extended, with center post elevated, to eight feet. With such a metal tripod it is important to keep the sliding parts free from dust and fine sand. The latter can burr the metal making it impossible to use the tripod without damage until the burrs are completely smoothed off.

FLASH

If flash equipment is to be used, there should be an extension cable of ten feet or longer. Photoflash lamps are bulky, but more practical than an electronic flash unless extensive use is expected. In many places the only batteries available are D-cells; any others needed should be brought along. If an electronic flash is used in a place where there is no electric current, it must either be charged from a car battery, in which case a special cable is needed, or adaptable for use with the easily available D-cells. Charging

Left: Over-all shot of the mosaic and altar in the Monastery of St. Catherine. A remarkable picture coverage made with the 21mm Super Angulon lens on a 35 mm camera. The monk in foreground was only three feet away and the mosaic on the ceiling 50 feet high. (Photo: Fred Anderegg). Below: Full view of the same mosaic after cleaning.

from lighting-line current is not as simple as it is at home. Foreign plugs are different from ours; their power may be anything from 110 to 220 or 250 volts and the current may be a-c, 50- or 60-cycle, or it may be d-c. Plugging a battery charger into the wrong power may either not work at all or blow the instrument to bits.

A special aluminum scaffold was used to obtain close-up views of the mosaic medallions.

CHANGING BAGS

Another necessity is a changing bag. On the field it acts as a small portable darkroom. If a film is torn or jammed in the camera, it can be

removed without loss of the film already exposed. Sheet-film holders can be loaded and unloaded in it. In it, too, roll film can be loaded onto the reel of a light-tight developing tank, and the tank closed before bringing it into the light. On many archeological expeditions such a changing bag has been the only darkroom I have used.

The archeological photograph is strictly a record picture. It must show, as clearly as possible, the details of the subject. Since any picture may be needed for publication, each should be of good contrast and resolution with care taken in the composition.

Lighting

As soon as the photographer is on site he must study the effect of the sun at various times of day and plan his photographs for optimum lighting. In most instances the sun at the back of the camera should be avoided; this also applies to heavy shadows cast by the sun at an oblique angle. When photographing low walls, backlighting is often very effective. In areas where the sunlight does not fall on the subject properly, the light reflected from white clouds will sometimes serve to fill in the shadows and give better relief.

On-site work is often done in closed covered areas, or places where there is not direct light from the sun. If the area to be photographed can be closed off from most extraneous light, light can be brought into the scene by mirrors and directed on the area to be photographed by a reflector. The reflector should be swung back and forth, painting the wall with light.

For small areas flash can be used. If there is relief, the angle of the light must be somewhat oblique. In such cases the distance to be divided into the guide number is measured from the subject to the flash and not from the subject to the camera. Often such sidelighting needs an additional half stop or more exposure. Both the angle and the exposure can best be determined by experiment.

On flat unvarnished surfaces the

Close-up of the head of Christ showing the geometric pattern of the tesserae, so typical of Byzantine art. Photographed using the Sinar view camera on scaffold. (Photo: Fred Anderegg)

picture can be made with the flash set on the camera, but even in these cases the textures of the subject is retained better by having the light coming from an angle. When the flash is held some distance behind the camera, the illumination will be more even.

Multiple flashes can be used with the shutter set at "Time." This method has been used frequently in lighting larger areas where a wide-angle lens and small diaphragm opening were necessary. An electronic flash, if so used, will substitute for flood-lighting equipment if there is no movement in the subject.

Excellent illumination can also be obtained from a kerosene pressure lamp. (Gasoline lamps are not recommended, as the necessary un-

Site of the Inanna Temple excavated to the Protoliterate period. Iraq: Nippur.
(Photo: The Oriental Institute, University of Chicago)

leaded fuel is not available in many places.) In one tomb a large painted wall was photographed with kerosene illumination. Having set up the camera and opened the shutter, the photographer, with a black cloth fastened to the arm nearest the camera, walked slowly along the wall, lifting and lowering the lamp to get even illumination. The cloth kept the shadow of the photographer and the direct light of the lamp from the lens. Though a slow process, the results were superior to those obtained with flash. Light from a pressure lamp is quite yellow, and requires longer exposure than a meter reading would indicate; it cannot be used with color film.

PROPER IDENTIFICATION

Each photograph, when taken, must be recorded in the photographer's notebook, giving subject, location, compass direction, date, hour, and exposure data. The manner of locating any given point depends on the methods used by the director. It may be a room number, grid co-ordinate, or, especially for large structures, a general description. Where there is stratification,

the particular stratum must be recorded. As soon as possible, these field notes should be transferred to a permanent record. This will also give the identifying negative number which is written on the border of the negative in india ink, and also recorded on the back of the eventual print.

The photographer must check to see that the area photographed is clean, free from rubbish with all footprints obliterated. He should have the cooperation of the excavator in assuring that any object to be photographed in situ is easily identifiable, with all details visible. A scale, usually marked in centimeters, should be placed so that no part of the subject is obscured, but close enough to give information as to its size. Several scales should be on hand; a usable series is five centimeters, ten centimeters, or 25 centimeters, divided into one-centimeter sections up to ten centimeters and into five-centimeter sections for the remaining distance, and a one-meter wooden measure, two to three centimeters wide, marked in ten-centimeter sections alternately black and white. This scale should be prepared at the home base; the

smaller ones can be made by the expedition's draftsman on white posterboard.

In photographing large areas of the excavation, the choice of whether or not to include workmen is partly a matter of preference and partly of subject. In many instances people will add the photograph if they are doing their assigned task without obscuring the subject to be photographed. A certain amount of judicious direction will be required to keep them from going stiff and looking at the camera.

In photographing large areas of wall covered with relief, it is necessary that the negative be exactly parallel to the wall. Where the final print is to be used for publication, the meter scale can be placed below the scene and carefully leveled. Sometimes plumb lines are dropped at each side, and the camera adjusted until all lines show straight on the groundglass. The lines then can be removed before the photograph is taken. At other times the angle of the wall can be measured with an inclinometer, and the camera set at the same angle.

Where the photograph is to be used as the basis for a drawing, the verticals and horizontals are drawn with chalk at the edges of the area with the help of a carpenter's level. These lines are washed off later so as not to deface the monument. A grid, carefully ruled on the groundglass, serves as a guide to positioning the camera relative to the lines on the wall. Such ruled groundglass is available commercially in some sizes.

FILTERS

There should be on hand a set of filters; the minimum set includes K-2 (yellow), G (orange), A (red), and C-5 (blue). The first three will darken the clear sky, lighten colors the same as the filters, and give better rendition to yellowish or reddish soil or sand. The last will give the panchromatic film almost the same qualities as color-blind commercial film, darkening the yellows and reds. When photographing painted surfaces, a filter is frequently needed to give contrast.

Present panchromatic films tend

to render different light colors the same tone of gray. In the Tombs of the Kings at Luxor there are astronomical ceilings with light-yellow figures against a light-blue background. Here, an orange filter was used to darken the blue so that the resulting contrast made the figures visible on the negative. In some instances a second photograph made with a blue filter was needed to bring out certain details. Often a filter will help to bring out the painted design on pottery.

PHOTOGRAPHING OBJECTS

The photography of objects is an exacting task. Where there are several specimens of one type, group

Fred Anderegg uses a 35 mm camera for photographing inscriptions on 6th-century beams under the church roof with George Forsyth, Director of the Kelsey Museum, University of Michigan.

pictures may be taken. The arrangement should be symmetrical as far as other considerations will allow. For light objects the photographic dark cloth will make a good background. One authority on early botanical remains mounts his specimens, especially grains, on a mesh of fine black thread over a black-lined pill box.

A large black-lined box is an excellent backdrop for larger objects. It must be deep enough so that the back receives no direct light and large enough that the objects being photographed, when viewed on the groundglass, will be within its area.

A white cloth sheet or matte paper serves well as a background for dark objects. The same material may be used to cover the stand on which the objects are placed. The background should be far enough

distant so that no shadow falls on it.

Small objects may be laid on a sheet of groundglass supported at the corners, with white paper some distance below. The glass should be so positioned before a door or window that no direct sunlight will fall upon it. The amount of shadow can be controlled somewhat by the height of the light opening above the groundglass. When such things as coins, medals, or seals are being photographed, be sure that the light falls from the upper left. Do not turn the object upside down to make focusing easier; the resulting reversal of light and shadow will make raised detail appear sunk and vice versa. This is an error that is often committed by inexperienced photographers.

The illumination of statuary and

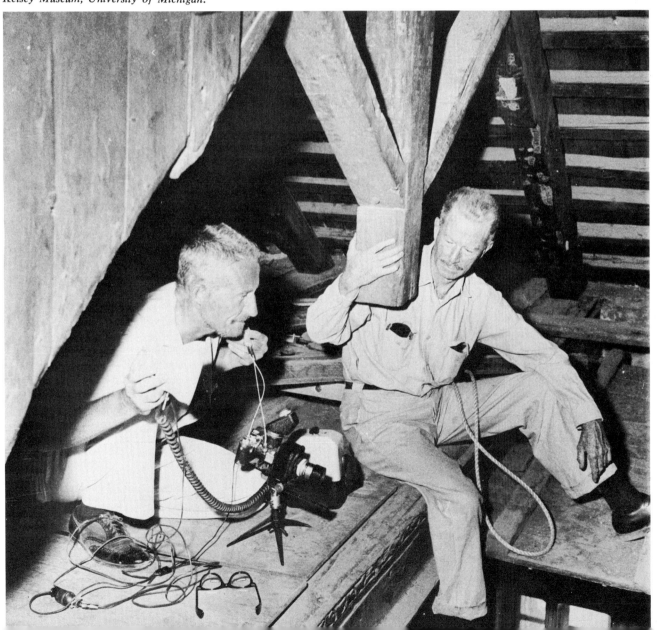

other large objects requires patience and ingenuity. In the sun, a reflector will help to lighten the shadows. Within a room, working with the light entering through doors or windows, a softer effect may be obtained. One must experiment with reflectors and baffles to get the optimum illumination.

PHOTOGRAPHY IN THE FIELD

It is of the greatest importance to make photographic records of all stages of the excavation and of all objects. The very process of excavation destroys the evidence of stratification, walls, and the position of objects. It may be that better photographs of various objects can be made in the studio but this is no reason to neglect photography in the field. The photographs thus obtained will be a great help in recalling details when the final report is written. A good photograph will often tell more than a page of printed description.

Most film comes with recommendations for exposure and development. These should be followed without modification until experience shows that a change is advisable. For low light intensities it is advisable to use a meter at all times.

Different makes of meters will give different readings under identical conditions. One should depend on the readings of one, changing the recommended exposure rating only when necessary, after examination of the results.

DEVELOPMENT IN THE FIELD

Equipment and Supplies

Ready-mixed formulas are preferred to those requiring mixing from bulk chemicals. Dry chemicals transport more easily than liquid. Plastic storage bottles not only eliminate the problem of breakage, but can be squeezed to keep air from the solutions and eliminate oxidization. All other equipment should be unbreakable if possible.

Developing equipment will vary with the situation. Roll film and 35 mm film will be developed in tanks, and it is as easy to develop two rolls at a time as one. Air-tight, stainless-steel tanks can be completely immersed in water for temperature control, and can be turned over and rotated for agitation. Many plastic tanks and reels will shatter when dropped.

Procedure

Where sheet film is used, tray development is the most convenient.

A stick about 3/8-inches square placed under the middle of the tray makes agitation simple. Developing should be done in complete darkness, with the time based on a time-temperature chart. After the film has been in the stop bath for a minute or two, with agitation, lights can be turned on. Fixing time should not be more than twice the time to clear.

With such fine-grain developers as Microdol and D-76, the replenisher should be added in the recommended amount to the developer solution before the developer just used is poured back from the tank. All excess should be discarded, and deficiencies made up from fresh developer. With this replenishing, 30 rolls of 36-exposure 35 mm film can be developed per quart of developer and replenisher with no change in developing time.

A widely used developer for sheet film, DK-50, will process about 56 sheets of 4×5-inch film, with an increase of ten percent in time for each seven sheets developed. However, in tray development the solution should be discarded after each period of use even though the exhaustion point has not been reached. The stock developer will keep much better if mixed double strength, one gallon of developing formula to only two quarts of water, and then diluted to working strength as needed.

When the time to clear film in the fixing bath reaches five minutes at 68 F, it should be discarded. A good test of fixer exhaustion is a drop or two of four-percent potassium-iodide solution in the fixing bath; if a milky precipitate forms, the bath should be discarded. However, a test should first be made of the water; if much organic matter is dissolved in it, the same reaction may occur and thus cannot be used as a test.

In making prints, exposure should be such that full development takes place within the recom-

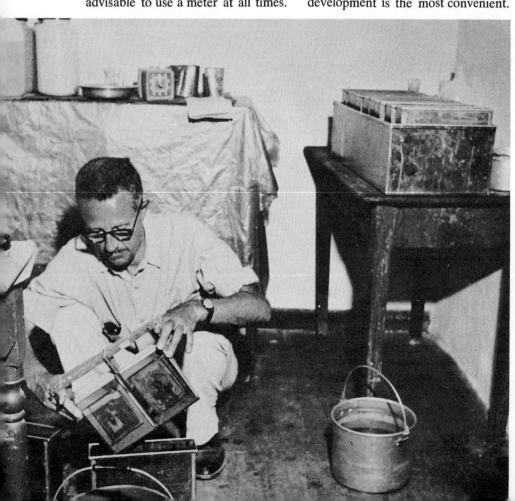

Processing 5×7 Ektachrome without running water at the Monastery of St. Catherine, shows the real problems that must be overcome for some types of archeological field work.

mended time. When proper development is reached, the process comes almost to a standstill for 15 seconds or more. Further development will occur after a longer time, but stains may result. After a drain of a few seconds the print should be placed in a fresh stop bath for about a minute and then in a tray of running water. When about ten prints have accumulated, they should be placed in a fixing bath with constant agitation, about four minutes for contact papers and three minutes for projection papers. Discard the fixing bath as soon as the test shows exhaustion. Do not fix film and prints in the same bath.

*Water Supply and
Temperature Control*

Water supply and temperature control are frequently serious problems in the field. Where water is not available in ample amounts through the tap, film can be washed in six to eight changes of water, giving five minutes of constant agitation to each change. Brackish or salt water can be used for all but the last two changes. A failure to wash sufficiently can be the cause of the ultimate deterioration of the film. A final 30-second bath in a two-percent Photoflo solution, or a few pinches of a detergent such as Dreft helps in even drying. Too much wetting agent may leave streaks on the negative, especially with roll film.

In cold weather it is easy to heat the developer by immersion of tray or tank in warmer water; the solution must be raised to the desired temperature before developing begins. In hot weather it is much more difficult to cool solutions; usually ice will not be available. Often developing must be done at dawn, the coolest part of the day. Water stored in a tank on a roof may get very hot during the day, and its use must be avoided. The porous water jars used in the Near East, placed in the shade, will cool the water considerably, especially if there is a breeze. They also serve as excellent filters for muddy water.

In tray development the addition of 100 grams (three ounces) of sodium sulfate per liter (quart) of

such a developer as DK-50 keeps the sheets of film from sticking together when first put in the tray, which may happen at temperatures of over 70 F. Each sheet should be put in separately and kept moving as the next one is introduced. With this solution one can develop up to a temperature of 110 F. Time of development is 50 percent longer than indicated for normal development on a time-temperature chart. The curve can be extended for high temperatures. Above 80 F, the developed film should be placed in a stop-hardening bath of 30 grams (one ounce) potassium chrome alum and 100 grams (three ounces) sodium sulfate per liter (quart) of water for four to five minutes, with constant agitation for the first minute.

Polaroid Film

A darkroom will be unnecessary when using Polaroid 55 P/N film, which gives both print and negative in 20 seconds. The negative requires the minimum of additional processing, which is done in full light.

Polaroid film is very valuable to archeological photography. In excavation, when a group of objects is found in one spot, a record must be made of their position before they are moved. It has been the practice for the excavator to make a sketch showing the position of the objects with each piece numbered for identification. Now that a print is immediately available, it can be pasted in the excavator's field notebook, with lines leading to identifying numbers at the side. (The surface of a Polaroid print will take either pencil or ink.)

Color Films

Developing color films is best left to professional laboratories. In countries where exposed film cannot be mailed to a foreign address, it can be kept under refrigeration in a tightly sealed plastic bag. If the humidity is low when the film is refrigerated, no harm will ensue. Unexposed color film should also be kept refrigerated. If must be brought to outside temperature before exposure.

Sometimes emergency situations require the development of color

film on the spot. For the best results development should be at the recommended temperature, but I have developed color film at temperatures from 62 to 75 F. More recently, the processing kits for both color films have been changed to work at higher recommended temperature. All Kodak Ektachrome and Ektacolor kits are now designed to work at 75 F, and Anscochrome can now be normally processed at 80 F. Even in the tropics or the desert, it should not be too difficult to maintain these temperatures in solutions for the short time needed for processing. Incidentally, the higher temperatures shorten the entire processing time of color films considerably.

Twice I have found it necessary to test-develop color film to determine correct exposure by flashlamp. Once was in the Syrian desert with the air temperature over 100 F. The solutions were cooled in water from a deep well at 72 F, and a second exposure made, once by sunlight and once by pressure lantern. In Egyptian Nubia, the developing was done at dawn, second exposure by sunlight, and for lack of any other water supply for washing, the reel was hung on a string in the Nile. While the resulting transparencies were somewhat dirt-streaked, they gave the information desired.

It is wise to bracket exposures of color film for important subjects. This is especially necessary if the conditions are unusual, and if the resulting transparency is to be used for publication.

Color photography will be used for pictures shown in lectures about the excavation. Whether still or movie, these must be carefully planned to give the best possible story to the general public. Since many expeditions are made possible only through public support, this part of the archeologist's work is very important. For movie work a 16 mm camera should be used; 8 mm will not usually give pictures of the quality necessary for exhibition to a large audience. Furthermore, satisfactory duplicates cannot be made from 8 mm, nor can it be enlarged to 35 mm for theatrical showing.

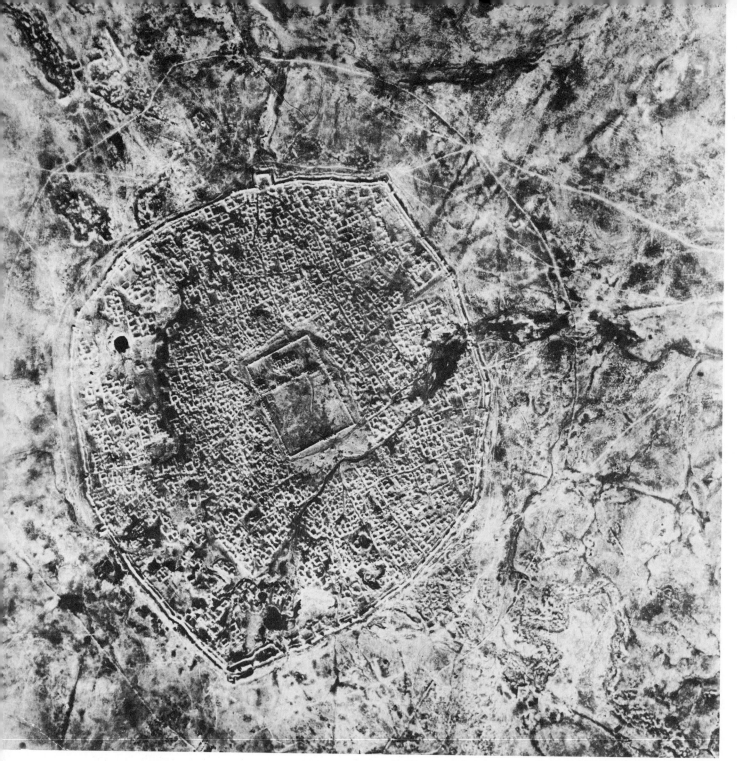

An aerial photo reveals the complete area of the now deserted Iraqi city of Hatra which flourished early in the Christian Era. (Photo: Aerofilms, London)

PHOTOGRAPHY AND THE ARCHEOLOGIST

Part III: PHOTOGRAPHY FROM THE AIR IN ARCHEOLOGICAL EXPLORATION

DAVID LINTON
Photographer, Writer
[This section provides a broad basis for understanding the importance of aerial photography when used in conjunction with archeological exploration.]
• *Also see: Aerial Photography.*

TWENTIETH-CENTURY SCIENCE HAS added a number of significant new tools to the archeologist's arsenal. Among them are electronic devices that can detect underground cavities, techniques for dating substances by the decay of radioactive isotopes, and vastly improved equipment for working under water. The most important new tool, however, is aerial photography. It has added hundreds of sites to the list of known or suspected finds and greatly increased our information about others. It has cut years from the time needed to investigate some sites. Because of aerial photography there is now a large "backlog" of sites waiting to be investigated when funds and personnel are available.

Aerial photography is important not only in the discovery of new sites, but also in mapping and studying known ones. It can show an ancient settlement in its total context, with fortifications, roads, water supply, and field systems—in short, as close as we can come to seeing it as a functioning entity. It can even help the scientist decide where *not* to look on the ground, by eliminating terrain that was unsuitable for habitation by a particular people or at a particular time.

A military expert was recently asked how much information a skilled photointerpreter could extract from a reconnaissance photo taken from an altitude of 40,000 feet. "Well," he replied, "we can tell whether a household uses a rotary-type lawn mower and whether it has a telephone and an underground septic tank." In archeology we might add that under the most favorable conditions the same interpreter could detect analagous details a thousand years after the household had been destroyed.

PATTERNS OF LIFE

Man's traces last for incredibly long periods because building alters the fertility of the land and sometimes its shape as well. The distinctive pattern of man's work makes it stand out from its natural surroundings when seen in aerial pho-

tographs. Straight lines and right angles usually mean human construction. Sometimes the dimensions and method of construction identify the builders. The Romans, for example, had rigidly prescribed sizes for roads and fields. Traces of their work can still be seen all over the once-Roman world, contrasting with the irregular artifacts of less-disciplined peoples. Similarly, the Mayas built elevated highways in Yucatan and although these roads have been completely overgrown by jungle, the trees growing on them are taller

X-ray phenomena in aerial photography. A lost city in Iran, invisible and unsuspected from the ground, appears in a tracery of foundations and wall vestiges in this aerial photograph. (Photo: Courtesy Oriental Institute, University of Chicago)

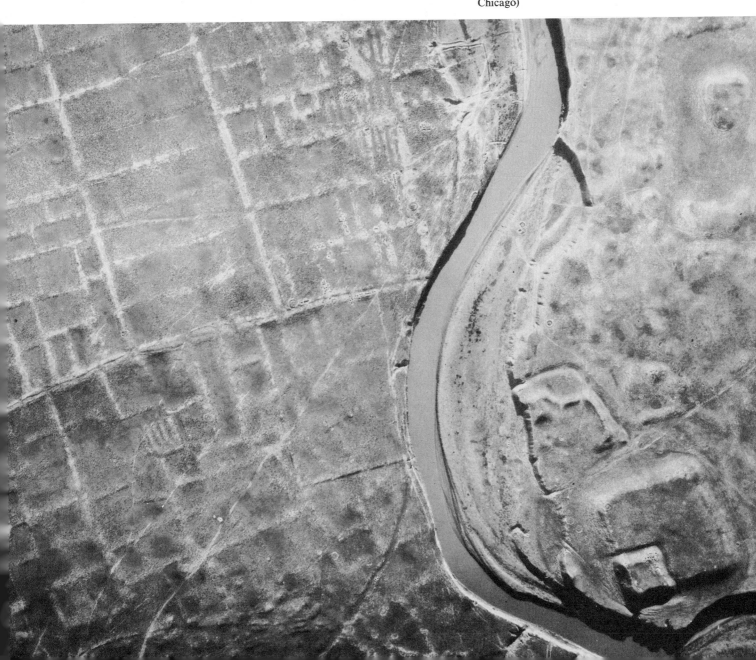

than their neighbors. The roads can thus be easily traced in aerial photos.

Such relief marks are easier to see, of course, where there are no plants to obscure them. In the dry Middle East, the sites of ancient cities are marked by mounds, and ancient field systems by their pattern of irrigation ditches. In some desert sites there is a rare kind of reserve relief; the irrigation ditches are now higher than the surrounding fields because the compacted and hardened earth in them remained while the wind eroded the softer ploughed fields.

Relief traces, obviously, do not show up well when the sun is directly overhead. They can be seen best when lighted from a low angle, and sometimes only at one time of

Aerial photographs revealed the large concentric earthworks of this early (400 B.C.) mound at Poverty Point, Louisiana. This site was obscured by cultivation on the ground and was thought to be a natural formation until its true nature was detected from this aerial photograph. (Photo: Mississippi River Commission, U.S. Army Corps of Engineers)

Ancient earthworks and building sites, Little Sodbury, Gloucester, England. The low-angle lighting helps to emphasize the lines in this oblique aerial photograph. (Photo: Aerofilms, London)

the year. In lands that are occasionally flooded, relief marks may appear when a few inches of water cover the lower parts of the landscape, leaving the higher parts dry. The same effect can occur when a light snow is followed by sufficient wind to blow the snow of the higher parts and drift it into the depressions.

Other kinds of traces may persist long after the ground has been leveled—for example, where stone walls have been used to separate fields or retain terraces. The walls may have been gone for centuries, but the stones are usually still in the soil and erosion will reveal their straight lines.

PLANT MARKS

Construction that has been not only leveled but buried as well may still show its traces in the form of plant marks. Plant marks are the most frequent and most important source of archeological information to appear in aerial photographs. They result from the differential effects of ancient construction on the fertility of the soil. Negative plant marks are seen where man has made the soil less fertile; positive ones where he has made it more so.

Traces of all these types may go

completely unnoticed for centuries; they are so big that their pattern cannot be perceived from ground level. The slight variations in color and height of plants that make up most plant marks are almost never detected at close range, but they may be obvious when seen from the greater distance and more comprehensive point-of-view of the aerial camera.

Negative plant marks are seen where buried pavements, stone walls, or foundations interfere with the roots of plants growing above them. Such marks are most likely

Even when the land is plowed over, the early Roman road in the center can be traced from the air. (Photo: Aerofilms, London)

to appear in a dry year, when water is scarce at the surface and plant roots have to go deeper to get it. A complete "map" of the Roman town of Caistor in Norfolk, England, turned up in the form of plant marks in an RAF photograph taken in 1929. Hundreds of Etruscan stone tombs in Italy have been located by similar plant marks.

Positive plant marks appear above ancient ditches, farmyards, and watercourses where the land has been made more fertile. Often the mere turning over of the subsoil is enough to create a channel for underground moisture that will make marks lasting for centuries. The ditches that surrounded neolithic settlements in Europe are still

recognizable in the form of plant marks for this reason.

Occasionally plant marks are produced by chemical changes in the soil. Ancient-settlement sites are rich in phosphates because of the high proportion of organic matter, and phosphates are good fertilizer. Sometimes the lime from the mortar of ancient stone walls will neutralize an acid soil, producing a more fertile spot. In places where there is no vegetation, or where it has been ploughed under, ancient construction may appear in the form of soil marks—differences in the color of the soil due to moisture, chemical content, or concentrations of stone.

Aerial photography can even be

helpful in locating sites that are now under water. Because water is so much less transparent than air, only those sites lying in shallow water, 50 feet deep or less, can be recorded effectively, but this is a valuable contribution because coastlines have sunk in many parts of the world so that former seaports are now submerged. The Roman resort of Baiae, near modern Naples, has been mapped from the air although it is now under 30 feet of water. Aerial photography has also helped in the study of the pirate stronghold of Port Royal near Kingston, Jamaica.

After a suspected site has been spotted in an aerial photo, a painstaking field investigation is necessary to establish its origin and importance. Aerial photography can help in this phase too, by providing plans and measurements, by relating various parts of a site to each other, and by recording outlying details that might otherwise go unnoticed.

OBLIQUE AND VERTICAL PHOTOS

Aerial photographs are divided into two types—oblique and vertical. Obliques are those taken at an angle to the ground and are most useful for reconnaissance and studying details of a known site. Vertical photos are taken straight down and are used for making maps.

Few scientific institutions have the resources to undertake aerial photography of their own, but extensive files of verticals already exist. More than half of the earth's land surface has been photographed at least once and many areas, obviously, have been photographed repeatedly. Most of these photographs have never been examined by an archeologist and no one knows how much might be added to our knowledge of early peoples if they were. We do know that one of the most important finds in the United States, the huge Indian mound at Poverty Point, Louisiana was made by Dr. James A. Ford of the American Museum of Natural History through a systematic study of aerial photographs from the files of the Missis-

Celtic field system in England is revealed from the air. The dark lines are due to subsoil having been turned over for ditches; the light lines are the old ridges. The present field has been leveled off for cultivation. (Photo: Aerofilms, London)

sippi River Commission.

Government mapping and geological agencies are the prime sources of air photos, but state highway departments, oil companies, lumber and power companies, and flood-control and soil-conservation agencies all have extensive libraries of them. Most of the photos in these libraries are verticals. They are made by special cameras that make exposures at regular intervals as the plane flies along. The views overlap so that there are always at least two pictures of every spot on the ground. Using this overlap,

These stony burial mounds were discovered by soil marks in the aerial photo and aided in excavation of the site of ancient Gordion in Turkey. (Photo: University Museum, Philadelphia)

the map maker measures vertical distances in much the same way that we see in three dimensions by using two eyes.

The scientists looking for archeological traces can see these verticals in three dimensions by looking at them through a simple stereoscope, not very different from the one grandfather had in his parlor. The relief is exaggerated because the distance between the successive positions of the plane is much greater than the distance between a person's eyes. This exaggeration is often helpful in bringing out relief marks.

Vertical photographs derive much of their usefulness from the ground control used with them—that is, the system for relating the picture to known points on the ground. It usually requires surveying parties

on the ground and complex computations in the laboratory. Scientists would, therefore, be best advised to rely on existing verticals for which the ground-control work has already been done.

Obliques are useful for a closer study of a known or suspected site, and the scientist can profitably make them himself. They are by far the most pleasing sort of aerial photos to look at and can be most informative if taken from the right angle at the right time. They can be made successfully with any type of camera and from almost any aircraft. In most places it is possible to drive out to a local airfield and to hire a small plane to fly over nearby country. Longer sorties can be arranged with air-taxi services or bush pilots.

RICHARD V. LUSBY / *Neon Wilderness*

RICHARD GROSS / *A Day to Remember*

HORN / GRINER / *A Foggy Day*

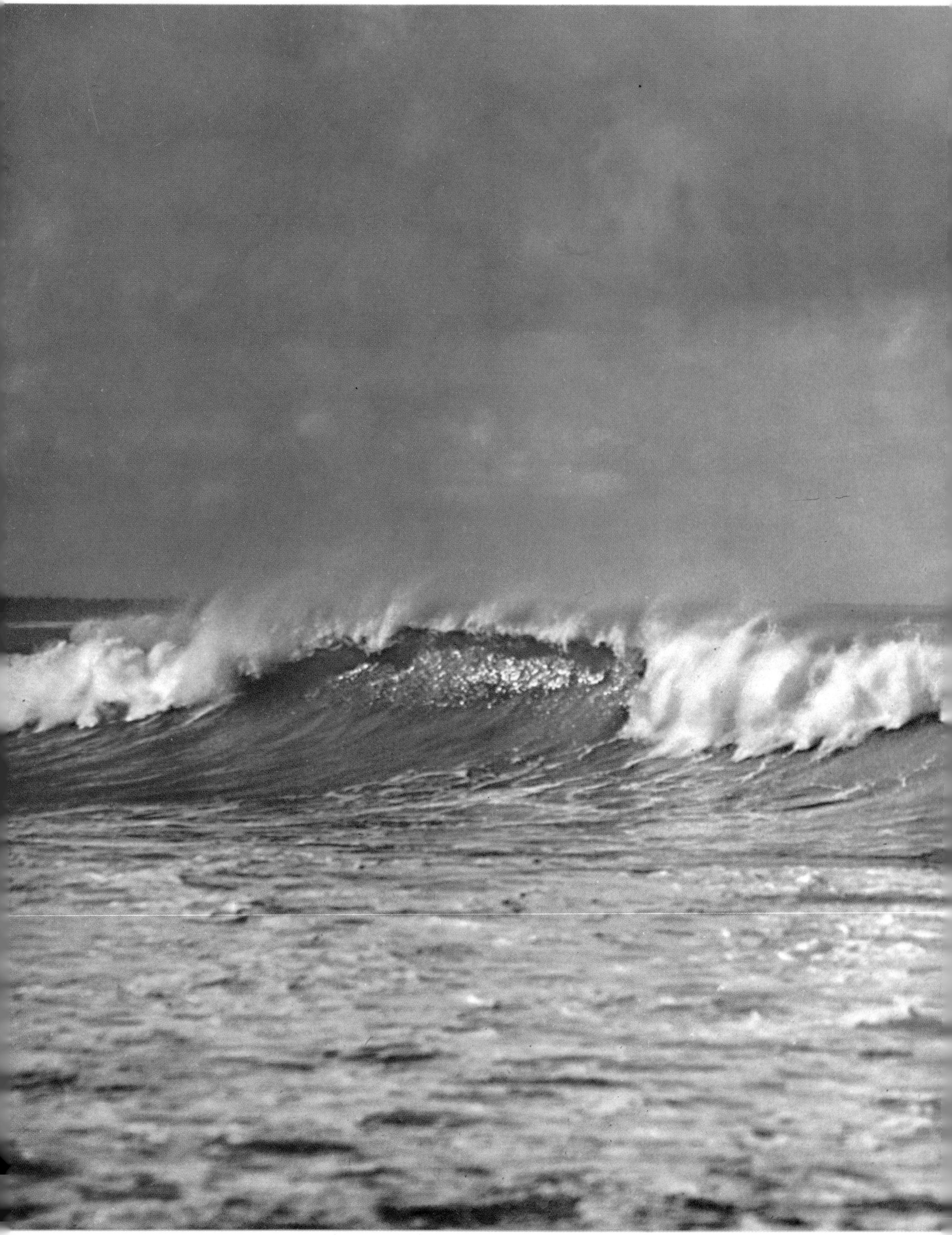

PHOTOGRAPHY AND THE SMALL CAMERA

PETER STACKPOLE
Former Staff Photographer,
Life *Magazine*

[The author has pioneered the small-camera field from the early days of the Model-A Leica. In this article he covers some of the history as well as the present trends in 35 mm photography.]
All photographs by the author, courtesy *Life,* copyright Time, Inc.
• *Also see: Reflex Cameras, Subminiature Cameras.*

TO WRITE PROPERLY ABOUT THE many changes and improvements I have witnessed during the 34 years in which I have became intimately acquainted with the 35 mm camera would require several volumes. Merely recording the highlights of technical achievements in this field during those many years would read like the story of the automobile or the airplane. Yet, in spite of the tremendous improvements in photographic tools, it's entirely possible for a competent photographer today to use a 1928 Model A Leica with the original Elmar lens and produce, under favorable light conditions, as fine a photograph as he might take under the same conditions with the most expensive and modern equipment available.

The most modern equipment, however, has, first of all, eliminated most of the guesswork; secondly, it has enabled the photographer to work under almost any light condition. Finally, the multitude of longer-range lenses, portable electronic-flash equipment, automatic-sequence and remote-control attachments, ultra-wide-angle lenses, and a host of other valuable aids make possible almost any type of photograph.

PROGRESS OF 35 MM PHOTOGRAPHY

During the mid-30's and early 40's, a small handful of us were rather self-consciously endeavoring to achieve technical standards to match the quality we admired in larger camera work. We were enthusiastic die-hards when it came to showing the world a different kind of photography—a kind that could only be achieved with the small camera.

Aside from the earlier recogni-

tion by a few magazine editors of the merits of "candid photography" during the mid-30's, there was little enthusiasm for such pictures in the nation's newpapers, in advertising, or among the professionals who were well-established with their larger cameras. But little by little the concept of reporting with the camera took hold. Dr. Ehrich Solomon had shown the way in German magazines years before the possibilities of a photojournalistic approach to photography were accepted in this country. Starting in 1936 with the emergence of *Life* magazine, which was soon joined by other picture magazines, the boom in 35 mm photography was on.

GERMAN AND JAPANESE CAMERAS

For a 10-year period, including several war years, German-made 35 mm equipment, which was often hard to find, had almost completely dominated the 35 mm market. It wasn't until shortly after the war that we became aware of the Japanese products, much of which closely resembled the leading German types. Shortly after V-J Day, Japanese equipment began to show original improvements and new features instead of being mere copies of other equipment. In a surprisingly short time, the quality of the Japanese product became well known among photographers.

Thanks to this keen competition between the Germans and the Japanese, the photographer enjoyed all the advantages that fine high-precision equipment could provide. Films improved equally as fast as the equipment, as did developing formulas and techniques. With all these improvements, the photojournalist was able to broaden his scope as never before, giving the picture magazines a new vitality. While I

Left: Ensenada yacht race. A good example of action and the use of a Leica with a 35mm wide-angle lens. The photographer had to hang on to something solid and at the same time operate the camera.

Right: A 1000mm long-focus lens on the Praktina camera produced this close-up shot of General MacArthur during an address at the Waldorf Hotel in New York.

never think of equipment as being anything more than necessary tools which would become meaningless without a photographer's imagination, creative ability, and experience, it is certain that new and improved equipment can often make the hitherto impossible or difficult picture a reality.

SINGLE-LENS REFLEX

It was 1950 before anyone began to realize that there could possibly be any great additional improvement to the 35 mm camera. The lenses were fast, film could be shift-

ed quickly, cameras were synchronized for flash and strobe, and viewfinders were getting bigger. Our longest lens was 135mm—because this was the longest lens that would still operate with the rangefinder, What more could one want?

However, a different type of 35 mm camera began to be seen in camera stores, although only a few of us gave it much thought. It was an East German product called the Contax S. It didn't seem to look very strong, a string worked the mirror, and it appeared rather expensive for what it was.

The price went down, however, when the Contax S was soon followed by the Pentacon, the Hexicon, the Consul, and many other similar single-lens reflex models.

We began to experiment with these, seeing immediately that they were fine for portraits and longerlens work, but we hesitated to use them on rugged assignments where reliability counts. The introduction of the Praktina, with its finer lenses, greater solidity, and better features started a sure trend towards the single-lens reflex, a trend even more firmly fixed by such cameras as the Pentax and the Nikon F. The limitations of the rangefinder camera gradually became apparent, with the result that the single-lens reflex is now the dominant camera

The small camera, and high-speed lenses, and available-light techniques have brought a new look to stage and floor-show coverage. Shown is a scene from "Pal Joey."

system on the market today.

The present boom in the popularity of the single-lens reflex may have been sparked by the professionals who quickly recognized the merits of this new system. But there is no doubt that the photographic neophyte who discovered he could view through the lens and get pictures exactly as he saw them caused the single-lens reflex concept to skyrocket to its present popularity.

With the single-lens reflex, the photographer can first regulate the *f*-stop and see whether a long depth of field with universal sharpness is preferable to a short depth of field allowing distant and closer objects to be out of focus. With rangefinder cameras, this can be no more than a guess as depth of field cannot be seen visually. The shutter speed in the single-lens reflex is determined after selecting the proper *f*-stop. Of course, when proper action-stopping is of prime

Ketch Ticonderoga in Bermuda race. Only a 28mm wide-angle lens could cover this scene at such close quarters.

importance, then the *f*-stop is the second consideration.

LENSES

Assuming one owns a Nikon F and several of the 23 lenses to be had for such a camera (including zoom lenses), there is practically nothing visible that can't be photographed. Wide-angle lenses, such as the 21mm and the 28mm, may save the day when working in close quarters. The 21mm is so short it can't operate with the reflex system, but with such depth of field, guess focus is adequate. With the 28mm, accurate focus on the groundglass is aided by a split-image finder. It's often difficult to see focus changes in lenses so short that the image always looks sharp. Here again, the focus scale becomes

a double check, but few focusing errors can be made with these lenses except when working with the lens wide open.

The range from 35mm to 1000mm brings out the real joys of the single-lens reflex because one sees the changes in focus more definitely in this band. Many of us prefer a clear groundglass without the split-image feature, especially when using longer lenses—say from 200mm to 1000mm. In this range the split-image system tends to go black when stopping down, disrupting proper viewing. Even in doing portraits with an 85mm or 105mm lens on other reflex cameras, I prefer a clear groundglass so that no area interferes with the entire viewing.

Now that easier handling of lenses longer than 135mm is possible on the single-lens reflex, "How long a lens can one hand hold?" is a question frequently asked. I'd say 300mm with ease, using $1/200$ of a second or faster. 400mm is possible using $1/500$, but is awkward to hold. I've used a 500mm handheld, aided by a Kenyon Gyro Stabilizer, a device with two high-speed flywheels which tends to remove unsteadiness in hand-held photography. Here holding up the total weight was the worst problem.

Owning 23 lenses for one camera might sound like a high price to pay for achieving versatility. One solution to this problem, of course, is the zoom lens, which is showing steady improvement. Already a simple and compact zoom lens for the Nikon F, with a range from 43mm to 86mm, is able to cover the most often used focal lengths in 35 mm photography, thus eliminating several fixed lenses. Another range from 85mm to 200mm takes care of the next most useful range and eliminates still more fixed lenses. The zoom

Left: *Public gatherings would be difficult to cover without the variety of focal lengths available in the 35 mm format. The 1952 Republican convention in Chicago is seen in this 300mm-lens close-up of the New York delegation.*

Right: *Cold Cat. The 35 mm camera is handy for quick action when the unexpected picture turns up.*

lens and the motor drive for rapid sequence are an unbeatable combination in sports photography.

LIGHTING

Since the $f/2$ or faster lenses are standard "normal" lenses on most new cameras today and films are faster than ever before, with wide latitude and reasonably fine grain, the available-light photographer is everywhere. This is as it should be. Most attempts to substitute or augment lighting tend to rob the picture of realism—either the lighting isn't believable, or the fuss in arranging it tends to make the subject self-conscious.

In doing portraits outdoors, back-lighting is usually best because it enables the subject to keep his eyes open without squinting. Small folding reflectors with dull-silver leaf can be used to give slight fill without throwing off the balance between shadow and highlight. Most attempts to fill the shadow with flash in outdoor portraiture give an

unnatural effect, but achieve a picture that satisfies the average taste.

In news photography there have been many instances when the better pictures were made with available light, while most of the photographers present used flash on camera. Sometimes, however, the opposite is true when lighting conditions and movement didn't allow the available-light man to function properly. In such conditions I recommend portable electronic flash held on a short extension at arm's length over the camera; this eliminates shadows and tends to substitute for room lighting, particularly when used as a bounce light. Bounce light, however, is effective only in smaller rooms. Flash on camera directed at the subject is the poorest of all lighting techniques.

ALTERNATIVES TO 35 MM

In these 34 years of close association with the many changes and trends in 35 mm photography, I've never held the belief that all photography should be done with the 35. The improvements in larger equipment may not have been as spectacular, but the frequency with which one finds subject matter more suited to larger cameras never ends.

I own 4 × 5 equipment and would use it more often, except that I've found a way to do it with 2¼ × 3¼ equipment and see little difference in the final results. For pictures in which perspective correction is needed, I find the Plaubel Paco Jr., a view camera with roll-film back, a compact and valuable instrument.

The selection of 120 films for black-and-white and color is great, and no loading of holders is required. Enlargements from 2¼ × 3¼ to 11 × 14 approximate the results obtained with a 4 × 5 negative. When ultra-wide-angle pictures are needed, I find the Veriwide camera helpful. For full-page cover portraits in color, I use the Hasselblad 1000 F with 180mm lens. I'm well aware that just as fine a

Precarious action scenes require fast camera work and a series of pictures in rapid sucession with the 35 mm camera.

reproduction could be made with a 35 mm single-lens reflex, but it's easier to sell a picture to an editor if he sees it in a larger size.

THE FUTURE OF 35 MM

In venturing a prediction of improvements to come I'd say that most of them will be in 120-format equipment. Already great strides have been made in shutter design with each lens having its own Compur-type shutter. This eliminates the problem of synchronizing electronic flash at higher shutter speeds, which cannot be done with focal-plane shutters. Holding 2¼ × 2¼ cameras steady for the slower focal-plane shutter speeds was never easy, but now the built-into-the-lens mechanical shutters will eliminate this problem. There is much room for more 2¼ × 2¼ cameras having penta-prisms, and I look for more activity in the 70 mm size.

In the 35 mm field we'll see a built-in exposure-meter system which measures the actual amount of light entering the lens when pointed at the intended subject. There will be further automation in the medium-priced cameras, but I doubt that the professional will accept complete automation on top-priced cameras in place of semi-automatic selective setting of his cameras. There will be further improvements in zoom lenses, with some increase in larger f-stops. There will be more rapid-wind motorized equipment available.

I question whether we'll ever see my "dream camera"—a single-lens reflex using 35 mm film without sprocket holes, which make use of this freed area so that the more usable proportion of 4 to 5 is framed on the film. Most lenses on present 35 mm equipment would cover the extra area and the only problem would be in proper film metering. The camera need be only a little larger. Undoubtedly it is a film-marketing problem that prevents this camera from being built.

Finally, we'll see a "foolproof" all-purpose film in which almost any exposure is a good one—and this will surely prove to many that any fool can take a picture.

PHOTOJOURNALISM

ARTHUR GOLDSMITH
Editor, Famous Photographers School Westport, Conn.
[This article discusses the status of contemporary photojournalism against the broad background of its early history. Current photojournalistic techniques are explained and appraised by a widely experienced editor-author who is intimately acquainted with the problems—and promises—of the field.]
• *Also see: Available Light; Magnum Photos, Inc.; Photography and the Small Camera.*

A PHOTOJOURNALIST IS ONE WHO reports with a camera. He may be a staff photographer for a small-town newspaper, the representative of a giant picture magazine, or a free lancer on assignment for an educational book publisher. His job is to communicate, using pictures rather than words—to relate the facts, and perhaps to comment on them. He and his camera are eye-witnesses to events that will be shared with other people at other times. If he is a good craftsman as well as an honest and accurate reporter, he will try to organize his images so they are clear, vivid, and interesting. But above all, like any responsible journalist, he must seek to tell the truth as he sees it.

A photojournalist is a photographer, but he is also a member of a complex team, including picture editors, art directors, layout men, caption writers, and graphic arts technicians. The end product towards which he works is not just a photographic print but a reproduction of that print on the printed page. Without publication, means of reproduction, and an audience, there is no such thing as photojournalism.

In terms of media, there have been two main streams of photojournalism in the few score years it has existed—newspaper photography (often called press photography) and magazine photojournalism. Of the two, magazine photojournalism has generally set the highest standards, been the most imaginative, and has most fully exploited photography's ability to communicate in depth as well as by sheer shock appeal.

The word "photojournalist" sometimes is used only to mean "magazine photographer." However, the distinction is a somewhat artificial one. Many top magazine photographers began their careers on newspapers, and some newspapers have achieved effective and creative picture reporting that rivals the best that magazines have done. In the following survey, we will consider both newspaper and magazine photographers as parts of what is essentially the same tradition.

THE ROOTS OF PHOTOJOURNALISM

Man communicated with pictures long before the invention of writing —at least since Stone Age artists of 10,000 years ago decorated the walls of French caves with animal pictures.

The ancient civilizations of the Middle East produced a visual art that richly documented the times. A wall painting on the tomb of an Egyptian king or a fresco in a Cretan palace may have been executed for ceremonial or decorative reasons, but it can give us today an impression of how people lived then. The artists who created them were not only good craftsmen but also discerning reporters.

Picture reportage designed to inform, amuse, or inflame a large popular audience only became possible with the invention of the printing press. Etchings, lithographs, mezzotints, and other graphic media could be reproduced relatively quickly and cheaply, and many artists turned to these methods of communication. The prototypes of modern photojournalists were men like Hogarth with his caricatures

of 18th-century London, Goya with his nightmarish images of war, and Daumier who ridiculed the failings of contemporary French society with devastating effect.

The invention of photography early in the 19th century provided a powerful new tool for documenting and commenting on people and events, although it would be several decades before the photographer-reporter largely replaced the artist-reporter. Photography in those early days was such a slow process, and required such cumbersome equipment, that it was impractical for "location" coverage of fast-moving events. The artist with his sketch pad had a great advantage over the photographer with his "glass-eyed monster" and baggage train

A guided missile, caught in mid-air, can be seen in clearer detail by a camera than by the unaided human eye. An important aspect of contemporary photojournalism is in reporting on the new technology of the space and atom age. (Courtesy United States Air Force)

of darkroom equipment. Also, once a picture was taken, it had to be made into an engraving by hand before it could be reproduced.

Early Pioneers.

Despite these difficulties, there were men willing to try the impractical: Friedrich Stelzner and Hermann Biow photographed the charred ruins of Hamburg after a devastating fire in 1842; leaders of the abortive Irish rebellion of 1848 were portrayed in jail under sentence of death; the reopening of the Crystal Palace in London in 1854 and the visit to England of France's Napoleon III in 1855 were documented by the camera.

In 1855, Roger Fenton, founder of the Royal Photographic Society, set out to cover the Crimean war with 36 cases of photographic equipment, a stock of 700 glass plates, a wine-merchant's wagon converted into portable living quarters and darkroom, a driver, an assistant, and harnesses for three horses. Contrary to popular belief, Fenton was not, strictly speaking, the first war photographer. According to historian Helmut Gernsheim, that honor belongs to Karl von Szathmari, a Bucharest amateur photographer, who took pictures of the Russian army two years before Fenton photographed the British. However, Fenton is the first to leave a memorable and enduring photographic record of a war.

Fenton carried on, despite frustrating difficulties, until an attack of cholera ultimately sent him back to England. His pictures aroused great interest among a public hungry for first-hand reports from the fighting front. The shortest exposure Fenton could make was three seconds, which ruled out any

The ruins of Richmond, photographed by Mathew B. Brady, are part of the vivid historical report that Brady and his team of cameramen produced during the Civil War. The burnt-out buildings, silhouetted against a blank sky, form a jagged design that suggests the destructiveness of all war. (Courtesy Museum of Modern Art)

instantaneous "snapshot" photography of action. Also, perhaps on instructions from the British government, he avoided showing dead bodies or the shambles after a battle. But his views of Army life in the field are powerful and revealing. The face of war had been portrayed with a realism and detail heretofore impossible with the camera successfully filling its new role as an eyewitness of history.

The potency of photography as a means of communication and persuasion was vividly demonstrated in the United States five years later.

The introduction of roll-film and "snapshot" cameras in the 1880's opened up a new world to photojournalists. This amateur snapshot, taken with a No. 1 Kodak camera, is a charming early example of available-light photography, later to become a vital part of photojournalistic technique. (Courtesy George Eastman House)

Presidential candidate Abraham Lincoln stopped in to have his portrait taken at the New York studio of Mathew Brady on the same day he was to make a speech at Cooper Union. Later, Lincoln commented that the Brady portrait and the Cooper Union speech made him President. Certainly, both helped dispel the impression many people had of Lincoln as an uncouth and ignorant backwoods politician. Finding a suitable "campaign portrait" has been a vital concern to most office-seekers ever since.

When the Civil War broke out, Brady covered it effectively and on a very large scale. Brady organized the first photographic-news syndicate. He invested the then enormous sum of $100,000 to outfit a crew of 20 war photographers, the most famous of them being Alexander Gardiner. The work done by Brady and his cameramen is monumental in scope and magnificent in effect, including portraits of fighting men from privates to generals, the aftermath of bloody battles, intimate scenes of camp life, and shattered Southern cities. This first attempt at a comprehensive photographic coverage on a large scale ended in financial disaster for Brady, but time has vindicated his belief that the pictures would become a national historical treasure.

Striking photojournalistic pictures were made during the 1860's and 1870's—a wrecked German troop train during the Franco-Prussian war, Parisian demonstrators beside a statue they had toppled after the Franch defeat, and crowds milling in the rain at a British election. These pictures had a news value and visual power that would have sent them over the wire or given them a spread in major picture-magazines had these media existed, but at that time, the only means of reproducing them was slow and expensive.

Photojournalism, except in the most rudimentary form, could not exist until the means were devised to reproduce photographs quickly and on a mass scale.

Snapshots and Halftones.

Two major improvements in technology, fast "dry" plates and film, and the halftone engraving process, took photojournalism out of its primitive stage.

With the old wet-collodion process, the photographer had to coat his own plate, expose it, and process it on the spot before the collodion dried. The new "dry" plates, first available in the late 1870's, offered much greater convenience. The photographer could buy the sensitized plates from the manufacturer, shoot his pictures, and then turn them over to someone else for developing at a later date. No longer was it necessary for a roving photographer to bring along his darkroom, as Fenton and Brady had to do.

The new plates were much faster, too. Soon it became possible to make "snapshot" exposures of $1/50$ of a second and less under good lighting conditions. A new dimension was added to photography—

Lewis Hine, an early documentary photographer, continued his work into the Depression. This photograph of an unemployed man, symbolizes the hopelessness and resignation of those troubled years. Contemporary photojournalism has been strongly influenced by the social and economic awareness of Hine and other documentary photographers who used a camera, rather than written words, to report on the problems of their time. (Courtesy George Eastman House)

the ability to catch life in the midst of its flow, to select and capture a thin slice of time, and to record expression or action at its peak of intensity. Out of this was to grow the concept of the "decisive moment," of great importance in future photojournalistic theory and practice.

Methods were found for coating the fast new emulsions on a roll of paper, and than on a flexible base of nitrocellulose. Light, compact, easy-to-operate "hand" cameras utilizing roll film began to appear in great numbers. Although designed to appeal to amateurs, they ultimately would be adapted to the needs of professional photojournalists. Roll film enabled the photographer to take a number of exposures in quick succession, a method essential to the fluid coverage of the modern picture story. However, it required decades of trial and error and imaginative experimenting before these advances could be fully exploited.

Simultaneous with the remarkable advances in picture taking, came a revolutionary improvement in picture reproduction. Before the halftone process was made practical, a photograph had to be drawn

During World War II, much effective photojournalism was done by official armed-services photographers, many of whom had worked for newspapers or magazines before the war. This moving and richly detailed picture makes the viewer an eyewitness to an incident shortly after the Allied invasion of Sicily. It was one of the most widely reprinted photographs of the year. (U.S. Army Photograph)

A classic photojournalistic picture is this shot of the Hindenburg crashing in flames at Lakehurst, New Jersey in 1937. An unforgettable image of one of the decade's most spectacular tragedies. It was taken by AP staff photographer Murray Becker and has been called one of the great news pictures of all time. (Courtesy the Associated Press)

by hand on a block of wood or piece of zinc. Now it became possible to produce an engraving much more quickly by photomechanical means, working directly from the photograph. The key to the process was a "screen" which broke up the continuous tone of the photograph into a pattern of tiny dots, some large, some small. When viewed from normal distance on the newspaper page, the printed dots tended to blend together, thus simulating the continuous tones of the original photograph.

On March 4, 1880, *The New York Daily Graphic* published the first newspaper halftone reproduction, a photograph of "Shanty-

A pioneer in candid, available-light photography was Dr. Erich Salomon. During a visit to the United States, Salomon visited William Randolph Hearst at the publisher's palatial ranch in California, and took this intimate view of Hearst studying dispatches from the editors of his many newspapers. (Courtesy Peter Hunter and Magnum Photos, Inc.)

town," a squatter's camp in New York, by H. J. Newton. This event marked a decisive step forward for photojournalism, but it was many years before the process was widely adapted.

THE AGE OF YELLOW JOURNALISM

The first burgeoning of photographic journalism took place during the closing years of the 19th and the early years of the 20th century. Newspaper publishers in the United States and Great Britain had discovered that there was an avid audience for pictures. Weekly newspapers such as *Frank Leslie's Illustrated Newspaper* and *Harper's Weekly* in the United States and the *Illustrated London News* in England used engravings long before the halftone process was made practical. Then daily newspapers began to run pictures as part of their regular fare, Joseph Pulitzer's *New York World,* and London's *Daily Graphic* being two outstanding pioneers.

By 1900 photographs reproduced by halftone had largely supplanted the woodcut, large newspapers were adding photographers as permanent members of the staff, and the lavish use of pictures was an essential ingredient of the crude, sensational, but vital brand of "yellow journalism" that had come into being. It was an age of ferocious circulation battles between the titans of newspaper publishing, of scoops and glamourous "special correspondents," and sometimes of outright photographic fakery. There was a public reaction against the most flamboyant abuses of newspapers, the faking and the often brutal invasion of privacy to get a picture or story, but for better or worse, a tradition had been set. In the tabloid newspapers and the picture magazines of a later era, the use of sensational pictures to shock, startle, and titillate the

reader would continue to be part of photojournalism.

PHOTOGRAPHY AS ART

Other influences also were at work that would have a profound effect on the thinking and working methods of future generations of photojournalists. There was growing emphasis on photography as a creative medium, a form of art that could express emotion and inner psychological states as well as record surface reality.

Alfred Stieglitz was a germinal figure in this movement. Stieglitz went to Germany in 1881 to study engineering, but took up photography instead. During the remainder of his life he fought for the recognition of photography as an art form in its own right, not merely as a second-rate substitute for painting. He organized the Photo-Secession movement in 1902 to advance photography as a means of creative expression, and published in *Camera Work* (1902 to 1917) the pictures of many skilled and sensitive photographers.

Although Stieglitz was primarily interested in "pictorialism," in photography as a fine art, his influence on photojournalism has been great. Students and followers, such as Edward Steichen, were to find ways to apply his ideas to the practical world of magazine publishing, setting new standards of taste, imagination, and technical competence.

PHOTOGRAPHY AS A SOCIAL AND ECONOMIC DOCUMENT

Still another trend had an important influence on the future growth of photojournalism. This was the work of such documentary photographers as Lewis W. Hine and Jacob A. Riis in the early years of the century, and the Farm Security Administration photographers during the Depression.

The purpose of the documentary photographers was to report and comment on the facts of social economic life they found around them. In spirit, many of them were reformers in the muckraking tradition; by exposing the evils of the day to public view they hoped to abolish them. They often used a direct, sharply focused, realistic style of photography, and the best of their work has great emotional and visual impact.

Hine was a crusading sociologist who turned to the camera so that he could more vividly expose the exploitation of child labor in American factories. His photographs helped arouse public opinion and contributed to the passing of child labor laws. Riis was a newspaper man who, like Hine, chose to use a camera to tell his story with greater realism and conviction than words alone could give. He exposed the "misery and vice" of New York slums in a remarkable series of photographs that are as vivid and moving today as when he first took them.

A gentler, less angry documenter of "things as they are" was the Frenchman, Eugène Atget, who turned to photography in middle age after an undistinguished career as a sailor, actor, and comedian. Atget's pictures of Paris street scenes, markets, window displays, brothels, tradesmen, and crowds are as realistic as they are intensely poetic, while his photographs of San Francisco's Chinatown and the aftermath of the great earthquake and fire are important historical documents. Atget combined human sympathy with a precise eye for visual organization, two qualities that future photojournalists would highly prize.

Hine, Riis, and Atget in their own ways contributed to the birth of a new form, the picture essay or group of related photographs, showing different aspects of a theme or subject. The picture essay is a report in depth, communicating in richer, more searching detail than any single picture could. But there was as yet no published media

The camera was an eyewitness to this moving incident during a bloody uprising at the Puerto Cabello naval base in Venezuela in 1962. Photographer Hector Rondon caught a navy chaplain and parish priest, Monsignor Padilla, as he comforted a dying soldier amid the gunfire of a clash between rebels and government troops. The photograph won the Pulitzer Prizer for 1963. (Courtesy the Associated Press)

Perhaps the most celebrated war photograph ever taken was Joe Rosenthal's shot of U.S. Marines raising the American flag on Iwo Jima during World War II. Its powerful symbolism won it instant acclaim. The picture was awarded the Pulitzer Prize in 1945. (Courtesy the Associated Press)

for presenting their work to the public in appropriate form. In general, photographs were still thought of as units, illustrations you dropped in to spice up the written word.

Documentary photography had its Golden Age during the bitter Depression years in the United States. At that time, Roy E. Stryker, an instructor in economics from Columbia, came to Washington to head up the newly created photographic unit of the Farm Security Administration. Stryker hired, trained, and inspired a group of talented young photographers, including Walker Evans, Dorothea Lange, Russell Lee, Gordon Parks, and Arthur Rothstein, to report on the effects of the Depression. Many of the FSA photographers later became active figures in the

photojournalism of the 40's, 50's and 60's.

As the time went on, the scope of the FSA photography unit increased. Its goal became to do a de-

Left: *Another compelling image of war is this photograph of Korean refugees swarming over the shattered girders of a bridge at Pyongyang. It won the Pulitzer Prize in 1951 for the photographer, Max Desfor.* (Courtesy the Associated Press)

Below: *Sometimes a single, dramatic photojournalistic picture can sum up the essence of a news event. Such was the case with "Leap to Freedom," a shot of an East German border guard jumping over a barbed-wire barricade to West Berlin. The photographer, Peter Leibing, had been tipped off that an East German soldier had signaled to spectators on the West Berlin side of the barrier that he was going to make a break. Leibing waited for an hour and a half until the defecting soldier saw his chance, ran to the barbed wire, and leaped over. The photographer caught the action precisely at its peak, and got one of the most memorable pictures of the Cold War.* (Courtesy the Associated Press)

tailed and comprehensive photographic "portrait" of contemporary U.S. life. Not only the Southern sharecroppers, the dustbowl farms, or the California migrant workers, but also the towns of New England, the cities of the Midwest, and the great urban centers of the East were photographed with precision and sensitivity. No nation in history ever had its "pictures taken" so many times and from so many angles as the United States in the 30's and early 40's. The documentation continued through the war years, then stopped. On file at the Library of Congress are the fruits of this labor, a priceless treasure for future historians.

The work of the documentary photographers gave photography a serious meaning and a stature it did not have before. It was not only a fine art, nor merely a means

for catching a reader's eye with a sensational but ephemeral image. It was a rich and powerful method of communicating. It could reveal and comment on the complex, disturbing problems of contemporary life. It could educate and persuade. This understanding is basic to modern photojournalism.

THE BIRTH OF MODERN PHOTOJOURNALISM

The right techniques, men, media and markets coincided in time to initiate modern photojournalism. This cross-fertilization took place in Europe and the United States in the two decades after World War I.

At the end of the war the public was more picture-conscious than ever before. Amateur photography enjoyed a boom that it had not seen since the early days of the Kodak roll-film camera with its "you push the button and we'll do

the rest" simplicity. Every tourist seemed to carry a camera, and amateurs banded together in clubs, devoting their weekends to photographing picturesque old mills, wagon wheels, winding roads, and models dressed up like beggars.

The reading public was hungry for pictures, too, and was fed by new tabloid-size picture newspapers such as the New York *Daily News*, founded in 1919. News-picture services distributed photographs to all parts of the country, and eventually the world. Sunday "roto" sections, usually printed in sepia ink, and national illustrated Sunday supplements such as *American Weekly* and *This Week* enlarged the flood of printed images.

But something was lacking. The scope of news photography has been increased by the invention of flashbulbs (far safer, more convenient,

The potent symbolic quality of a good photojournalistic picture, its ability to sum up the essence of a time and place in a vivid image, is shown in this photograph by Henri Cartier-Bresson. The one-legged man, stumping through the bomb-scarred streets of Hamburg, Germany, is an eloquent comment on early post World War II Europe. (Courtesy Magnum Photos, Inc.)

and reliable than flash powder), but the quality and content of most news pictures continued at the same deadly level of banality. The news photographer of that day was essentially a "one-shot" man. Under the pressure of deadlines and impelled by a desire to scoop his rivals, he usually had time only to rush to the event, blast away with

This photograph exemplifies Dr. Salomon's genius for gaining entree into the most exalted circles, and in recording people without their being aware of his camera. The time: 1931. The place: a car on a special train en route to a Seven-Power Conference in London. The people, left to right: Philippe Berthelot, General Secretary of the French Foreign Office; Dr. Heinrich Bruening, German chancellor; Camille Hymans, Belgian Foreign Minister; Aristide Briand, French Foreign Minister; Pierre Laval, French Premier, and Frances-Poncet, advisor to Laval. Intimate, behind-the-scenes views like this delighted the public and made Salomon's work much in demand. (Courtesy Peter Hunter and Magnum Photos, Inc.)

Photography has the power to report the news in concrete, human terms. The plight of refugees from Communist China, required to turn back to their homeland by Hong Kong authorities, took on a vivid, personal meaning to millions of viewers who saw this picture of 19-year-old Lee Ying stifling her sobs in a handkerchief. The picture was taken by P.C. Lee shortly after the girl was halted by British soldiers for illegal entry. She and 3000 other refugees were returned to Communist Chinese territory the next day, but this picture stirred up more comment and awareness of the problem than any word report could do. (Courtesy the Associated Press)

flashbulb and camera, and hurry back to the office. Small wonder, then, that so many news pictures were trite, static, and superficial.

A significant break with tradition took place in Weimar, Germany, where photographic activity was at its busiest. Here, Kurt Safranski, manager of a chain of magazines published by Ullstein, began to experiment with fresher, more effective ways to use photographs in the two magazines *Illustrite* and *Die Dame*. Promising photographers were assigned to cover stories in depth, and given the time and resources to accomplish this. They were encouraged to shoot candidly, by available light, for a more spontaneous and dynamic kind of picture. The resulting photographs often were published in groups or in sequence, telling their story with a minimum of accompanying words.

Among the regular contributers to Ullstein was a suave and charming ex-lawyer named Erich Salomon. Able to speak seven languages, and perfectly at ease in white tie and tails, Salomon was an expert at gaining entree to the most intimate meetings and socal gatherings of statesmen, diplomats, and heads of state. Once inside, he used a small camera with a fast lens (early in his career, an Ermanox, which utilized glass plates; later, a Leica, with 35 mm film), enabling him to shoot unobtrusively by available light. His candid, intimate pictures of Europe's top officials delighted the public, giving a vivid sense of being on the scene. They were refreshingly different from the conventional, contrived news picture made by flash, and soon no conference at a European capital was considered complete without the presence of Salomon and his funny little camera.

Another pioneer in these early days of available-light photojournalism was Alfred Eisenstaedt. A

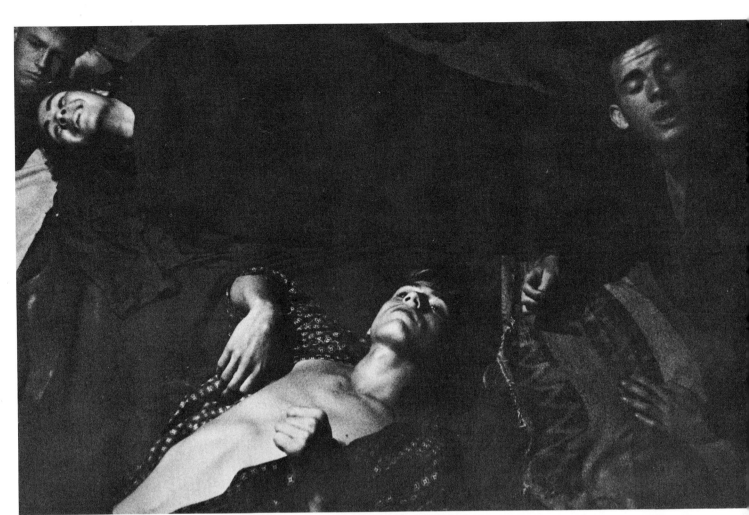

button-and-belt salesman, Eisenstaedt was also an enthusiastic photographer. Impressed by his work, Safranski persuaded him to become a full-time professional photographer. Eisenstaedt who also worked with a small camera and available light combined a strong sense of pictorial design with warm human understanding. A humble little man with great pride in his craft, he was able to establish friendly contact with all manner and stages of men and women. His reputation grew in Germany and Europe until with Hitler's rise to power, he, like so many talented photographers, sought refuge in the United States, there to continue his work with *Life* magazine.

A technical innovation was central to this new brand of photography that was quietly revolutionizing photojournalism. It was the invention of the "miniature"

camera. The word, "photojournalism" had not even been coined when Oskar Barnack, a technician at the E. Leitz optical goods factory in Wetzlar, Germany, built the first 35 mm still camera. His purpose was to construct an instrument that would enable him to run inexpensive exposure tests on small strips of 35 mm motion-picture film. To his surprise, the instrument produced pictures of surprisingly high technical quality.

World War I interrupted further perfection of the device, but development was resumed after the war, and in 1924, at the Leipzig Fair, the first Leica was introduced.

It met with mixed reactions ranging from delight to ridicule, but the "miniature" camera quickly caught on. It was regarded by many as a toy or gadget, a fascinating device for an amateur to play with but scarcely suitable for serious

or professional work. Photographers vied with each other in producing fine-grain blowups of enormous size from the tiny negatives, or in catching often vulgar and pointless candid pictures of people. But a minority of imaginative amateurs and professionals understood the instrument's remarkable potential.

Its small size and light weight gave the photographer great mobility, and its fast lens permitted unobtrusive available-light shooting, even with the relatively slow films then on the market. Its eye-level viewing made it an extension of the photographer's own vision, and its 36-exposure film load and rapidity of operation allowed a fluid,

The two photographs on these pages are taken from Cornell Capa's poignant, tension-packed picture essay on the problems of old age. For this assignment Capa employed small-camera methods that have since become the trademark of realistic interpretive reporting. (Photographs courtesy Magnum Photos, Inc.)

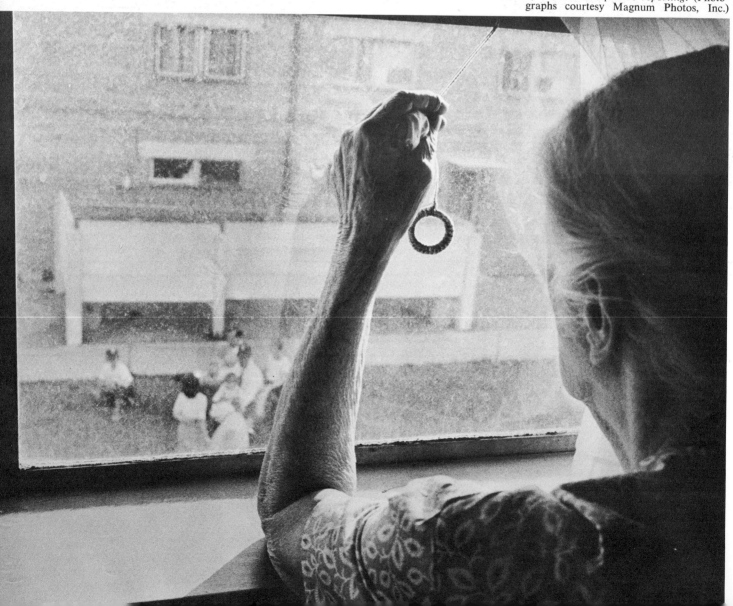

spontaneous kind of shooting akin to motion-picture technique. In skilled hands, it could produce vivid, realistic images plucked from the midst of life. For men such as Salomon and Eisenstaedt it offered exciting possibilities.

Another photographer, a young Frenchman named Henri Cartier-Bresson was also intrigued by the new camera. He began to experiment with it while convalescing from a bout of tropical fever, and found that it opened an electrifying new world of vision. First as an amateur, then on assignment for illustrated magazines, he took precisely composed "snapshots" in Europe and America. Fascinated by photography's ability to slice off an instant of time, he developed an uncanny ability to catch the

precise moment when moving elements in a scene coalesced into a meaningful, well-organized pattern. His work and his philosophy of photography later articulated in *The Decisive Moment* were to have a strong influence on his contemporaries.

THE RISE OF THE GIANT PICTURE MAGAZINES

Life magazine first appeared on the newsstand with an issue dated November 23, 1936. It combined innovations and traditional features, and in some of its early issues looked rather like an enormously bloated Sunday roto section. But it was a smash hit from the start, as through a hectic trial-and-error period its photographers, editors, and layout people gradually began

to evolve a more coherent and effective form.

Never had photographs been used on such a scale, and never had the photographer's role on a publication been given more importance or prestige. The original staff included Alfred Eisenstaedt, Margaret Bourke-White, Thomas McAvoy, and Peter Stackpole; soon other talented photographers were hired as the burgeoning magazine increased the scope of its staff coverage.

The *Life* staff photographer, glamourous, far-traveling, and presumably highly paid, became an archetypical figure in the magazine publishing field. He was often envied, usually respected, and sometimes even resented, but he became the idol of thousands of aspiring

young photojournalists.

At *Life* the techniques experimented with by Safranski in Germany were repeated and refined on a large scale. With the resources of a wealthy and powerful publication behind them, talented photographers were given days, weeks, and even months to carry out their assignments. They were urged to dig deep, to bring back pictures that got beneath the surface of personality or event, pictures that told a story in striking and unexpected images. *Life* staffers and stringers literally covered the world, and as the march of events moved ever closer to war there was no lack of big stories to cover. With all its faults, and the new publication had many, the world had never before been so fully and richly reported by pictures as on its pages.

Close on the heels of *Life* appeared *Look* and a host of lesser imitators. After a period of sensationalism, *Look* found its own highly successful style of photojournalism. Emphasizing the human side of the news, *Look* photographers often worked for warm, intimate close-ups, and a candid "family-album" kind of picture story. Whereas the *Life* photographer utilized a researcher or researchers in a strictly secondary role as assistant, *Look* developed a systems of photographer-writer teams for the production of major stories and essays.

Not only did new and important markets for photography appear,

A single picture can rarely reveal more than a limited aspect of a personality, place, or event. Therefore, the modern photojournalist is less a one-shot man than the typical press photographer of a generation or so ago. He is interested in shooting picture stories or picture essays—a number of related pictures that explore his subject in depth. A lively and penetrating example of this is Burt Glinn's photographic profile of the dynamic entertainer, Sammy Davis, Jr. Glinn's purpose was not just to make a series of interesting pictures of Davis, but also to reveal something about his motives and emotions. The pictures on these and the following pages show some of the facets of "What Makes Sammy Run" that Glinn caught with his camera. Even without captions they are strongly journalistic pictures, communicating and commenting through the visual media alone. (All photographs: Burt Glinn courtesy Magnum Photos, Inc.)

but existing publications became more picture-conscious and began to use photographs more widely. To fill the growing need for good photographs, a new type of photojournalist emerged—the magazine photographer. Whether "on staff" or working as a free lancer, he made his living primarily by shooting and selling pictures to magazines. The opportunity to do creative work, the greater prestige, and the relatively higher pay of magazine photography attracted many newcomers and enticed many of the more ambitious and talented newspaper photographers into the rapidly-growing field.

WORLD WAR II

World War II curtailed the supply of paper and clamped a temporary ceiling on magazine circulation. It was, however, an exciting

time for photojournalists. Sometimes as civilian war correspondents, sometimes as uniformed
members of the armed forces, they
continued their work on a global
scale. Particularly brilliant work
was done by Navy photographers
(many of them former photojournalists) under the direction of ex-
fashion photographer Edward Steichen. It is generally thought that
the single greatest combat photog-

rapher was Robert Capa.

The quantity of photographs
taken dwarfed anything seen before,
and the quality of much of the
coverage was magnificent. The violent panorama of war was documented in all its ramifications from
vertical shots through open bomb-
bay doors to pictures made through
the periscope of a submerged sub-
marine. The camera, as eyewitness
to history, recorded the drama,

heroism, horror, and shambles in
such detail that picture historians
have not yet completed the task
of cataloging the results.

PHOTOJOURNALISM IN THE POST-WAR WORLD

At first, the post-war world was
full of promise for magazine publishers and photojournalists. The
war had stimulated the public's
already hearty appetite for pictures,
and the hunger persisted. There
was a powerful, backed-up demand
for periodicals, and almost every
magazine's circulation began to
soar.

Picture agencies such as Pix and
Black Star were busy supplying
photographs and picture stories
from stock, and in lining up assignments for their teams of free lancers. Robert Capa, Henri Cartier-
Bresson, David Seymour, William
Vandivert, and others formed a new
cooperative-picture agency called
Magnum. Magazines hired new staff
photographers, and the free lance
market supported many ambitious
youngsters as well as established
professionals. New, important picture markets appeared, including
Holiday and *Sports Illustrated*.

But about midway in the 50's,
it became apparent that the magazine business, until then the chief
source of income for most free
lance photojournalists, was in deep
trouble. Caught in a squeeze between rising production costs and
TV competition for advertising dollars, many publications ran in the
red. When *Colliers* and *Woman's
Home Companion* folded, the double
blow had a shattering effect on
morale. It meant not only a loss
of good markets, but a weakening
of confidence in the future of magazine publishing.

McCall's seemed to buck the
trend. Under the dramatic leader-
ship of Herbert Mays, its circulation increased as huge sums were
spent on photography. However,
the magazine tended to use a decorative, "art director's" brand of pictures, and provided little outlet for
photojournalists. Later, *Coronet*
folded and even the huge and vener-
able Curtis Publishing Company
seemed to teeter on the brink of ruin.

However, while some magazines folded, other markets appeared in such specialized publications as *American Heritage, TV Guide,* and special magazines for the fast-growing fields of electronics, space technology, and medicine. Also, a number of publishers went in for picture books in a big way. Many were financial flops, quickly landing on the remainder counters of cut-rate book stores, but some were highly successful. *Life,* for example, launched a vast and very profitable book-publishing division that drew heavily from the photographic files of the magazine, used *Life* staff photographers, and hired outside free lancers.

Industry, public relations, and even advertising favored the photojournalistic approach. The "Family of Man" show, put together by Edward Steichen for the Museum of Modern Art, publicized the work of many fine photojournalists and helped sell picture buyers on the value of candid, journalistic photography. A few corporations, notably Standard Oil of New Jersey, had long used good magazine photographers to report on the human aspect of its world-wide activities. More and more corporations followed this example. So if the magazine photographer found fewer old-timers to buy his work, a number of new and lucrative, doors had opened for him.

The Picture Essay.

During this period, the picture story, a sequence of related pictures with a distinct story line, seemed to languish after a promising start. The history of the picture story has been that of an idea in search of a form. Few photographers or picture editors agree as to precisely what the ingredients of a picture story should be, or how it should be presented. However, three basic forms can be recognized.

The first of these is the picture sequence, a series of related pictures showing the unfolding of an event in time. The subject usually is simple, and the number of pictures might range anywhere from a pair ("before" and "after," cause and effect, and so on) to several.

In its effect, the picture story is similar to a selection of stills taken from a strip of motion-picture film. The picture sequence can be amusing (a baseball fan's cup of beer spilling onto the head of an outfielder, to take one famous example) or charged with drama (the recovery of a manned spaced capsule). However, it is a limited form. Often luck and alertness are more important than the photographer's imagination or understanding in

shooting this kind of picture story.

A second form is found in the complex picture story. In the sense we use the word here, "complex" means complex in comparison to the picture sequence. This type of picture story also extends in time: it must have a beginning, a middle, and an end. But it covers a more complicated type of event, and usually a longer period of time than the simple picture sequence.

Typical of this form are the

"life in a day of" picture stories. The camera follows a subject, a New York career girl, for instance, or a Kentucky coal miner, or a U.N. diplomat, from morning until night. The story might require a layout of several pages. If well done, the picture story gives the viewer a vivid sense of participation, of actually sharing the experiences of the subject. Eugene W. Smith's "Country Doctor" story is an outstanding example of photojournalism in this vein.

Leonard McCombe used this photojournalistic technique to produce a fictional love story. Told through photographs and a minimum of text, *You Are My Love,* provoked considerable comment at the time of its publication (1952), but little further has been attempted with this approach.

A third form is the picture essay, which is a picture report in depth. It differs from both the simple picture sequence and the complex picture story in that it does not follow a sequence in time. The pictures are related, showing different aspects of a common subject or theme. But they do not illustrate the unfolding of an event to a climax or conclusion.

The picture essay is capable of rich, profound, and beautiful expression. Perhaps the most ambitious picture essay by a single photographer to date is Eugene Smith's massive "Pittsburgh Story"—an attempt to portray the psychological landscape of a city as well as its physical features. In expanded form, the picture essay becomes a picture book, for example, *The Europeans,* Henri Cartier-Bresson's brilliant survey of the human condition in post-war Europe.

TRENDS AND TECHNIQUES

The 40's and 50's were years during which photojournalists became more aware of their tradition and more self-conscious about their role. A number of free lancers banded together to form the American Society of Magazine Photographers. Although not restricted exclusively to photojournalists, the Society has always emphasized the needs of this group.

The ASMP set up widely-accepted codes of ethics and payment for the industry, held picture exhibitions, and published members' photographs in picture annuals. Its official magazine, *Infinity,* has sometimes missed its deadlines, but has often been provocative and usually interesting. The ASMP was less effective in its attempt to function as a labor union with collective-bargaining power. The collapse of many major magazine markets rendered this aspect of its work practically meaningless.

Newspaper photography lagged behind the demonstrated potential of picture communication. Exceptional publications such as the *Milwaukee Journal,* the *Denver Post,* and the *Charlotte Observer* used pictures imaginatively. However, far into the 50's, the 4×5 press camera, flash, and the one-shot approach continued to provide a majority of news and feature pictures

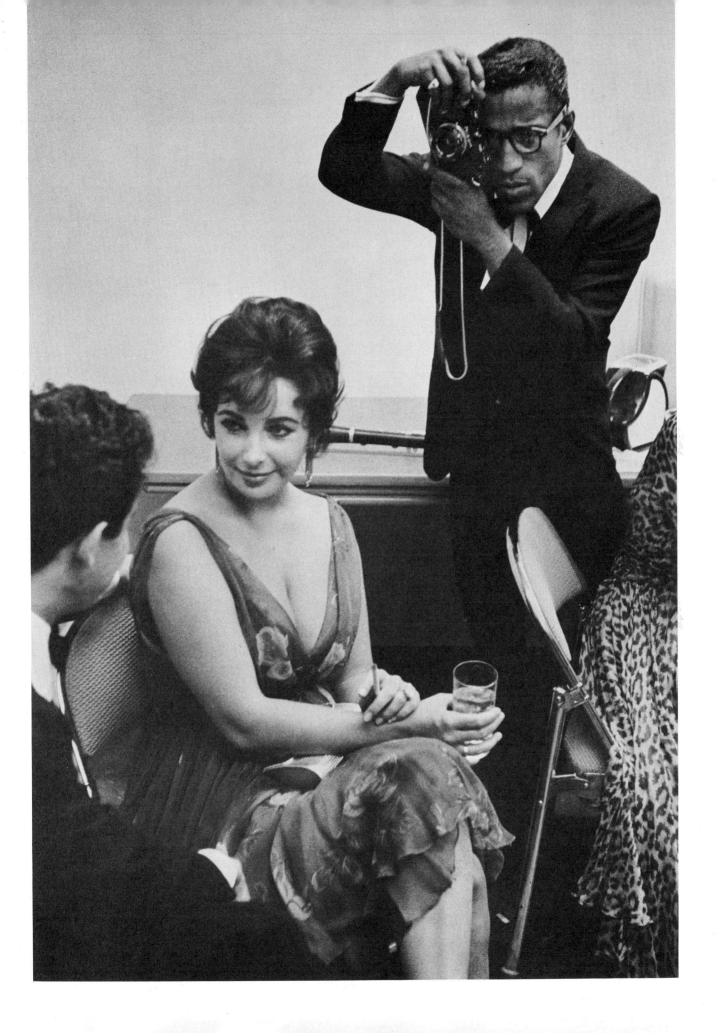

appearing in the daily press and going out over the wire.

Gradually, however, the more fruitful techniques of magazine photographers were adapted as a new generation of newspaper photographers and picture editors began to take over. The threat of TV also stimulated many publishers into a belated appreciation of the importance of good, fresh picture reporting. By the 60's, many photographers on the wire services were using mobile, rapid-firing 35 mm, roll-film, and 70 mm cameras. Staff photographers for a large number of newspapers, small-town as well as metropolitan, were shooting multiple-picture coverages by available light. They were proving that a local basketball game or a city council meeting could be reported with pictures in a more vivid, meaningful, and sincere way than before.

At the beginning of the post-World-War II era, flash was a highly favored technique among many magazine photographers. Tricky multiple-flash effects, razor-sharp pictures, and speedlight's astonishing ability to freeze the most violent motion were highly prized qualities. Despite the work of pioneers in small-camera techniques, few picture editors would risk assigning a man to cover a major story by available light only. The technical results were too uncertain, even if available-light shooting did often bring a realism and spontaneity that could be achieved by no other means.

However, a new generation of devoted, even fanatical, available-light photojournalists was coming along. They insisted on a direct approach, on removing the barriers that separated the person or event from the photographer's response to it. Sometimes the results they got were all "soot-and-chalk," with coarse grain and blurred images. But their work often had a vitality that was missing in the work of more orthodox craftsmen.

Among this new group were Ernst Haas and Dennis Stock of Magnum, free lancers Louis Stettner and Robert Frank, and the late Ed Feingersh and Dan Weiner, to name a few. Wilson Hicks, *Life* Managing Editor, hired Leonard McCombe on a contract forbidding the use of flash or flood on assignment. Eugene W. Smith did outstanding work with a 35 mm camera, and the combat pictures of the Korean War by David Douglas Duncan established his reputation as a top photojournalist.

By the 60's, technical improvements in films, developers, and lenses had so improved the quality

The picture book became an increasingly important outlet for the work of photojournalists during the 50's. Many photographers found in books a wider scope for their work than they could obtain in the more limited space of a magazine picture essay. This poetic and charming picture is from Wayne Miller's The World is Young, *an extended picture essay on the experiences of growing up in a modern American town. The subjects: his own four children. (Courtesy Magnum Photos, Inc.)*

of available-light photography that it became much more widely accepted. Its advantages were recognized and sought after by imaginative picture-buyers in industry and advertising, as well as on magazines. Available-light photography became an accepted tool of most photojournalists.

It was only one tool among many, however. Other technical improvements increased the scope of effects and images that could be captured with a camera. For example, "fisheye" super wide-angle lenses gave a panoramic view. Variable-focal-length "zoom" lenses allowed a photographer to shift quickly from a medium shot to a close-up, or from a long shot to a medium shot. Motorized backs permitted rapid-sequence photography. A photojournalist armed with the proper equipment, could "see" an event in a way that was impossible for a human eyewitness. But just as it took decades for photographers to exploit the technological revolution of the 1870's and 1880's, it would require much experimenting and imagination before these new techniques would be fully mastered.

Color photography is a good case in point. Although color materials and methods were vastly improved during this period, few photo-

tojournalists found a way to use color effectively in their work. Ernst Haas photographed lovely, poetic picture essays on New York and other subjects in color, and George Silk, Eliot Elisofon, and Gordon Parks of *Life* did effective journalistic work in the medium. But for the most part, color rarely seemed to strengthen a photojournalistic story, except for scenic and travel subjects.

The greatest challenge facing the photojournalist today is competition from television. TV can report events while they are happening, and in images that move. A photojournalist, using a still camera, can't compete with this "instant reporting." A television image is one step closer to reality than the still picture. It recreates an event in time, whereas the still picture can only pull an isolated moment out of time.

However, the television image is fleeting; the still-picture image endures. The still picture has qualities that make it worth a viewer's careful study, and that may make it live for a long time.

A still picture, as communication, can distill the essence of an event or personality. This single image can't tell all the truth, but it can give a deep, flashing insight into some aspect of reality. Henri Car-

tier-Bresson's one-legged war victim in Hamburg, Bruce Davidson's Old Woman of Montmartre, or Werner Bischof's Peruvian Piper are all "journalistic" pictures with this enduring quality that seems to depend on a photographer of uncommon talent being totally absorbed in a subject he feels very strongly about.

A good journalistic picture does more than just tell a story. It also has a symbolic quality. To take a simple example, an amateur photographer's snapshot of Johnny is just a record of Johnny, no more and no less. As such it's interesting only to people who know Johnny. But Wayne Miller's photograph of his daughter running by a pond's edge is not only a record of one little girl—it's also a symbol of all children running free and happy across an expanding universe they have not yet discovered to be hostile.

This concentration and symbolic meaning are qualities that make the best photojournalistic pictures worth coming back to, time and time again, long after the television image has faded from the screen. The photojournalist of the future will need to emphasize these enduring qualities; his images will have to tell more, and tell it more effectively than television can do if his work as an eyewitness to history is to survive.

Dramatic accident photographs are always in demand and are quickly serviced to a vast newspaper audience. The horse spill shown here not only was widely circulated, but took several prizes in press photographers' competitions. Made at Belmont Park, in 1943, with a 5×7 press camera, an 8¼-inch lens, in 1/350 of a second, at f/8. (Photo: John Rooney / Associated Press)

PHOTOJOURNALISM AND ITS DEVELOPMENT

EDWARD STANLEY
Writer, formerly Executive News Photo Editor for the Associated Press

[This article touches on the history of photojournalism and discusses at length the various means and techniques employed in the gathering and distribution of the news photo. The operation and development of the large wire services is also covered in detail.]

The news in pictorial form is older than many realize, as this picture made in 1857 testifies. Francis Frith, called the "wandering photographer," was one of the most prolific workers in this field during the 1850's. He made this straight forward view of the Sphinx on a wet collodion negative, from which a 6½×9-inch toned silver print was made. (Photo: Francis Frith, Courtesy A. E. Marshall Collection)

• *Also see: Agencies, Photographic; News Photography; Picture Series; Selling Photographs.*

PHOTOJOURNALISM IS EASILY THE most robust and spectacular of all the developments in modern journalism. Cursed at the start with a bad reputation as a result of its association in the public mind with the more lurid type of crime and its sensational pictorial presentation, it is only within the past few decades that photojournalism has achieved anything like adult standing in the profession. For a long time it was indeed the underprivileged and misunderstood child of the press. But today photojournalism is here to stay. One has only to consider the immense amount of money, running into millions of dollars annually, that is spent for the collection and distribution of news photos, and the effects of these photos on the ever-increasing circulation of our major newspapers and magazines.

BEGINNINGS OF NEWS PHOTOGRAPHY

The circulation-building possibilities of pictorial material were first recognized by Joseph Pulitzer. He brought the first pictures into a modern newspaper shortly after he acquired the old *New York World.* He had only woodcuts to offer, but the circulation spurted, nevertheless. On the day of Grant's funeral, Pulitzer sold a record 250,000 newspapers. That was in 1885.

Five years earlier, Stephen Horgan's halftone process was perfected and used for the first time with the appearance, in *The New York Daily Graphic,* of the now famous "Shantytown Scene." Gradually

An anxious moment at President Kennedy's inaugural was the basis for this interest-compelling picture. The cause of the anxiety was smoke from a flash fire at the speaker's rostrum but Life *photographer Joe Scherschel correctly reasoned that the greater interest lay in the reaction of his well-known and highly photogenic subjects.* (Photo: Courtesy Life, copyright Time, Inc., 1961)

other newspapers began reproducing photographs, and by 1897 the circulation of *The Sunday World,* which was crammed with pictures, had risen to 600,000. Pulitzer, incidentally, originated the X-marks-the-spot technique which is with us still. The X is now supplanted by arrows or circles.

Hearst battled Pulitzer in the use of pictures, and during the Spanish-American war the competition between the two was fierce. Hearst once astounded conservative publishers by chartering a special train to rush the Jeffries-Johnson fight pictures from Carson City, Nevada to San Francisco.

In the early part of the century photoengraving became commer-cially available and economically feasible. With this development came the demand for speed and still more speed. Trains or fast horses were sometimes employed in relays to rush pictures to anxious editors in distant cities.

The first picture syndicates came in the early 1900's—Bain's, which was chiefly concerned with events in and near New York, then American press, followed by Underwood and Underwood and many others.

In 1913 the late Adolph Ochs, publisher of *The New York Times,* investigated the development of the rotogravure press while abroad, and ordered two such presses shipped to this country. Early the following year the first rotogravure supplement in the United States made its appearance in *The New York Times.* A gain of 100,000 in circulation was reported. The *Times'* success led to the introduction of gravure supplements in many metropolitan newspapers in America. *The Tabloid.*

During World War I, pictures came into wider general use, but never equalled the prominence they enjoyed in England. There Lord Northcliffe had established *The London Mirror,* the world's first illustrated tabloid daily, and probably the greatest single spur news photography has ever had. Northcliffe, influenced by the success of the pictorial weeklies in England, set up a staff of photographers and engaged photographer-journalists as correspondents in all parts of the world.

In June of 1919, *The Illustrated Daily News* was established in New York, and at first seemed intended as a feature and sports publication. Its name was later changed by dropping "Illustrated"—today it is just *The Daily News,* and has the largest circulation of any newspaper in America. Its content changed as experience was gained, and its appeal broadened. By and large, however, *The Daily News* seems to have passed its period of exploration with the pictorial form, and in that respect offers few surprises.

The success of *The Daily News*

The circulation-building possibilities of picture material were first recognized by Joseph Pulitzer, in 1885. The annual Pulitzer Prize in News Photography is a major event and honor. This picture of the fatal stabbing of Japanese socialist leader Inejiro Asanuma won the prize in 1960. (Photo: Yasushi Nagao / The Mainichi Newspapers of Tokyo)

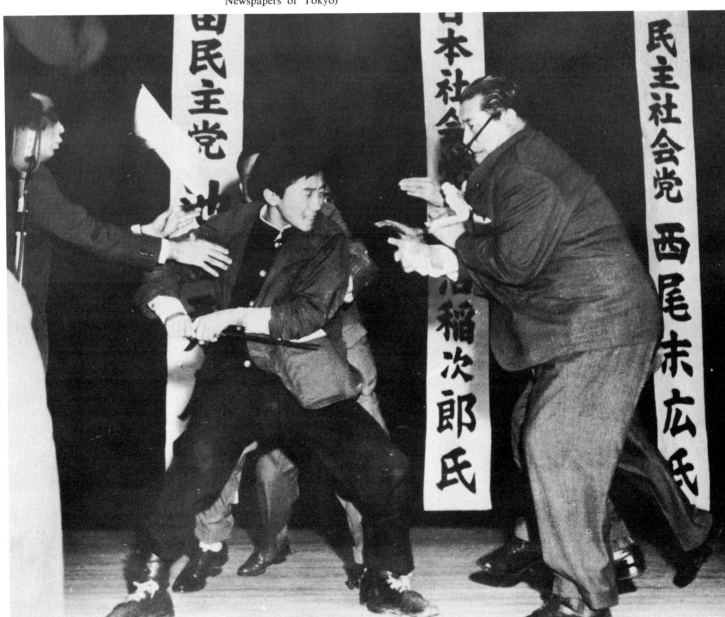

boomed the news picture as a powerful circulation builder, and picture tabloids sprang up in all parts of the country, but few were successful. Some newspapers built their own photoengraving plants, subscribed to one of the larger picture syndicates, hired staff photographers, built darkrooms, and bought equipment. Speed became the keyword, and competition was keen.

GETTING THE NEWS PHOTO

Newspapers usually employed their own staff of cameramen for local news; the syndicates opened bureaus in the key cities, with staff photographers on the job from coast to coast. Able free lance photographers in the smaller cities and outlying districts were encouraged by the syndicates to send in their material.

Hundreds of the smaller dailies, weeklies, and semi-weeklies contracted for the mat services which were built up by the syndicates. For a nominal price, the picture page in the matrix form would be received by the smaller newspapers, all prepared and ready for casting. Cables and wires were speeding the news; ships, trains, and planes were bringing the pictures. Chartering trains to expedite the news picture became an everyday occurrence, and with the first airmail, the big syndicates turned to planes to get the first picture in on a big story.

As speed became more essential, experiments were conducted in many quarters to transmit pictures by wire, utilizing the existing telephone and telegraph facilities. In 1921 *The New York World* made a successful picture transmission to *The St. Louis Post-Dispatch* using a telephone circuit, and in 1923, the first telegraphed pictures of the Japanese earthquake were sent from Seattle to Los Angeles, Chicago, and New York. The following year the American Telephone and Telegraph Company sent pictures of the Republican convention in Cleveland to test telephone-wire transmission.

In December of the same year, RCA gave a public demonstration of picture transmission by radio from England. In Europe, as in the U.S., wired transmission of pictures was taking a firm hold.

In New York two inventors working for a picture syndicate in-

An important part of camera journalism is in the coverage of sports. For this action-packed close-up of pro football, the use of fast films and telephoto lens is essential. (Photo: Robert Riger, from his book The Pros)

A spot-news photo which shows how a photographer's imagination can make a feature out of an insignificant news item. This was a small chicken-farm fire with not much damage, but the photographer found the lone survivor walking around. He put it in the foreground, used a low shooting angle for emphasis on the chicken, but filled up the background with activity around the burning building. The staff photographer made the front page of his own paper plus the prestige of having the wire services pick it up. (Photo: Rodger Hamilton / Columbus Dispatch)

vented a process called Telepix, and on New Year's Day of 1925, they successfully sent a picture of the Rose Bowl football game in Los Angeles to New York and Chicago simultaneously over the Western Union wires. This system reduced the image to telegraphic dots and dashes which were then sent over the telegraphic wire and retranslated to form the original picture at the receiving end.

Though Telepix was syndicated to quite a number of large cities, A.T.&T. carried on its experiments

Above: *Dramatic close-up of driver in peril.*

Above: *Car smashes into ground as fence-leaners watch.*

Below: *Car bounces in air, clearly shows driver in seat.*

using a photoelectric cell to translate light and shadows of pictures into sound impulses which could be sent over the telephone lines, and then reconverted into light beams. In a test on March 4, 1925, pictures were transmitted from Washington to New York and San Francisco. A.T.&T. then added more cities to its list, opening its commercial service to the public on April 4, 1925. It charged $50 for a 5×7 transmission from New York to Chicago; $100 from New York to San Francisco. Boston was added to the service in November of the same year and later Cleveland and Atlanta.

But facsimile was to win out over the dot-and-dash method of transmission. Telephoto, as the A.T.&T. system was called, remained in existence for several years, but its results were not too impressive and service was first curtailed and then abandoned while the idea underwent further laboratory research.

As mentioned above, December, 1924 was another important date in the history of news photography. At this time RCA opened its New York offices to the public for a demonstration of a small machine which was able to receive a picture transmitted through the ether across the Atlantic from its offices in Marconi House in London. In less than two years, Captain R.H. Ranger, then an RCA engineer, had developed this remarkable piece of apparatus—a machine to send pictures by radio.

The first spot-news picture that was ordered and received by a syndicate in this country was transmitted from London to New York on March 5, 1925, and showed the body of President Ebert of Germany lying in state. It took only 25 minutes for the actual transmission

Sometimes a unique skill and ingenuity in using his equipment turns a photographer into a specialist. Such a person is John Crozier, on-call staffman for the Indianapolis Star, *whose specialty is shooting crack-up sequences without a motorized camera or rapid-wind equipment. All pictures in this accident sequence, frames 16 through 21, were taken with a Leica M2 using the standard film advance lever and a 90mm Elmar lens; 1/1000 of a second and at f/11.*

of the picture. Five days later, the original of the same photograph reached New York on the Aquitania.

WIREPHOTO NETWORKS

While all this was going on the quality of the news photograph improved sharply. With the increased demand for news pictures, photographers and their editors began to explore new fields, and picture reporting flourished on the more varied diet. Kent Cooper, the aggressive general manager of the Associated Press, had predicted to his Board of Directors in 1924 that one day they would transmit news pictures over a great network, side by side with the text report.

Cooper, always an innovator, had followed the first experiments with fascinated interest, and when the Bell laboratories, in 1934, showed him some almost perfect prints they had received over their new machines, he was determined to set up a network for the Associated Press.

The details accomplished, the AP's Wirephoto network began operation on New Year's Day, 1935. It comprised 10,000 miles of high fidelity wire and had receiving and sending stations in 24 leading cities. (The first picture transmitted was of an airplane accident in the Adirondacks.) Many improvements have followed the original set—the machines became smaller, less expensive to build and operate, and the participating memberships increased.

Other services quickly followed the Associated Press. International News Photos, Acme, and Times Wide-World each developed its own system. Under Charles M. Graves, Wide-World Photos (then a subsidiary of *The New York Times*) fathered the development of portable transmitters that did not require a network wire for operation.

In 1941 the Wide-World photo service was taken over by the AP while later the Acme Service became part of the United Press. Subsequently UP and INS merged into the present UPI organization, with the current UPI Newspictures organization one result of that change.

The technical advances that have made it possible for pictures of news events to flash across the continent have counted more than any single factor in making photo-news reporting a major interest of American newspapers. It logically follows that the greatest sources of news in picture form are the organizations which distribute newsphotos by wire, and these organizations, of which there now are two, AP and UPI, are part of great news organizations.

Growth of these major picture organizations since World War II has been phenomenal. From its modest start in 1935, for example, the AP's Wirephoto system by 1962 delivered direct picture-wire service to more than 600 newspapers and television stations, extending over some 40,000 miles of leased wire, with some 30 state networks in

Above: *Car up-ended, driver's arm in dramatic upthrust.*

Below: *Back on ground, wheels flying, car comes to rest.*

addition to the main national facility. In 1960 the AP established the first internationally leased picture-wire system in Europe, serving major cities in 11 countries.

These major picture agencies have bureaus with editors, managers, and varying numbers of photographers located at strategic points throughout this country, and around the world. The Associated Press, for example, maintains newsphoto bureaus in dozens of cities the world over. In addition, the services of photographers employed by member newspapers are available to the service, and there are the usual arrangements with free lance photographic correspondents in all parts of the country. In many states the agency has at least one such "stringer" in every county seat. Thus, the photographic resources upon which the service can call in any part of the country run into thousands of men and women. In addition, the AP operates two foreign subsidiaries which collect and distribute its pictures abroad.

FREE LANCERS VS. STAFFERS

Staff photographers in the field, or operating from the head office, bear the brunt of the assignments. They are perhaps more responsive to editorial direction than free lancers, and they are also familiar with the requirements of the service. Generally they are also better photographers, since that is their professional occupation.

Free lancers are very important in the life of a photo service, but by and large, the bulk of the great news pictures—and these are incapable of being posed—are taken by professionals. It seems to be a matter of "know how." When the zeppelin, *Hindenburg*, exploded at Lakehurst, not a single press photographer lost his stride, and for once there were enough shots to satisfy any editor. But of all the

The photography of world-famous personalities is an everyday event for the press cameraman who learns to work at a hectic pace, hemmed in by his co-workers, and working against a tight deadline. Some idea of the number of press photographers, and the variety of equipment used, can be seen in this picture as shutters click on President De Gaulle during President Kennedy's visit to France, 1961. Made with a 35 mm camera, on fast pan film. (Photo: Don Steffen, Gamma)

amateur photographers on hand, only two or three got pictures good enough to be published.

NEWSPHOTO ROUTINE

The customary route of a news photo taken, say, in New York City by a staff photographer would be as follows:

A wet print, or sometimes a developed negative, is examined by an editor. He determines its news interest, decides what subscribers should receive it, and the size print that should be delivered. If retouching is required, a glossy print goes to the artist. Meanwhile the caption has been written and the picture either scheduled, as in the case of the AP, or offered to subscribers by telegraph in the case of the other services. If the picture is to be serviced by mail, the captions will be mimeographed for attachment to the photograph.

By and large, the pattern of photo coverage has followed that of spot news. It is erratic, seldom predictable, and requires a constant readiness on the part of an agency to cover anything, anywhere, without knowing whether it will be a ship in distress, a school bus caught in a blizzard, a plane lost in the mountains, or a portrait of a 4-H Club Winner.

NEWSPHOTO REQUIREMENTS

The major market for pictures is, of course, the daily newspaper. Their requirements cover almost every conceivable field, but their greatest need is for spot-news pictures.

A spot-news picture must answer the same questions that a news story must answer. It is only a fragment of an action, and it must therefore tell its story as clearly and completely as possible, because there is no second paragraph, no "turn to page 16," to help out a news picture's failings. Either it tells its story or it doesn't.

All of the careful technique a photographer can learn is needed in a news picture. Composition, definition, and angle are as important in a picture as punctuation and grammar is in a news story.

A news picture must have news

The press photographer must be able to handle his equipment quickly and surely so he can concentrate on the action before him which sometimes shifts with lightning speed. This photo, catching a typical Kennedy gesture, was taken during the late president's visit to Paris in 1961. (Photo. Don Steffen, Gamma)

interest. An auto accident may be interesting in its own locality and dull elsewhere, but a crack train plunging into a flooded river is news anywhere.

A news picture must have action and human appeal when it can, and be composed with a thought to the limited reproduction facilities of newspapers, which print at high speed on cheap paper. The picture must be understandable. Just as a reporter strives to tell his facts in a new and interesting way, so must the photographer constantly seek a fresh approach.

Above all, a news picture must be completely honest. There is no place for any other kind of news photograph. A false photograph and its maker fall into the same category as the reporter who colors and falsifies his story.

EDUCATIONAL AND DOCUMENTARY PICTURES

The enormous expansion of the use of pictures to tell news stories has had its repercussions in other fields, particularly in the field of education and social documentation. In the final analysis these are news pictures.

The government, for example, in endeavoring to make understandable the necessity for soil conservation, has found photographs to be a dramatic propaganda medium. The Department of Agriculture probably makes the widest use of the photograph, but other divisions of government, such as the Office of Education and the Public Health Service are also large users.

There are a number of independent photographers operating in this field, as well. Some are searching out their own subjects, others working on assignments from foundations and other organizations. An examination of books of photographs published in the last dozen years will show how important the field has become.

The American and European press make rather different uses of pictures. Until recently the European tendency had been toward feature and off-the-news pictures. The U.S. press found only straight-news

Left: *The more ingenuity a photographer displays in angling his shots, the more able he is to meet the stiff competition of his fellow workers. Here Bill Stahl shoots from the window of an East Side tenement for an unusual spectator view of the principals in a "Cinderella" romance—pianist Anthony di Bonaventura, son of an immigrant barber, and his bride, Sara Delano Roosevelt, F.D. R's granddaughter and adopted Witney heiress. The newlyweds face a battery of news cameras after their wedding in New York.* (Photo: New York Mirror)

Below: *The portable electronic-flash units are largely responsible for the improvement in quality and action of sports-events photography. Good use of electronic flash and a water-level angle give this swimming picture a new look.* Photo:(G. A. Smallsreed, Jr. / Columbus Dispatch)

pictures of interest. With improvement of American newsphoto technique, however, the European has tended to follow the American lead.

The exception to this is found in the Germany of the 1930's. Here photographers were government directed to produce propaganda photographs to help build the legend of Nazi invincibility.

THE FUTURE OF PHOTOJOURNALISM

Photojournalism is a rapidly growing field. The small-town news-

paper, once limited to syndicate material purchased in stereo-mat form, now uses local pictures, thanks to the introduction of the Fairchild Scan-A-Graver, which makes a plastic printing plate from a photograph in a matter of minutes. Many small-town newspapers, even weeklies, are using the Scan-A-Graver in conjunction with the Polaroid camera. With this combination, no darkroom is needed, and pictures can be taken and processed to printing plates up to half an hour

before press time.

Portable wirephoto machines that can be plugged into telephone lines anywhere in the country are available, and many newspapers and magazines have them. These machines can be sent with the photographer to almost any distant event, and pictures can be back in the office as soon as they are developed.

Radio transmission has kept pace, and pictures are received from abroad by the thousands. Other means of getting pictures are even more outlandish—on occasion, a newspaper has photographed the coverage of an event right off the screen of a TV set, getting its pictures without even sending a man out of the office. The legality of this trick is in question, but the possibility of setting up private circuits for this pupose is not at all remote.

The technical problems of taking pictures and distributing them are pretty well solved. But the emphasis in photojournalism, in any case, is not and never has been on the technical aspects. The essence of photojournalism is in the editorial and the news content. While the chief responsibilitty lies with the photographer, picture editors have been sharpening their technique, too. The last few years have been years of great experimentation in the newspaper field and some of the rewards of this experimentation are now beginning to appear.

Photographs will improve as photographers study their craft and have better equipment available. But tomorrow's photographer must be more than merely technically competent. As the world in which we live changes, news interests change, too. Today people are far more interested in the social developments which affect their lives, and the photographer must know *why* he is taking his picture. A picture is worth 1000 words only when a picture has something to say. And apart from accident, a picture only repeats what the photographer was able to see. Tomorrow's photographer, if he is to hold a mirror to his world, must be a photojournalist.

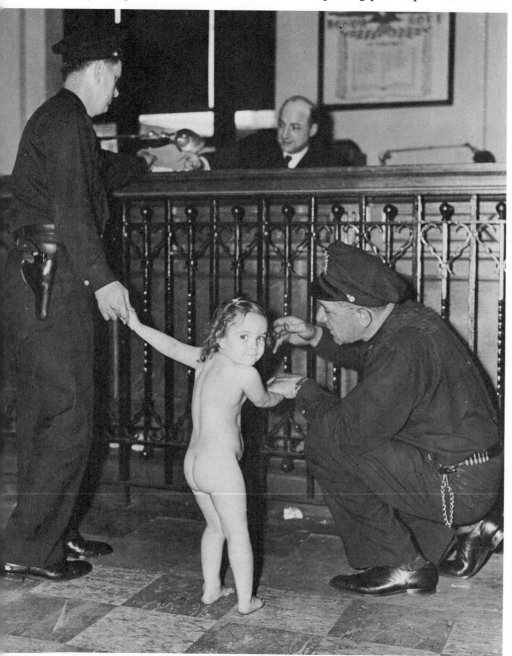

Typical of camera-journalism feature photographs, this one is part of the hot-weather theme. (Photo: Bill Stahl / New York Mirror)

LAPLAND   **PAL NILS NILSSON**

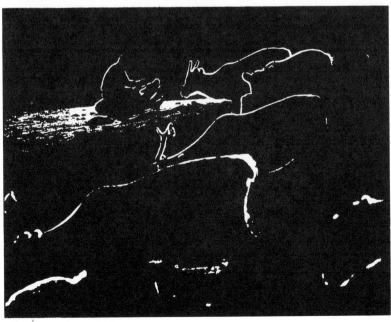

This scene of reindeer and their herder in Lapland, immediately commands attention because of the dramatic way in which the lighting has been used to define the compositional arrangement of the figures. The position of the deer, extending from foreground to background, leads the eye directly to the man and deer in the far background (the smallest but most important figures in the shot). By deliberately under-exposing so that each of the figures appears as a black form without detail but outlined in white, the photographer has reduced this picture to its essentials. The head in the lower right balances with the figure in the upper left and the diagonal line of the other deer (with the farthest one pointing directly at the man) serve to tie these two areas together.

MILWAUKEE JOURNAL

Left: **HERO'S WELCOME.** Friends and townspeople wait for General Douglas MacArthur at his homestead in Milwaukee. Speed Graphic 4X5 and Super Panchro Press Type B film exposed at **f**/6.3 for 1/100 of a second. (Photo: George Koshollek, Jr.)

Below: **THE JUDGES.** Putting their heads together helps decide flower-show winner. Speed Graphic 4X5 with medium pan film. (Photo: Robert Boyd)

Top Left: **COMING-OUT PARTY.** After a long wait, patient photographer got his shot of the first public appearance of this lion cub. Speed Graphic and strobe. Super Pan Press film exposed for 1/60 of a second at **f**/8. (Photo: Hugo Gorski)

Top Right: **CRIES OF PAIN.** Only boy out of three to survive after being struck down by a car. Leica M3 with 35mm Summicron **f**/2 lens. Panatomic-X exposed at **f**/11 for 1/100 of a second. (Photo: Foster C. Stanfield)

Bottom Right: **STRANGE ILLUSION.** Marquette University in one of its last years of football runs a typical losing play. The five Marquette men (dark jerseys) seem to be running interference for the opposition. Leica M3 with 135mm Hektor **f**/4.5 lens. (Photo: James G. Conklin)

PHOTOMECHANICAL PRINTING PROCESSES

ERWIN S. KOVAL
Graphic Arts Consultant

[The pleasure experienced by a photographer in viewing the results of his creative efforts as a finished black-and-white print or as a color transparency, is exceeded only by the thrill in seeing that same original photograph faithfully reproduced in a magazine, newspaper, or other printed medium. While it is not essential that the photographer also be an expert on the graphic arts, a basic knowledge and understanding of photomechanical processes can be beneficial, particularly to anyone who hopes to have his work ultimately published.]

• *Also see: Preparing Photographs for Publication, Silk-Screen Printing.*

EXCEPT FOR SEVERAL RELATIVELY specialized methods, such as collotype or silk screen, which are limited to fairly short runs, most reproductions in quantity are accomplished by one of three major methods: *relief* printing, more commonly referred to as *letterpress; planographic* printing, generally termed *lithography, photo-offset,* or simply *offset;* and *intaglio* or *gravure.* Conservatively speaking, these three basic methods account for perhaps 98 percent of all printing today. While the type, size, and speed of the particular equipment used may vary considerably within each category, the basic reproduction technique will be the same.

COMPARISON OF METHODS

Not too many years ago, definite differences existed in the quality obtainable by each of the three methods, and this quality difference was often the governing factor in deciding which process to use for a particular reproduction. For work involving very fine reproduction, either letterpress or gravure was used, depending largely on the kind of paper to be printed and the quantity involved. Most printers and publishers considered lithography, or photo offset, a definitely inferior method, its only saving grace being that it was less costly, particularly when large numbers of illustrations were involved. In recent years, however, due to technological advances, lithography has been improved to the point where today its quality is at least equal to that of fine letterpress work. Because of numerous other advantages it offers, the process has in many instances supplanted the relief process as a standard method for many types of work.

Some of these advantages include the ease and speed of preparing plates for the press, the ability to print fine details on rough or textured paper, and the generally higher production speeds of offset presses competing with comparable-size letterpress equipment.

In broad terms, no one of the three major processes can be said to be better than the others per se. Each offers certain advantages which make it the best method to use for a particular job. The following more detailed explanations of each process may help point up the relative merits of each.

THE LETTERPRESS PROCESS

Taking its name from its method of transferring the ink to the paper, i.e., the actual physical contact of the letter(s) pressing or touching the paper, this method is the oldest, most universally practiced, and

Photoengraving of a portrait without the use of the halftone screen. Only two tones—black and white—are possible.

The halftone screen, which enables the photoengraver to convert the continuous tonal scale into printing surfaces.

An enlargement of the halftone dot formation which permits reproduction of all tones of the original copy.

Reproduction of the same portrait by use of the halftone screen, recreating all the tonal values of the original copy.

A precision camera for large-map reproduction. (Photo: Rand McNally & Co.)

most generally familiar. Gutenberg, the "inventor" of modern printing (because he is believed to be the first to use movable and thus reusable type) was a letterpress printer, but centuries before him the Chinese were printing by letterpress. They cut relief images into wooden blocks, inked the raised surfaces and pressed it against a sheet of paper or other material. This principle still applies today, although the technique of creating the printing material and the method of ink transfer (press equipment) have been improved.

Depending upon a variety of factors, including size, quantity, quality, and the nature of the end product, letterpress printing is done on specific kinds of press equipment. Letterheads or announcements might best be printed on a small "job" platen press, but a

daily newspaper or best-seller book produced on a large, high-speed rotary press. In either case, since the image material, whether original type or a duplicate plate of the original, is in relief and the reproduction is obtained by direct contact of this material with the paper, the process is letterpress.

An adaptation of letterpress printing termed *flexography* is a relatively new and rapidly growing speciality. It differs from conventional letterpress principally in that rubber rather than metal printing plates and special, highly volatile inks are used. Flexography's great advantage is its ability to print on flexible materials such as foil, polyethylene and other plastics, cellophane films, and glassine papers. Its growth has paralleled the increasing usage of these materials

in the packaging field, and the process is also making inroads into the book manufacturing industry.

Normally, letterpress printing is done by arranging type and/or illustrative matter (halftones or line "cuts") together with necessary blank spacing material, in a metal frame or form, called a *chase*.

Regardless of whether the form is *all-type* (individual letters set by hand or machine composition), or a *mixed form* (including individual types, machine composition, cuts, plates, and so on), all these elements are the same height at the image plane—.918" or *type-high*. All type-casting machines automatically produce material of this standard printing height. Halftones or line cuts, which are considerably less thick to conserve weight and material, are brought up to standard

Photocomposing machine for making large offset-printing plates. (Photo: Rand McNally & Co.)

height by mounting on wood or metal blocks.

Minor variations in height on the various elements are corrected before final printing by *make-ready,* which consists essentially of building up the low areas by placing some additional material, generally a special kind of tissue paper, under them. Special additional make-ready also is often required on halftone illustrations.

For most short-run job work, the original form is put on the press, but where large quantities are involved, as for magazines and newspapers, duplicate printing plates are made of the original.

Duplicate Plates

For newspaper work, which usually is run on a rotary press where the printing is curved to fit snugly around a cylinder, a *stereotype* is made. The original form is placed in a special molding device, usually a hydraulic press, and a sheet of papier-maché-like material, termed a *matrix,* impressed against the relief printing surface. The molded *mat* is then placed in a casting box, curved to match the cylinder circumference, and molten type metal poured in. The resulting stereotype plate is then trimmed and *routed* large blank nonprinting areas gouged out even deeper to insure that they do not act as a printing-image surface), and the plate fastened on the newspaper press, ready to be inked and run.

Stereotype plates are quite satisfactory for reproducing newspaper type and line work, and halftone illustrations of 55- or 65-line screen, but for finer-quality work, other kinds of duplicate plates are required. Of these, the most common is the *electrotype,* a duplicate plate capable of reproducing the finest detail in any original.

An electrotype is produced by making a duplicate mold of the original material, using a microcrystalline wax, pure lead, or, most recently, a vinyl-resin material. This mold is carefully stripped away from the original (previously coated with graphite or some other coating to facilitate separation). The mold's image surface is sprayed with a silver spray only a few millionths of an inch thick. The mold material itself is nonelectroconductive, whereas this silver coating is highly so. The mold is then placed in a special tank, direct current is introduced, and by means of electrolysis, a thin layer of pure copper is slowly transferred to the silver-coated surface of the mold. After several hours, the copper deposits build up to the point where the entire mold area is filled, resulting in a thin *shell* which is a perfect duplicate of the original form.

This shell is backed up by a lead or plastic sheet, or bonded to a preformed aluminum or magnesium base (to reduce over-all weight of the finished plate), the back milled to make the finished plate the desired working thickness, dead metal in the nonprinting areas routed out, and other finishing operations performed. Extra wearing properties may be added by nickel or chromium plating the finished surfaces; plates so treated are capable of running several-million impressions.

For many years the major drawback of the electrotype was its heavy weight, due to the lead backing, but recent efforts to produce a plastic-backed, aluminum-reinforced electrotype have been highly successful and many magazine printers, for example, are now using such plates.

Rubber and Plastic Plates

The use of rubber plates in letterpress printing, including flexography, is still confined largely to work which does not necessitate fine halftone reproduction, although progress also is being made in overcoming this handicap. Some European-developed plates, which incorporate a laminate or rely on a sandwich principle (consisting of various layers) to eliminate stretch or distortion, are said to be capable of printing halftones up to 120-line screen.

Much more rapid has been the improvement of various types of plastic duplicate plates, which are extremely light compared to electrotypes or stereotypes and can be made much more easily. Several which have developed within the past few years start out as a monomer or vinyl-liquid material. This viscous material is simply poured into a matrix and polymerized or thermoset. Developed initially for the book printing field, these plates are expected to have wider applications in other fields, particularly since they are reported capable of reproducing faithfully halftones up

to 133-line screens.

Dycril Original Plates

Another type of relief plate which is rapidly gaining favor is DuPont's Dycril photopolymer printing plate, which can be used for flatbed, rotary, and wrap-around letterpress printing, or for *letterset,* which is an improved method of dry-offset work.

Unlike duplicate plates, which are created by first making a mold or matrix and then using the latter as a master to produce any desired quantity of duplicates, all Dycril plates are originals. Instead of a mold or matrix, a photographic negative is the starting point for Dycril platemaking, and although any number of identical plates may be reproduced from a given negative, all of them will be originals.

Dycril consists of a layer of photosensitive plastic (a photopolymer) bonded to a metal support (steel for flexible plates, aluminum for rigid ones). When conditioned in a carbon-dioxide atmosphere, the photopolymer reacts to light, which must be intense. A plate is made by placing a sheet of raw, conditioned Dycril in a special vacuum frame in contact with a negative and exposing to intense light for 2½ minutes. (The technique, apart from special equipment required, is similar to making a photographic contact print.) The exposure changes the chemical structure of the photopolymer in relation to the amount of light coming through the negative, again as in making a photographic print.

After exposure the plate is "developed" by placing it in a special wash-out unit which sprays the plate with an extremely mild solution of water and caustic soda. Exposed portions have been hardened and are impervious to the wash; the unexposed portions remain soft and are washed away, leaving an extremely sharp and clear relief image. The resulting plate, taking less than 20 minutes to make, can then be mounted, if required, and run immediately.

Its light weight, high fidelity of reproduction (including extremely fine-screen halftones), and speed of preparation are plus factors in fa-

vor of Dycril, and outweigh its relatively high initial cost. Its popularity among quality printers is steadily increasing and the recent availability of the flexible Dycril material in sizes up to 40×76 inches is expected to implement the development of special wrap-around rotary presses. The latter, utilizing flexible relief plates, would thus be capable of competing on an economic basis with comparable-size lithographic equipment.

THE PLANOGRAPHIC PROCESS

As opposed to the raised relief surface in letterpress and the depressed surface of intaglio, the planographic process utilizes a smooth or flat printing surface. There are several methods of planographic printing, all based on the principle of grease repelling water.

The original method, *stone lithography,* is generally credited to an Austrian musician, Alois Senefelder, who is said to have discovered the basic principle in 1796 while seeking a less expensive method of reproducing the scores of his musical compositions. He, and others who refined the method, used wax or grease crayons to draw their designs or lettering on smooth stone slabs. These were coated first with water and then with greasy ink. The greasy design areas attracted and held the ink and repelled the water, while conversely the wet, open stone areas repelled the ink. When a sheet of paper was placed on the surface, the drawn image was transferred to it; the slab re-wet and re-inked, and the process repeated.

Basically the same principle is employed today, except that the stone slabs have been replaced by thin metal plates, and the images are placed on the plates by photographic and chemical means. The term *photolithography* is therefore more correct for almost all present-day commercial planographic methods, as is *offset lithography.* This latter term, or simply *offset,* has come into wide usage because modern lithographic presses do not transfer the image directly from the plate to the paper (as in letterpress), but instead first transfer the image from the plate to a rubber or composition blanket which in turn offsets it to the paper. Still another common term is *web offset*, the name given to the process when the paper to be printed is placed on the press as a roll, rather than as a stack of individual sheets, and travels through the special press as a continuous ribbon or web. Because of the higher production speeds possible in this type of lithographic printing, and other economic factors involved (roll paper costing less than sheets, for example), web-offset printing has become one of the fastest-growing segments of the printing industry. Many periodical printers and publishers, including a large number of smaller newspapers, are switching from traditional rotary letterpress to web offset.

Lithography is being used more and more for all types of printing jobs. Less than a quarter of a century ago, the number of printers who offered offset services as compared to letterpress was a mere handful. Today over 80 percent of all commercial printing establishments are so-called combination shops, offering both letterpress and lithography.

This tremendous growth of lithography as a commercial process stems from a number of factors, not the least of which is the fact that more time, effort, and money have been put into its research and development than in any other method. As a result of these efforts and corresponding technological developments, what was once considered by many people as a secondary and inferior process is today competing vigorously with other printing methods. Vastly improved plates, presses, inks, paper, films, and chemicals, and more skilled craftsmen, have all contributed to this progress.

In the last decade, the appearance on the market of the so-called presensitized plates has been one of the major reasons for the increasing popularity of the process. Previously, the printer himself had to coat the surface of the plate with a photosensitive material (usually an albumin-bichromate

solution) just prior to usage. This might be comparable to a photographer having to sensitize his own film just before exposure. While not a particularly complicated technique, coating a plate nevertheless involved extra equipment, effort, and skills, and the results were not always consistent in quality. The appearance of presensitized plates, uniform in quality from one batch to the next, and requiring only exposure and simple processing to make them ready to run on a press, opened new vistas for the average printer.

In many respects, lithography involves more photographic principles and techniques than any of the other major processes. A copy camera (usually a great deal larger than a hand or studio camera), lighting equipment, a darkroom (usually built so that the back of the camera extends directly into it), and film and processing chemicals are essential for large-scale lithographic work. On the other hand, many small printers have only an offset press, and obtain their finished plates, ready to run, from a trade shop specializing in platemaking.

The copy or process camera, generally capable of enlarging or reducing, first photographs the material (termed *copy*) to be reproduced. Either a line or screened-halftone negative is made to the proper size. After drying, the negatives are *stripped* to *flats,* which is lithographic terminology for fastening them in their proper place on large sheets of opaque masking paper corresponding in size to the total plate area. Holes or windows are cut out of this masking material so that only the desired area to be printed shows through. In some cases, one flat is made of only the line negatives and another of the halftones, but often both can be combined on one.

The flat is then turned over and placed, emulsion side down, on top of the sensitized plate in a vacuum frame to insure perfect over-all contact, and exposed to an arc lamp. The photosensitive surface of the standard albumin plate responds to this exposure by becom-

ing slightly hardened and insoluble in water where exposed. Next, the plate is rubbed with a so-called developing ink, which adheres to the exposed portions and repels the water with which the plate is next rinsed, to remove the nonexposed, nonprinting sensitized areas. Since these clean areas would attract either water or ink afterwards, they are coated with a gum-arabic solution which absorbs water only. The plate, which incidentally is "right-reading," is then ready to put on the press and be run.

Deep-Etch Plates

When extremely long runs are desired, the deep-etch plate is often made. A slightly different sensitized plate coating is used, and a positive rather than a negative film is used for the exposure. The result of this is that the areas affected are exactly opposite to those exposed and consequently hardened when making a standard surface plate. At this point, instead of developing by rubbing up with ink, a water rinse is used to remove the unexposed portions. The hardened areas remain and act as a protective coating when a weak acid is applied to etch away the unprotected portions (corresponding to the black portions of the original image). After this etching, which really is not deep enough to be termed a true intaglio, the plate is dried and inked. The hardened areas are then cleaned off by brushing away the insoluble coating, and recoated with a gum-arabic solution, which naturally is repelled from the etched, inked surfaces. Thus the plate now presents a positive image, the same as a standard plate, and hence is put on the press and run the same way.

Press Equipment

Most offset presses are of the rotary type, which means that the plate extends almost completely around the circumference of a cylinder, leaving only a small gap between the two ends of the plate. This circumference also corresponds to one dimension of the largest sheet capable of being printed. Thus, each time the cylinder

Fairchild Scan-A-Graver makes a finished engraving directly on a special plastic material without the usual copy photography or use of chemicals. The plate is ready for printing when the scanning process is finished on this machine.

makes a complete revolution, one impression is made, and the feeding in of the paper is so synchronized that sheets follow one another practically without interruption. In the case of web offset (or rotary letterpress, which also utilizes a continuous roll) the nonprinting area between each complete impression area, lengthwise, is called the *cutoff,* and it is on this line or gap that the web is later automatically cut into separate sheets.

In contact with the plate cylinder are other, smaller cylinders (dampening rollers) whose purpose is to keep the plate wet. These rollers are usually covered with an absorb-

ent material such as molleton cloth, and revolve in a trough filled with *fountain solution.* Also touching the plate, after it has been wet by the dampening rollers, is another roller carrying ink which it has picked up, usually via a series of *distribution rollers,* from the ink fountain.

Based on the lithographic principle of water repelling grease and vice versa, the nonprinting plate surface attracts more water which in turn repels the printing ink previously deposited by the ink roller, while the greasy image surface, having repelled the fountain solution, takes on, absorbs, and carries

the ink coating.

At this point the plate makes contact with another revolving cylinder, exactly the same size in circumference, covered with a smooth rubber or composition surface known as the *blanket.* The ink from the image area is transferred (offset) to this blanket, which in turn is revolving against a third large *impression cylinder.* The paper passes between the blanket and the impression cylinder, the ink is again offset to the paper, and the entire process repeated continuously for as many impressions as can be printed before the plate wears out. Depending on the type of plate and press, this can be anywhere from as few as several hundred or thousand

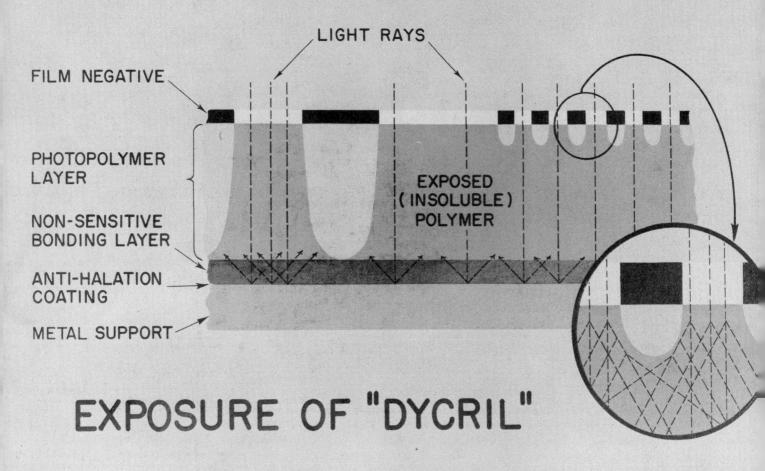

LIGHT RAYS

FILM NEGATIVE

PHOTOPOLYMER
LAYER

NON-SENSITIVE
BONDING LAYER

ANTI-HALATION
COATING

METAL SUPPORT

EXPOSED
(INSOLUBLE)
POLYMER

EXPOSURE OF "DYCRIL"

Schematic cross-section of a Dycril plate during exposure. Plate consists of three layers: metal support, nonsensitive bonding layer, and photosensitive plastic. Ultraviolet light passing through transparent areas of negative penetrates photosensitive plastic, with bounced and scattered light causing pyramidal-shaped character. Unexposed plastic remains soluble and washes out. Nonsensitive bonding layer prevents washout down to metal support. Effect on text matter is shown in left portion of drawing. In halftone areas, right, scattered and bounced light provides strong, interlocked bases (see enlarged section, inset lower right) for dots, with no washout to bonding layer depth.

up to almost a million. The basic lithographic process, however, is essentially the same, whether the press is a small office "duplicator" capable of printing sheets no larger than 8½ × 11 inches, or a mammoth, million-dollar web-offset publication press printing rolls of paper up to 77 inches wide at speeds of 2500 feet per minute.

THE INTAGLIO PROCESS

The third major printing method is intaglio or gravure and is generally acknowledged to be the finest in terms of pictorial-quality reproduction. Gravure is perhaps the most expensive method in terms of the equipment and materials needed, and hence not economical-

ly feasible for short-run jobs. Unless expense is no object, gravure is generally not called upon for runs of under a half-million impressions. On the other hand, when very large quantities are involved, it may prove to be more economical on a per-unit basis than either of the other two processes.

The higher costs of gravure stem from preparation of a complete metal cylinder, which must be etched

out to provide a printing image *below* the surface. In printing, these thousands of tiny holes or depressions making up the image are filled with ink as the cylinder revolves in a huge trough; the excess ink on the nonprinting surface is wiped off by a *doctor blade,* and the ink pulled out of the holes and transferred to the paper surface by capillary action and great pressure.

Tone, or gradation, is achieved by making the ink depressions relatively shallow or deep, while the smoothness of the surface is retained by means of a screen pattern. This screen pattern, however, is not the same kind as is used in making halftones for letterpress or lithography. The latter, examined under a glass, retain a definite screen, whereas a gravure image so examined shows less of the screen pattern and appears to be almost a continuous tone. It is this characteristic which makes the process so ideal for high-quality photographic reproductions, because the printed image resembles so closely the original.

As with the other methods, minor variations exist for the different kinds of intaglio printing, for ex-

ample, rotogravure or photogravure, sheet-fed gravure, or copper and steel engraving, but the principle of preparation is basically the same for all.

The first step in rotogravure, for example, is the creation of a continuous-tone negative (unscreened) on special film, which may incorporate a matte surface on the emulsion side to permit ease of pencil retouching. From this negative a positive transparent film is made. This positive is then placed in contact with a so-called transfer paper (sometimes termed *carbon tissue*) containing a photosensitive gelatin surface.

By means of powerful arc-lamp exposure, the gelatin is made insoluble to different depths, proportional to the light reaching it

through the positive film. The latter is then removed and replaced with a film carrying the desired gravure screen (usually 150 lines per inch), and another exposure made. This screening exposure hardens the gelatin in the open portions of the screen, forming a superimposed cross-hatch ruling over the entire area.

The transfer paper is next soaked in water and placed upon the copper cylinder on which the image is to be etched, with the gelatin side down. By revolving the cylinder slowly in a tank of warm water, the nonexposed or least-exposed portions of the gelatin

The Chandler & Price New Model-N Press is made in 8×12, 10×15, and 12×18 chase sizes. This is a hand-fed press, used in commercial plants, schools, and institutions.

(next to the paper backing) become soft and melt, whereupon the paper can be removed completely to leave a gelatin coating on the cylinder.

Next, the water bath is replaced with a chemical solution (ferric chloride or perchloride of iron), and as this solution permeates the gelatin, it attacks the copper and dissolves it away. The thinner portions of the gelatin (representing shadows in the original subject) permit faster penetration of the solution and hence a deeper etch in these areas. Actually, the depth of the etch becomes directly proportional to the original illustration—highlight areas are shallow, shadow areas are deep. It is these areas which will later be filled with a proportional amount of ink for transfer to the paper surface.

At this point the necessity of the screen should be apparent. The regular cross hatch pattern formed by it distinctly separates the image elements during printing, so that the ink is held in the depressions and does not run together or smear.

PHOTOGRAPHIC HALFTONES

In both letterpress and photolithography, the reproduction of continuous-tone photographic illustrations is made possible through the use of *screened halftones*. The purpose of the screen is to provide a printing surface of varying tonal gradations corresponding to the original. (Were a screen not used, the copy negative and plate would produce a silhouette effect when printed, half black and half white, depending on whether the original tonal gradation copied was above or below 50 percent on a gray scale.) These varying tonal gradations are recreated in printing by simply varying the amount of ink laid down in either the white or black areas. In highlight areas, very little ink is deposited; in shadow areas, a proportionately greater amount is laid down by the rollers. In effect, an optical illusion is created; the printed photograph is actually a pattern of tiny dots of varying sizes, but when viewed at a distance, the effect is one of continuous tones.

The dot pattern which creates the required tonal gradation is usually built through the use of a cross-line screen placed in front of the negative when exposing the copy. The normal screen consists of a series of fine lines etched both vertically and horizontally on the glass. (For some types of halftone work, a sheet of transparent plastic incorporating a comparable cross-hatch pattern is placed in direct contact with the negative before exposure.) To a large extent the kind of paper the illustration will be printed on determines the coarseness or fineness of the screen used. For example, most newspapers use an uncoated, fairly rough paper (newsprint) and hence are limited to about 65-line (number of lines per inch) screens on their halftones. Magazines or advertising literature, printed on smooth coated papers, can print halftones of up to 300-line screen, but the average use 120-line.

As mentioned previously, the purpose of the screen is to break up the continuous tone of the original copy into a series of evenly spaced dots (which become the actual printing image or inked surface) with white space between them. The relation between the size of the dots and this white space is what creates the illusion of the tonal gradation. Hence, in highlight areas the printing dots are extremely small and are surrounded by proportionately large nonprinting white spaces between them, whereas in shadow areas the printing dots are relatively large and have very little white space surrounding them.

For both letterpress and lithography, the making of the basic halftone negative is essentially the same; original continuous copy is photographed using a halftone screen. The light, reflected through the screen from various parts of the copy, determines the relative size of the dots exposed on the negative—the more light reflected, the lighter (smaller) the dots and conversely, the less light reflected, the larger the dots. In both processes, the resulting negative is then used to create a printing plate.

In lithography, where the entire press plate is made at one time, usually more than one negative is involved—perhaps one or more line negatives of type material plus several halftones. Working on a glass-topped light table, the *stripper* marks on a sheet of opaque paper, the same size as the plate or slightly larger, the desired arrangement or layout. He then uses a razor blade or comparable cutting tool to cut away the paper and create windows or open areas to accommodate the negatives, which are held in place, emulsion side up, with strips of opaque cellophane tape. When completely *stripped up,* the paper sheet, or *flat,* thus serves two purposes—it supports the negatives in proper position, and masks out nonprinting image areas. The flat is then turned over, placed in a vacuum frame in contact with the sensitized plate, registered in position, and the exposure made.

Sometimes one flat is stripped up of type material only and a second flat made of the halftones. In this case, the plate is exposed twice, once for each flat, but because the type areas are masked out by the paper on the halftone flat, and the halftone areas masked out on the line flat, the final result is the same as if both elements had been combined in the same support. This technique is also used to effect a multiple exposure in the same areas of the plate, as in the case of applying a Benday tint. The latter is a device for applying an over-all screen of equal dot sizes for the purpose of reducing the density of the ink coverage in solid areas.

For making letterpress halftones, the copy negative also is exposed through a screen, but the negative material is much thinner than regular photographic film. The kind used for fine-screen copper halftones is supported on a secondary piece of base film during exposure and processing, then is stripped off and transferred to a glass support. For less critical zinc plates, such stripping is unnecessary, but the film itself is quite thin. The reason for the thinness is that prior to *printing down* on a sensitized cop-

Above: *Original Heidelberg cylinder press, 21×28, 4000 impressions per hour.*

Right: *Original Heidelberg platen press has a maximum printing speed of 5000 impressions per hour, automatic feed, 10×15 chase size.*

per or zinc plate, the negative must be reversed, i.e., turned upside down. This is necessary because the resultant image on the relief plate must be reversed in order to make the image read correctly when printed.

Zinc is generally used for the coarser-screen halftones, and copper for fine-screen work, although magnesium also is now being used extensively, as is Dycril. Working with copper or zinc, the photoengraver coats the polished smooth surface with a photosensitive colloid, (called hot-top or cold-top resists), which has the property of becoming hardened and insoluble in proportion to the amount of light it absorbs. Highlight areas (black on the negative) thus receive little exposure and are not hardened too much; shadow areas (white on the negative) get more exposure and are hardened and made insoluble proportionately. A special cold-top developer plus warm water (for the zinc) or plain warm water (for the copper plates) is then used to dissolve and remove the un-

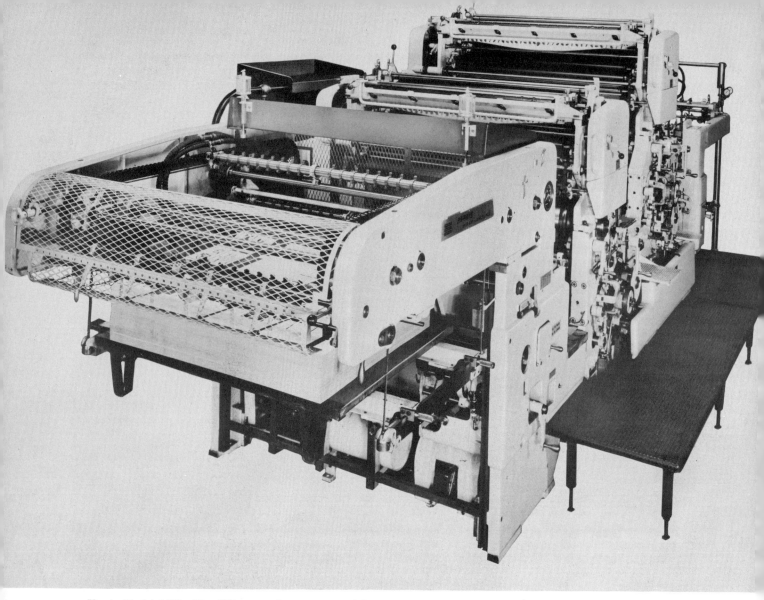

Harris Model 249L, 39×49½ two-color wrap-around letterpress.

hardened colloid, leaving the insoluble areas still protecting the plate surface.

Chemicals capable of deeply etching the metal are next applied, with the result that those portions which are no longer protected by the resist are eaten away. However, because the acids used attack the exposed metal not only downward or vertically, but also laterally or horizontally under the edges of the resist on the dot surfaces, the complete etching cannot be normally accomplished in one bite. Instead, a shallow etch is first made, and then a resin coating, known as *dragon's blood,* is applied with a brush to coat the edges of the dots. The resin is hardened by heat and the etching process repeated, usually four times, until the desired

depth of etch (22 to 25 thousandths of an inch) is reached.

Occasionally one portion of a plate will require more radical etching than another, in which case a *staging* solution is applied by brushing wherever further etching is not needed. This solution thus permits selective etching to be accomplished, after which it, and the protective resist, is removed with a solvent.

Until about 1950, photoengravers were forced to follow the above procedure, which produces extremely good halftone plates, but has many disadvantages, particularly in terms of the lengthy time required for repeated "bites" and attendant expense. Research and development toward a better method therefore led to the so-called *pow-*

derless, one bite etching technique. As the name implies, this patented machine process eliminates use of the traditional dragon's blood and achieves the desired depth of etch, without undercutting the dot edges, in one relatively fast etch. Developed originally for use with magnesium metal by the Dow Chemical Company and often referred to as the *Dow-Etch* process, it has recently been improved and refined to accomplish similar results on both zinc and copper.

Electronic Scanning

Still another method of plate preparation, which has gained tremendous acceptance in the last decade, completely eliminates conventional photomechanical or photochemical processes. This method employs an electromechanical technique known as *scanning* to produce either screened-halftone negatives for lithographic work, or finished letterpress plates.

The most common and perhaps best known of these electronic scanning devices is the Fairchild *Scan-A-Graver,* a commercial unit which has almost revolutionized the small-letterpress newspaper field by making possible fast and relatively inexpensive production of relief plates. Similar machines include the *Klischograph,* developed in Germany, and a newcomer—the *Photo Lathe.*

The Scan-A-Graver makes finished plates identical in size to the original photograph, up to an 8 × 10-inch maximum, but an improved and more sophisticated model, the *Scan-A-Sizer,* incorporates controls which permit limited reduction and enlargement of original copy, up to a maximum plate size of 18 × 20 inches. On either machine, a finished engraving is made directly on a special plastic material without recourse to intermediate copy photography or the use of chemicals. Also no special photoengraving skill or training is required; usually the photographer on a newspaper makes his own engravings.

Basically, the Scan-A-Graver consists of two related elements—

a photoelectric-scanning assembly and a mechanical-engraving portion. The photograph to be reproduced is wrapped around and fastened to one portion of a revolving cylinder, and the thin sheet of special plastic fastened around another portion. The scanning head, transmitting a pin-point beam of light, moves horizontally across the surface of the revolving copy at a fixed speed of from 65 to 120 lines per inch, while the engraving device, a heated stylus, penetrates the plastic sheet at the identical rate of travel.

The reflection of light from the copy is magnified electronically to create impulses which in turn govern the degree of penetration of the stylus into the plastic. Thus, on highlight portions of the original photograph or drawing, the impulse transmitted to the stylus is strong, creating a deeper penetration. The shadow areas, which reflect correspondingly less light, transmit a proportionately more shallow cut. Because the stylus does not rest continuously on the plastic surface, but instead is pulsating, a pattern is created automatically of untouched plastic, which in effect forms the halftone dots. Prior to starting, the operator, using a stroboscopic

magnifying microscope, adjusts the the maximum depth of the stylus penetration in both the highlight and shadow areas. Once adjusted, the machine then operates automatically, creating tonal gradation between the two extremes in terms of depth of stylus penetration and hence more or less plastic removed between the remaining surface image dots.

When the plate is completely engraved, it is trimmed with a knife or scissors all around and brought up to the same height as standard printing material by mounting it with double-backed Scotch tape on a block. Where it is used directly on the newspaper press, a blank space is left for it by putting an equivalent-sized piece of spacing material in the original form before making the mat. This creates a depression of exactly the right size and height in the stereotype plate to accept the plastic plate.

Normally, unmounted halftone plates must be positioned in the form before the mat is made. In the case of a Fairchild plastic plate, however, since its finished size is known beforehand, the engraving can take place while the remainder of the page is being made up, mat-

Harris Model 238, 25¾ × 38½ two-color offset press.

ted, and stereotyped, with the finished plate fastened in place before the press run commences.

Line Negatives

As opposed to halftones, which are necessary in order to reproduce the tonal gradations in continuous-tone original copy, line negatives are made when such gradations are unnecessary, i.e., for two-tone artwork, type, and similar high-contrast copy. Special film is used, which produces totally black (opaque) and white (clear) areas. Before platemaking, minor imperfections, such as tiny pinholes or scratches in the black portions, are corrected by *spotting* with an opaquing material. Over-all tonal gradations also can be introduced, by superimposing Benday screens, which have the effect of changing the tonal value of the black area from 100 percent (totally black) to a lesser percentage, or creating a desired pattern effect.

Color Printing

Up to this point, all explanations on halftone preparations have been in terms of single-color reproduction. When full-color copy is to be reproduced as black and white, only one negative and one plate are needed, but when this color copy is also to be reproduced in full color, additional steps in preparation and printing are required.

Full-color, or *process* printing from halftones normally is accomplished by using a set of four plates, one for each of the three basic colors—yellow, red, and blue —plus one for the black and white tones. To obtain these plates, the original copy must be *separated,* or broken down into the four elements, by photographing successively through filters.

The yellow plate is made by photographing through a blue filter (Wratten C-5) which blocks out the red and green. The red (actually magenta) plate is made through a green filter (Wratten B) which blocks out blue and red. And the blue (cyan) plate is made through a red (Wratten A) filter, which blocks out blue and green. Finally, a fourth shot is made through a light-yellow filter, which is used for the black *key* plate which adds depth to the shadows.

Each of these negatives is made through the normal halftone screen, to provide the dot pattern, but the screen is rotated at a different angle for each color. For example, the screen angles usually are 45 degrees for the black, 75 degrees for magenta (red), 90 degrees for yellow, and 105 degrees for cyan (blue). In this way the dots produced by the use of the screen will not touch or lie on top of each other, but will fall alongside each other instead—smaller and more widely separated in the highlight areas, larger and closer together in the shadow or dark areas. Examination of a full-color lithographic or letterpress reproduction under a strong magnifying glass will readily show this pattern. When viewed normally, however, the individual color dots are not apparent, so that the over-all illusion is one of continuous-tone color.

After the separation negatives are made, the same procedures are followed in making plates for either lithographic use or letterpress. *Register marks,* placed outside the actual copy area, are carried through from original to negatives to plates, to insure that in make-up and printing, each plate is positioned to print in the identical area on the sheet.

When an original illustration is made by photography, it may be separated automatically at the same time with the use of a one-shot color camera. This type of camera employs filters and prisms to break up the image into the four desired color-separated negatives. The size, weight, complexity, and cost of such cameras, however, normally preclude their use by most photographers, who rely instead on cameras producing color transparencies.

The color transparency is the most common source of original copy to be reproduced, but like reflection copy (color prints) it also requires separation. This can be accomplished in several dif-

ATF four-color web-offset publication press.

Blueprint: Photographic print made from lithographer's negatives, after stripping but before plates are made, used as a proof.

Body Type: Type used for main portion of a job, as opposed to display type, used for headlines.

Bold Face: Type set in a heavy face in contrast to normal light face.

Caption: Text describing illustration, usually placed adjacent to it.

Chase: Metal frame in which type and plates (a form) are locked-up for letterpress printing.

Coated Paper: Stock which has surface coating for a smooth and usually glossy surface.

Collotype: Special-purpose method of reproduction, using photogelatin; a variation of intaglio process. The collotype process does not use a halftone screen, reproduces continuous-tone illustrations with extreme fidelity.

Combination Plate: Halftone and line copy combined on one plate.

Continuous Tone: Tonal gradation without using halftone dots.

Copy: Original material (text or illustrations, or both) supplied for reproduction.

Cut: Slang term for a halftone or line plate in letterpress printing.

Cylinder Press: Letterpress machine with flat bed, on which the type form is placed, and large cylinder which rolls over it.

Deep Etch: In photoengraving, etching a plate deeper than normal to prevent nonprinting areas from filling in on certain kinds of work, such as envelopes; in lithography, a type of plate made for long-run work.

Direct Halftone: Halftone for which screen negative is made directly from the article to be reproduced, rather than from photograph or drawing.

Doctor Blade: Metal squeegee which wipes ink from nonprinting surface on gravure plate.

ferent ways, including mounting in the transparency holder of a camera to make continuous-tone separations; making direct halftone-separation negatives with a glass screen or gray contact screen; or using an enlarger instead of a camera to make the continuous-tone and halftone separations. Still another is separation via electronic scanning, using special machines which in one operation combine a photocell scanning device, electronic amplifiers, and a computer to accomplish color correction of each color plus a perfect black plate negative—all finished simultaneously. Once the separation negatives are obtained, however, by whatever method is employed, the platemaking process is identical to that used for straight black-and-white reproduction.

Base: Wood or metal used to mount letterpress plates.

Basis Weight: Weight of 500 sheets of standard-size paper. Basic standard size for book papers is 25×38; for writing (bond) and ledger papers, 17×22, for cover papers, 20×26.

Benday: Method of emphasizing portion of a line illustration by applying a screen pattern of dots, lines, etc.; named after its inventor, Benjamin Day.

Bleed: Copy or illustration which extends to edge of page, accomplished by printing oversize and trimming off excess paper.

Block: To mount an engraving or an electrotype on a wood or metal base to make it type-high, also the mount so employed; European equivalent of a photoengraving or cut.

A photograph with strong contrasts reproduces on the printed page with greater fidelity than one with a long or subtle tonal range. (Photo: Zeiss Ikon)

Dow-Etch Process: Patented method of photoengraving metal plates faster without having to apply dragon's blood; originally developed for magnesium, but now also used for zinc and copper plates.

Dragon's Blood: Special reddish powder which when heated melts to form an acid-resistant coating; used by photoengravers to protect sides of lines and halftone dots against undercutting by acid.

Dropout: Halftone from which screen dots are removed in highlight areas to provide pure whites.

Dry Offset: Printing method using a rubber blanket to transfer image to paper, as on lithographic press, but employing wrap-around relief plate in place of conventional offset plate.

Dummy: Sketched or paste-up plan of type and illustrations to guide printer.

Duotone: Color reproduction made from monochromatic original. Two halftone negatives are made at proper screen angles and plates etched to represent proper tone and color values. Key plate is then usually printed in a dark color for detail, and the other in light, flat tints.

Dycril: Trade name of DuPont's photopolymer printing plate, used for flatbed, rotary, and wrap-around letterpress or for letterset (improved dry offset).

Electrotype: Duplicate letterpress-printing plate, made from the original type and/or other elements by means of electrolytic process.

Engraving: Process of producing printing plates by some form of etching process.

Flat: Opaque material, usually goldenrod paper, which holds lithographic negatives stripped into position for platemaking.

Flatbed Press: Type of cylinder press, usually large, on which the form is placed in horizontal (flat) position, as opposed to a vertical press where chase is locked into position vertically, with the cylinder traveling up and down rather than back and forth.

Flop: Term to indicate that illustration is to print facing in the opposite direction.

Flush Blocking or Flush Mounting: Trimming a plate and mounting material so printing surface is flush with plate's edge.

Folio: Identifying number on a page.

Font: Assortment of different characters in given size and style of type.

Form: Type and other printing elements locked in chase and ready for press or electrotyping.

Foundry Type: Individual pieces of metal .918 inches in height with a letter or character cast in high relief on the face of each.

Fountain: On letterpress presses, through holding ink supply; on lithographic presses, trough holding the water called fountain solution.

Fugitive Colors: Colors or inks which are not permanent, fading or changing color after prolonged exposure. to light.

Furniture: Wood or metal blocks, less than type-high, used to fill out blank nonprinting areas in chase when locking-up type form.

Galley: Shallow metal tray used to hold type during composition or storage.

Galley Proof: Proof taken of type while it is still on tray, before it has been assembled into a page or other arrangement.

Halftone: Illustration reproduced by recreating original in the form of a pattern of tiny dots formed by photographing copy through halftone screen.

Highlight: Lightest or whitest tonal gradation in an illustration, represented in the printing plate by finest dot pattern or by absence of any screen.

Insert: Special page or signature, usually printed separately, designed for binding into a publication.

Key: To identify location or position of copy or illustration in a dummy, usually by means of letter symbols.

Key Plate: In multicolor printing, plate which carries the most detail and to which all the other plates are keyed or registered.

Layout: Basic conception of how a final page (or job) will look when finished.

Lockup: In letterpress printing, positioning a form in a chase, and securing with quoins.

Make-ready: Technique of preparing form for press, by making necessary register and/or optimum printing-height adjustments.

Make-up: To assemble proof elements on a dummy; to assemble type and/or other printing elements, following dummy, into a complete page or form.

Mat: Abbreviation for *matrix*.

Matrix: Molded papier-maché sheet from which stereotypes are cast; also the individual metal mold for letters and characters on type-casting machine.

Measure: Width, in picas, of type matter to be set.

Offset or Set-off: Freshly printed ink transferring from the face of one sheet to the back of another in the delivery pile; usually prevented by coating surface of printed sheet with anti-offset spray as it passes from press to delivery pile, or by passing sheet through drier.

Opaque: To block out nonprinting image areas on negative prior to making plate.

Patent Base: Metal base, usually steel or magnesium, on which electrotypes are mounted by means of special hooks or clamps.

Phototypesetting: Assembly of letters or characters automatically, using a special machine, resulting in a photographic negative or positive film (or paper) instead of metal; often termed cold-type composition, as opposed to hot-metal composition.

Pi: Type which through carelessness or improper handling has become mixed and is thus unusable until it is rearranged.

Pica: Standard unit of type measurement; there are approximately six picas to an inch.

Platen Press: Also sometimes called a job press, most simple kind of letterpress, employing a clam-shell or "clap-hands" technique;

the form of printing material and paper are brought together all at once to make a complete over-all impression.

Point: Abbreviation *pt.;* also a standard unit of type measurement, equivalent to .0138 inches; there are 12 points to a pica, 72 points to an inch.

Presensitized Plates: Commercial lithographic printing plates which require only exposure (*burning-in*) and development for use.

Process Plates: Two or more color plates, used in combination with each other to produce other colors and shades; *process printing* usually refers to full-color printing, using a set of four plates, yellow, red, blue, and black.

Progressive Proofs: Set of color proofs, made by the engraver, showing the impression of each color plate separately and then combined; these serve as an accurate color guide for printer, showing exact results at each step of process.

Quoins: Expandable devices used to tighten elements in a form or chase.

Reflection Copy: Artwork photographed directly by copy camera to produce negatives for plate-making.

Register: When printing from two or more plates, having separate impressions print in exact jux-

taposition; highly critical factor in color printing, to avoid various elements overlapping each other.

Reproduction Proofs: Also called repro proofs or repros; proofs pulled from type for specific purpose of photographic reproduction in offset lithography or gravure work.

Reverse: Printing effect opposite to normal, for example, white lettering on a black background.

Rotary Press: Press which uses curved printing plates fastened to a cylinder, with the paper, usually in web or continuous form, passing between the latter and another cylinder.

Routing: Removal of excess material in nonprinting areas of letterpress plate.

Scan-A-Graver: Name of Fairchild Graphic Equipment Company's electronic automatic engraving machine for making plastic letterpress plates.

Scanner: Electronic masking device used to produce color-corrected separation negatives for plate-making.

Separation Negatives: Set of negative images for color platemaking, obtained by breaking down full-color original into three primary colors plus black.

Short-Run 3-Color Process: Simplified, standardized method of color reproduction, developed by Eastman Kodak, which elimi-

OFFSET

Printing from a flat surface

Offset halftone dots print from a flat plate onto a rubber blanket which transfers them to paper.

GRAVURE

Printing from a sunken surface

Gravure halftone dots, etched into the plate, build up tones of varying ink thickness onto paper.

Letterpress is the oldest form of printing. The Chinese printed from woodblocks as early as 868 A.D. The invention of movable type in 1450 carried over the same principle. Letterpress halftone plates, etched into thousands of raised dots per square inch, varying in size to produce gradations of tone, are inked on their surfaces and pressed directly onto paper with pressures up to 1,200 pounds per square inch. The photomicrograph shows the sharp, clean result.

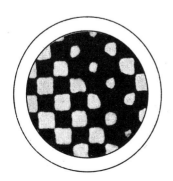

LETTERPRESS

Printing from a raised surface

nates black or "key" plate in process printing.

Signature: One section of magazine or book, usually obtained by folding a single large sheet, printed on both sides, into 8, 12, 16 or more pages.

Silhouette: Halftone illustration from which the screen on all normal background portions is removed, leaving only the image area in sharp relief.

Silk-Screen Process: Special-purpose graphic-arts reproduction process wherein thick ink or stencil (usually silk) consisting of solid and porous sections by means of a squeegee; used primarily to print on materials which cannot be run through a normal press.

Slug-Cast or Machine-Set Composition: Type matter which is assembled mechanically (as on a Linotype or Intertype machine) or by hand (as with Ludlow matrices) and then cast as one solid piece for each line.

Step and Repeat: Platemaking technique whereby a single unit or element is repositioned mechanically to produce photographically as many repetitions of it as are desired on one plate.

Stereotype: Duplicate printing plate made by casting, using a papier-maché matrix; generally limited to newspaper use.

Stripping: In lithography, the operation of affixing the various pieces of film in correct position on an opaque-paper support with areas cut out as needed; in photoengraving, the removal of collodion and stripfilm images from their temporary supports preparatory to transfer in an inverted position to a glass plate or flat.

Tint Block: Letterpress plate with a solid surface, used to print a light, flat color.

Type High: Standard height for letterpress-printing materials, .918 inch.

Up (as in 4-up, 8-up, and so on): Printing a given job in multiples of the designated number; for example, by printing four identical 8½ × 11 letterheads on a single 17 × 22 sheet, the press run for a 10,000 order would require only 2500 impressions.

Vignette: Halftone with background or portion of the illustration gradually shading off toward the edges, giving appearance of blending into surface of the paper.

Web Offset: Lithographic printing on a high-speed rotary press, on paper fed from a roll, in continuous form.

Wrap-around: Relatively new form of letterpress printing, using thin flexible relief plates which are wrapped around the cylinder in a manner similar to mounting lithographic press plates.

Xerography: Graphic-arts reproduction method which is electrical rather than chemical in nature.

Zinc Etching: Photoengraving, either halftone or line, on zinc; term almost always refers to line work.

□

PHOTOMETER

Strictly speaking, a photometer is an instrument which measures the intensity of a light source. Originally, the photometer accomplished this by comparing the light to be measured with a standard light, such as the standard candle (from which we get the term *candlepower*).

In its simplest version, the Bunsen photometer, the standard light, and the light to be tested were placed on the opposite sides of a test patch, which was simply a piece of thin paper with a tiny grease spot in the middle. If the light behind the paper were brighter, the grease spot appeared brighter than the paper. On the other hand, if the light in front were brighter, then the grease spot appeared as a dark patch. When the light on both sides was equal, the grease spot appeared to disappear altogether, or else appeared equally bright on both sides of the paper. The relative brightness of the light being tested could be calculated from the two distances—that is, of the standard and the light being tested—from the paper, by means of the inverse-square law.

Such photometers are still in use today for precise laboratory work. The grease spot has been replaced by more sensitive devices such as the Lummer-Brodhun cube, which is an arrangement of prisms producing a test field which is much more critical and therefore more accurate.

PHOTOMETERS AS EXPOSURE METERS

Strictly speaking, any photoelectric exposure meter is a photometer; however, the term is normally reserved for meters working on the comparison principle, such as the SEI Photometer. In this meter, a small electric lamp is used as a comparison, and the brightness of its filament varied until it seems to melt into the subject detail being viewed. It is obvious that this produces a very sensitive means of measuring the brightness of very small subject areas.

Early versions of the photometer, such as the prewar B & H Photometer, suffered from inaccuracy because the battery used for the lamp tended to run down rather rapidly and the instrument could not be accurately calibrated. Also different lamps gave different readings. In the SEI Photometer, this difficulty has been overcome by the inclusion of a sensitive photocell and a meter, which are used to set the brightness of the lamp to a standard value. The brightness of the filament image in the meter is controlled, not by the rheostat, but by a diaphragm. Thus the calibration of the meter does not change if a new lamp is required; the new lamp is merely adjusted by its rheostat until the meter indicates the correct brightness, and then exposure readings are made with the diaphragm.

ENLARGING PHOTOMETERS

A variety of photometers is available for measuring the brightness of the projected image on the enlarger easel. Some of the early ones worked on the same grease-spot principle as the Bunsen Photometer. They had a target on which the enlarger image was projected, and, in the middle of the target, a grease spot with a small lamp underneath.

In order to minimize differences in color which result from changing the brightness of the lamp with a rheostat, the comparison field was often colored green and a green lamp was used; this made color matching easier, and made the instrument more sensitive.

However, the brightness of the image on an enlarger easel is not very high, and it is nearly impossible to read the highlights (densest parts) of the image with one of these meters. They were usually calibrated for shadow readings, and a factor had to be introduced to compensate for negatives of differing density ranges.

Newer enlarging photometers use different balancing methods; in the Kinnard Spot-O-Matic, a photocell is used to indicate balance. Other enlarging photometers using highly sensitive photocells and amplifiers are available but are considerably more expensive.

PHOTOMICROGRAPHY

ROY M. ALLEN, D.SC.
Consultant on Metallurgy and Microscopy Specialist, Author of "The Miscroscope," "Photomicrography," and other books [A fascinating field for amateur photographers and an important adjunct of scientific photography is the photography of microscopic images. The basic technique with a standard compound microscope is explained by a man who has taken all kinds of photomicrographs with all manner of equipment. Included is a discussion of equipment, numerical-aperture magnification, technique with opaque and translucent objects, critical illumination, exposure, and use of filters. Also special photomicrographic fields.]

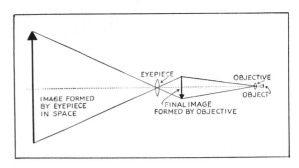

Figure 1. *The projected image as formed by the compound microscope.*

All photographs by the author.
• *Also see: Biological Photography; Electron Microscopy; Medical Photography; Micro- and Macrocinematography; Microscopic Movies; Polarizing-Microscope Technique With Color Photography.*

PHOTOGRAPHING ENLARGED IMAGES such as those observed visually in a microscope is possible because the optical system of the instrument is not essentially different in principle from an ordinary camera lens. Pictures taken through a microscope are known as photomicrographs. The older term micrograph is also frequently used, but in its broadest sense the term micrograph includes all enlarged reproductions of minute objects, regardless of how they are made.

Photography with a microscope can be simple or extremely complex. Essentially the microscope acts as a camera lens of short focal length projecting an image onto the film plane of the camera just as the ordinary camera lens would. Microscopic images may be obtained in two general ways: 1) With a camera, such as a view camera or a miniature, attached directly to the eyepiece of the microscope by a light-tight tube or sleeve, the camera lens having been removed. 2) With a permanent lens camera attached to the eyepiece of the microscope by a light-tight tube or sleeve, the camera lens being left in place and set at infinity.

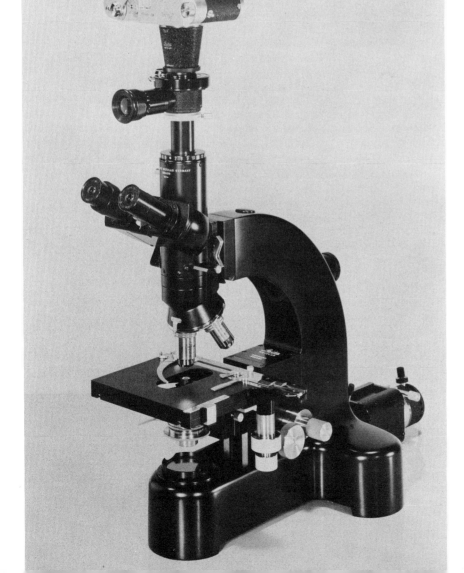

Figure 2. *Leitz Ortholux research microscope with 35 mm Micro Ibso attachment and the Leica camera.*

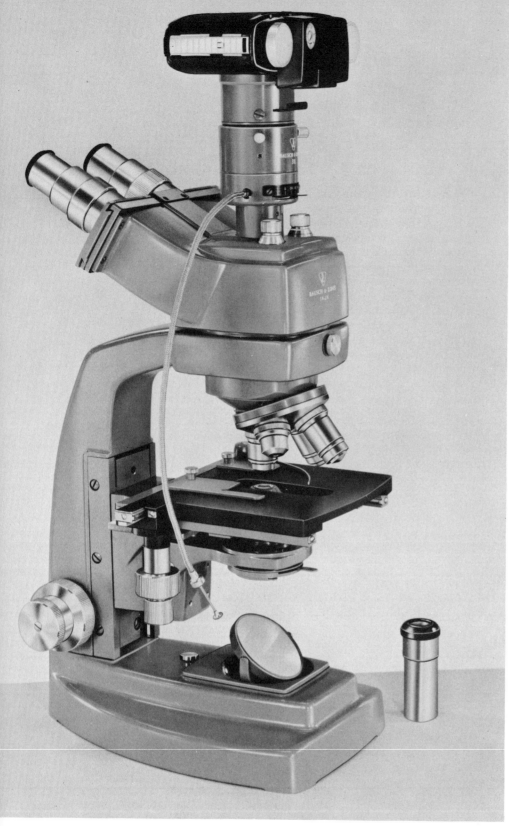

Bausch & Lomb model PVB-4 microscope with 35 mm camera in position.

Focusing. The ordinary compound microscope forms an image in the following way: the lens just above the specimen forms a real image in space within the microscope and this image is in turn further magnified by the eyepiece which forms the virtual image in the eye or a real image on the film plane. Focusing takes place on the microscope, first with the rough adjustment (which is like a bellows extension on the camera) and then with the fine-screw adjustment. When the image is in focus for the eye, it is never in perfect focus for the projected image in the camera. Refocusing is required, as the eye picks up the virtual image and the camera picks up the real image (Figure 1). For this reason, it is best to use a groundglass camera or one with a split-beam focusing finder.

The amount of extension between the camera, film, and eyepiece governs the amount of light reaching the film and the size of the image, but not to any noticeable degree the focus. Since the microscope can be focused for any projection distance, the camera portion can be anything from a miniature to an 8 × 10 camera with a bellow several feet long. Moreover, assuming a microscope with an inclination joint, the camera can be either a vertical or horizontal model. Each size and type of camera has its own advantages and disadvantages.

For some 35 mm cameras, the manufacturers provide accessory fittings to adapt them to a microscope. Figure 2 shows a Leica attached to a standard microscope by means of the Micro-Ibso attachment. This is the most elaborate and expensive type of fitting for the purpose. For those desiring simpler and less expensive outfits, other devices are available.

Special Cameras. Where greater flexibility in negative size, or magnification, is required and where a wide diversity in objects requires different treatment from one picture to the next, a camera designed especially for photomicrographic purposes is more practical.

Some manufacturers supply a simple fixed-focus metal camera, taking films or plates around the

PHOTOMICROGRAPHIC EQUIPMENT

The equipment required for photomicrography includes three separate units, the microscope, camera, and source of illumination. No matter how simple or complex an outfit may appear to be, it will be found to resolve itself into these three units.

3¼ × 4¼ size, which mounts directly on the top of the microscope in a manner similar to the Leica. These cameras are not expensive and have some advantages in that larger negatives result and roll film is not used. Still further specialization and flexibility are secured by using a separately mounted camera on an independent base. From this simple photomicrographic camera one can proceed to numerous more expensive models.

Recent developments in microscopic and photomicrographic equipment are along the lines of universal outfits. The microscope itself is incorporated in the design, together with the camera and illumination train, compactly constructed and with all parts properly aligned. Arrangements are provided for automatically shifting from one type of set-up to another so that practically all classes of work can be done with a minimum of effort.

Changes in the design of microscope stands in recent years have an important bearing on the type of camera, that is, vertical or horizontal, that must be employed. All professional stands of earlier vintage were equipped with an inclination joint enabling the microscope to be used in either a vertical or horizontal position. This has been largely eliminated in modern stands, which call for vertical positioning only. Users of older-model stands have the advantage that they can also use a horizontal camera, which makes it adaptable for homemade outfits where long bellows-view cameras, even up to 8 × 10 size, can be used.

THE ILLUMINATION UNIT

For visual microscopical work an intense light is not required or even desirable, but when the image is to be projected and photographed, a fairly strong illumination is needed.

While the arc lamp is the most

The Bausch & Lomb Type H camera is adaptable for taking vertical or horizontal photomicrographs. The camera may also be used for taking gross specimen photographs with a bellows extension up to 24 inches. The camera front has a removable lens board with flange carrying the light-tight chamber for connecting to the microscope.

powerful source of illumination for this work, and is required in exceptional kinds of photomicrographic work, for most purposes it is by no means the best. A concentrated-filament, gas-filled tungsten lamp of around 500-watt intensity is far more satisfactory. It is only in those cases where the outfit is made up of separate units, or the simple photomicrographic equipment does not include the illumination unit, that the type of lamp must be considered.

Usually 500-watt lamps have a light intensity of around 3200 K, the quality of light recommended for color photography. These lamps are satisfactory for color work, but if lower-wattage lamps are used,

special lamps (tungsten filament type) are available with definite 3200 K rating. Such lamps should be used for both transparent and indirect lighting of opaque objects for color photography. For black-and-white photomicrography they are not necessary.

Large research models and universal outfits are completely equipped with suitable lamps and accessory parts of the illumination system. For best results, the light source should be supplemented by at least a lamp condenser for projecting an image of the light source into the microscope substage condenser. Most manufacturers of microscopic equipment have suitable

designs of lamps available. These usually consist of a lamp housing within which the lamp is located; a focusing condenser and iris diaphragm are provided as a part of the unit. Also a filter holder may be included.

TYPES OF PHOTOMICROGRAPHIC WORK

All ordinary photomicrographic work can be divided into two general classes: 1) The photography of opaque objects by means of top illumination, or incident lighting, as it is usually called. 2) The photography of transparent objects, sections, smears, dispersions, and so on, by means of transmitted light.

Opaque Subjects. The only large class of materials falling into the first group is the metals, the study of which is a highly specialized type of work. Most other opaque objects are photographed at relatively low magnifications, and the illumination is oblique to the optic axis. This form of photomicrography is analogous to ordinary photography and subject to the same conditions as to highlights and shadows. With very uneven surfaces, more than one light may be necessary to soften shadows, or some form of diffusion of the light must be used. The principal source of illumination must be quite intense and preferably focused on the object by means of a lamp condenser. As a general proposition, panchromatic plates should be employed for this class of work to secure correct color rendering. As

in ordinary photography, the use of a yellow filter (K-2) is often a further aid. The filter can be placed either in the path of the light source or over the lens.

Transmitted Light. The entire design of the modern microscope (exclusive of metallographic models) is built around its use in connection with transmitted light, which is probably employed in connection with most microscopy. While, by analogy, this type of photomicrography might be likened to silhouette photography, such comparison does not convey a true idea of the results. Likening it to X-ray photography is a better illustration, since what is desired is a picture of the detailed internal structure of an object and not a black-and-white outline.

Occasionally some specialized object may benefit by a double exposure, first with transmitted light to reveal clear or translucent structure, followed by incident light to delineate surface structure.

THE SIMPLE MICROSCOPIC LENS

Before speaking of the actual technique of photomicrography, familiarity with the nature and operation of the microscope itself is desirable. By common consent, when one speaks of a microscope, a compound microscope is understood. From the strictly technical standpoint, however, there are two classes of microscopes, simple and compound.

A simple microscope consists of a single positive lens of relatively short focal length, or a combination of lenses functioning together as a single lens. To differentiate such simple microscopes from the compound type, they are given names such as magnifiers, loops, reading glasses, and the like. When used for low-power photomicrography they usually have the designation *micro*-attached to them as a prefix (for example, Micro-Tessar). Except in the case of reading glasses, the focal lengths of such lenses rarely exceed a couple of inches and may be as short as one-half inch. Magnification up to 25 or 50 diameters are feasible with the single lens, or simple microscope, in combination with a long-bellows camera. With

proper design of lens, it is even possible to go as high as 100 diameters.

Photographic lenses are also positive lenses. When one of short focal length is removed from the camera, it can be used as a simple microscope, and will yield an enlarged virtual image, by projection, an enlarged real image. The reason for this is that all positive lenses possess not one focus, but two, one on each side of the lens. These two foci are known as conjugate foci, and the exact position of each, as to distance from the optical center of the lens, depends on the position of the other.

In referring, therefore, to the focal length of a lens, as is customary in both camera and microscope work, the conjugate focus on one side is stated with the understanding that the other conjugate focus is at infinity, or some other predetermined distance. This is the principal focus. Since rays of light can proceed through a lens in either direction, they can emanate at infinity from a given object and, after passing through to the opposite side of the lens, form a real image of the object from which they originated, in the plane of the principal focus.

It is equally possible to have the rays start from an object located in the plane of the principal focus and form an image of the object at infinity. In the latter case, if the object is moved away from the lens, its image moves toward the lens. When the object plane reaches a distance from the lens equal to twice the focal length of the latter, the image has moved up to a position where it is situated twice the focal length on the opposite side of the lens. In every case, the size of the image is to the size of the object as the image distance is to the object distance.

This being true of all lenses, the same lens can be used to make a reduced picture of an object located a considerable distance away as in ordinary photography; to copy an object full size, as when both are located at twice the focal length; or to make an enlarged picture of an object when the object

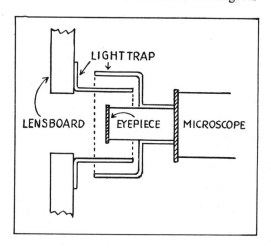

A single light trap for the connection between the lensless camera and the miscroscope eyepiece.

LIGHT TRAP

LENSBOARD   EYEPIECE   MICROSCOPE

is close to the lens and the image a considerable distance away, as in the case of photomicrography. The only requirement for the latter condition is the use of a sufficiently long bellows length on the camera. An approximation of the set-up for photomicrography is present in ordinary enlarging, where the image distance (the space between the lens and the enlarging paper) is greater than the distance between the lens and negative.

From a practical standpoint, it is usually not feasible to employ standard short-focus photographic lenses for photomicrographic purposes exactly as described. There are several reasons for this. The first, and most serious, is that a symmetrical lens has been assumed in explaining the theory and most modern lenses used for regular photography are not symmetrical. In making correction for the various aberrations present in a simple lens, the design of a lens is based upon the light passing through it in a given direction. Hence the lens may not yield the same quality of image if the object is brought so close that the object distance becomes less than the image distance, as required for making photomicrographs. In such case, the lens must be turned around on the camera lens board so that the back of the lens faces the object. This is not necessary when the lens is symmetrical, for example, a Dagor.

The second limitation on the use of ordinary lenses for photomicrographic purposes is that of available bellows length, which determines the amount of enlargement possible with a given lens. For low-power work which comes in the photomicrographic class, a 5 × 7 double-extension view camera equipped with the shortest available commercial lens represents about the limit. Some workers have made special cameras up to 12 feet long or more for the photographing of certain objects, such as insects and flowers.

Regardless of the actual camera length, it is obvious that for any given projection distance, the shorter the focal length of the lens used, the greater will be the magnifica-tion, since the shorter the focal length, the closer the object can come to the lens. According to the principle already enunciated, the greater the ratio between the object and image distance, the greater the ratio between object and image size. This is the basic principle prevailing throughout photomicrography, where extremely high magnifications are sometimes required.

Looked at from the viewpoint presented, it is evident that no radical difference exists between ordinary photography and low-power magnification in photomicrography.

THE COMPOUND MICROSCOPE

With a simple microscope, the limit of enlargement is reached long before science would wish to stop. It is at this point that the compound microscope enters the picture. Broadly speaking, the magnification of the compound microscope starts in the region where the single lens leaves off, or roughly 50 diameters.

The compound microscope is so-called because the magnification is obtained in two stages. By analogy it might be likened to a double arrangement of enlarging cameras where the first forms a magnified image of an object on its ground-glass focusing screen, this image becoming in turn the object upon which the second camera is focused. If each camera enlarged ten times, the ultimate picture would be 10 × 10 or 100 times enlarged.

In the microscope the first enlargement is made by the objective which forms its image at its rear conjugate focus lying within the tube. This image is formed in space, since no focusing screen is required for it. The eyepiece, or ocular, is the second enlarging lens. It picks up the image formed by the objective and further enlarges it.

THE OBJECTIVE

While in principle the objective is similar to any photographic lens computed for the light rays to enter it from the direction of the shorter conjugate focus, in practice there are several notable exceptions. The most obvious of these lies in the actual focal length of the lens, which

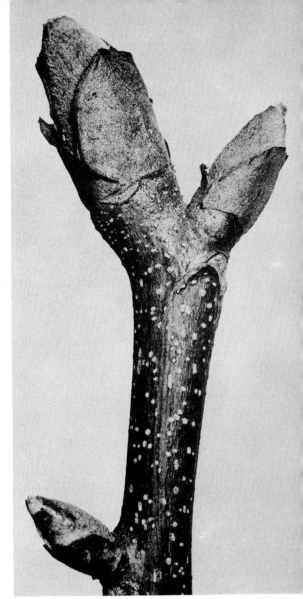

Terminal bud of hickory. 4× magnification.

in the case of objectives is designated the equivalent focus. This equivalent focus extends downward from the lower-power, longer-focus objectives, in a graded series, those under one inch usually running $^2/_3$ inch (16mm), $^1/_3$ inch (8mm), $^1/_6$ inch (4mm), $^1/_8$ inch (3 mm), $^1/_{12}$ inch (2mm) and $^1/_{16}$ inch (1.5mm).

Older vintages of lenses were usually stamped with the equivalent focus in either inches or millimeters, but the present practice is to stamp them with the initial magnification; that is, the size of the image formed at the rear conjugate focus, as compared to the size of the object. The magnifications for the standard tube length (160mm in American instruments) corresponding to the

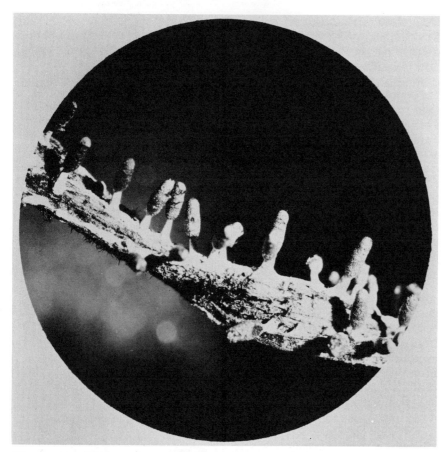

Myxomycete, Diachaea leucopodia. Sporangia on a minute piece of rotten wood.

various focal lengths, are substantially as follows:

1 inch (25mm)	6×
⅔ inch (16mm)	10×
⅓ inch (8mm)	20×
⅙ inch (4mm)	40×
⅛ inch (3mm)	60×
¹/₁₂ inch (2mm)	90×
¹/₁₆ inch (1.5mm)	120×

Note that a one-inch lens (25mm) is only rated as 6×, whereas ordinarily a one-inch lens would have a magnification of 10× based upon the accepted average distance of 10 inches for best viewing by the unaided eye, that is, ten inches divided by one inch equals 10×. The reason for the 6× magnification is that ordinary objectives are computed for 160mm tube length, instead of 250mm (10 inches), as was the case with early microscopes. As all American microscopes are designed for 160mm, this affects the initial magnification of all objectives; $^{160}/_{250}$ of 10× = 6× (approximately).

Photographic lenses are com-

puted to have one of their conjugate foci lie at infinity, but this is not the condition with microscope objectives. They are corrected for a definite projection distance, known as the optical-tube length, which must be such as will bring the image plane to the position of the diaphragm in the eyepiece. In the case of the higher powers (the shorter-focus lenses) this position is very critical; hence objectives alone should not be used for photomicrographic purposes, as is sometimes done by those unfamiliar with the optical theory of the microscope. It is true that an image will be formed at any projection distance, but the quality of the image will only be ideal at one position, which lies within the tube where it cannot be photographed without resorting to unusual expedients.

It is, however, possible to use objectives without an eyepiece for photographing, under one condition. A supplemental negative lens, in a Royal Society thread mounting, is

available for mounting in the older-vintage microscopes that are equipped with a threaded end on their draw tubes inside the microscope body. This lens corrects the objectives for infinity, making it, in effect, the equivalent of regular photographic lenses designed for enlarging purposes. It is unfortunate that modern microscopes do not have draw tubes. Such cannot be provided with a supplemental lens.

The magnification of the objective is not changed with the use of the supplemental lens; all that is accomplished is that it provides good images with any projection distance. The actual magnification obtained is the total projection distance from the objective to the position of the film in millimeters divided by 160, or, if computed in inches, divided by 6¼. On the whole, it does not appear to be worth while to use objectives alone for photographic purposes.

Objects to be examined under the higher powers of the microscope must be suitably prepared and mounted for the purpose. It is universal practive to cover these prepared objects with a thin glass plate known as a cover glass. The standard thickness adapted for these cover glasses is .18mm. Since, in ordinary microscopic work these covers are invariably present between the object and the objective, they become, in effect, a part of the optical system and the computation of the objective is based upon their presence. For this reason, ordinary microscopic objectives should not be used on uncovered objects.

NUMERICAL APERTURE

With the microscopic objective, requirements must be met which are not present in ordinary photographic work. This implies the use of terms not employed in connection with photographic lenses. The most important of these is numerical aperture, ordinarily written N.A.

In ordinary photography, the *f*-ratio of a lens is used exclusively as an indication of its speed. In visual microscopic work, speed is not a factor, although the characteristic which the *f*-ratio expresses (the light-gathering capacity of the lens) is of utmost importance. There is no purpose in enlarging an object unless additional detail is revealed thereby; hence there would be no reason for having an objective with an initial magnification of 40 times if it could not show any more detail than one of 20 times. This implies that a lens of $40\times$ enlargement must have a smaller circle of confusion than one of 20 times.

The term *numerical aperture* was coined by Ernest Abbé to provide a direct relationship between the resolving powers of various lenses. While analogous to the f-ratio, it is not computed in the same manner, since the numerical aperture is stated as the sine of one-half the angular aperture multiplied by the refractive index of the medium present between the objective and the cover glass. This latter factor is added so as to include oil-immersion lenses in the same series. Except when oil is present the numerical aperture must obviously be less than one; as the angle picked up by the objective cannot exceed 180 degrees, half of the angle must be less than 90 degrees, the sine of which is 1.

The numerical apertures of the objectives previously listed usually run about as follows, depending upon the type of correction, that is, whether achromat or apochromat:

$6\times$	.10—.15
$10\times$	.25—.30
$20\times$	.50—.65
$40\times$	.85—.95
	(oil immersion 1.00)
$60\times$	.85—.95
	(oil immersion up to 1.40)
$90\times$ (imm.)	1.20—1.40
$120\times$ (imm.)	1.30 N.A.

It may come as a surprise to pictorial photographers who believe they are working with the fastest possible lens, because theirs is considerably under $f/2$, to be told that such a lens is very slow, microscopically speaking. The N.A. of an $f/2$ lens is 0.24, while an $f/1$ lens rates an aperture of N.A. 0.45. Translating the numerical aperture of the highest commercial dry lens, 0.95 N.A. into an f-rating, we find

it is $f/0.16$, while a lens just under the theoretical limit of N.A. 1.00 reaches the amazing speed of $f/0.02$ —250 times faster than an $f/1$ lens, photographically speaking. The introduction of oil immersion, with its high refractive index, into the N.A. ratings above 1.00 results in an effective angle in excess of 180 degrees; hence these cannot be translated directly into equivalent f-ratings.

The numerical aperture of an objective is a direct indication of its resolving power, other conditions being equal. An N.A. of 0.80 will resolve twice the number of lines per inch that can be resolved by an N.A. of 0.40. Roughly speaking, the theoretical limit of the resolving power of a lens at the optical center of white light is reached at a magnification around 1000 times the numerical aperture. Thus, an objective with an N.A. of 0.85 can be used with beneficial results up to 850 diameters. Beyond this, empty magnification starts, although from a practical standpoint with

first-class objectives, photomicrographs can be taken far beyond this limit without noticeable ill effects.

Not only is the numerical aperture of value as an indication of the performance of the lens; it is also of extreme importance to the photomicrographer as one of the factors influencing the exposure time. In this respect it corresponds somewhat to the f-ratio in that the exposure is affected inversely as the square of the numerical aperture.

EYEPIECES

Eyepieces are optically simple compared to objectives. There are several different types, with different characteristics, but essentially the result obtained is the same, that is, they pick up the image formed by the objective and further enlarge it. This enlarged image is a virtual one in visual work, and a real image in projection or photographic work. Figure 1 shows diagrammatically the enlarged image obtained by the combination of objective and eyepiece when photographing with

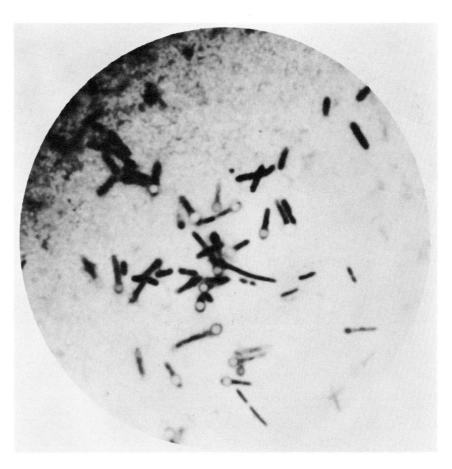

Figure 3. *Bacillus tetani, spore formation. Magnification is about 3000 times.*

a compound microscope. Eyepieces are available in various magnifying powers, the usual series being 5×, 7.5×, 10×, 12.5×, 15×, and 20×, although the average microscope is equipped with only two or three of the series. As any objective can be used with any eyepiece, a large number of magnifications is possible. It is customary for the manufacturer to assure that the proper type of eyepiece is furnished for the objectives with which the instrument is equipped, that is, Huygenian eyepieces for the achromatic series and Compensating eyepieces for the apochromatic.

MAGNIFICATION

Magnification implies the lineal relationship between the image and object and never a comparison of areas (which can be expressed, when required, by the square of the magnification). To illustrate, if a scale engraved in $1/100$ inch is photographed so the divisions are spaced one inch apart in the pic-

ture, the magnification would be 100× (or 100 diameters). It thus becomes a simple matter to determine magnifications photographically, since by the use of a stage micrometer (a minute scale graduated in $1/100$-millimeter divisions) the exact magnification for any combination of objective, eyepiece, and camera extension can be quickly determined.

As all three of these factors effect the magnification obtained in a photomicrograph, it is obvious that the marked magnification customarily placed on objectives and eyepieces cannot alone determine the resultant enlargement. These values can be multiplied together to obtain the visual magnification. For instance a 40× objective and a 10× eyepiece give a visual image of 400×. This image is identical with the size of the projected image on a plane ten inches from the eyepoint (the latter being located about a quarter of an inch from the eyepiece). To determine

the approximate ultimate magnification, resulting when a camera is used, this value must be multiplied by P divided by ten in which P is the projection distance in inches from eyepoint to plate. When this distance is less than ten inches, P divided by ten is less than unity and the magnification is less than the visual magnification. A projection distance in excess of ten inches gives a higher magnification than the visual magnification.

ZOOM MICROSCOPES

Until recent years it was necessary to combine given objectives with individual eyepieces to secure the desired magnification. Hence for visual work each combination resulted in gaps in magnification with no possibility of intermediate steps. Now the microscope manufacturers have incorporated the zoom principle used in movies and television. This involves additional optics located between the objective and the eyepiece, manipulated by an external knob. Thus magnification can be varied continuously over a fairly wide range without changing either the objective or eyepiece.

Zoom microscopes are an advantage for visual work where it is essential to be continuously examining objects at various magnifications. But from the critical-image standpoint zoom microscopes cannot be the equal of the old method of changing objectives or eyepieces over the entire range, since compromises in optical performance must be made. For photographic work, if flexible bellows length is available, the zoom microscopes are of no advantage, but with a fixed projection distance they are useful.

CRITICAL ILLUMINATION

Many of the problems of photomicrography are inherent in the objects to be photographed, but the basic principle upon which successful results in transmitted-light work are predicated has to do with the illumination used. It is not enough to project a beam of intense light into the microscope via the substage condenser and assume a proper exposure will then produce a good picture. For proper results, the

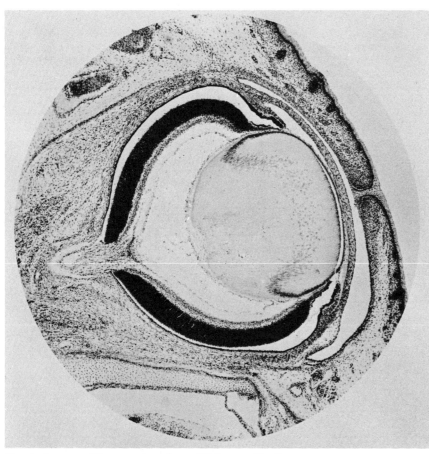

Developing eye. 30 mm rat embryo, 50× magnification.

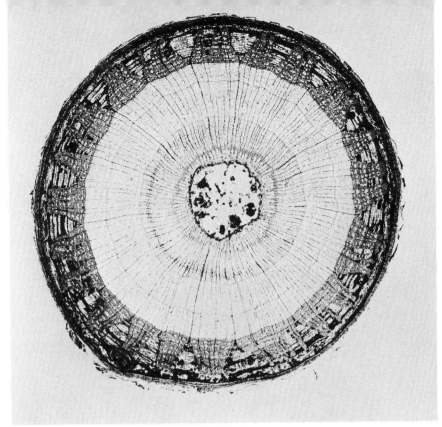

Figure 4. *Transverse section of a three-year old stem of Basswood.*

lighting must conform to definite conditions, known to the microscopist as critical illumination.

It has already been pointed out that resolution is related to the aperture of the objective. We must conceive of a solid cone of light rays proceeding from any single point in the object to the front lens of the objective. These are brought together by the objective at its rear focal plane to form an image of the point. The apex of the cone is the point in the object, the base is the area of the front lens, and the height is the distance from the object to the front lens. Underneath the object is the substage condenser, which is similar to an objective but turned around so that its shorter conjugate focus is also toward the object. If therefore, substantially parallel rays of light are projected into the condenser from beneath, they will come to a focus to form an image of the source of light.

The first step in the formation of critical lighting is to focus this image of the light source on the plane of the object, which will then be illuminated by a cone of light similar to that between the object and objective. The angle of the cone, or, technically, the aperture, is controlled by an iris diaphragm located beneath the condenser. To adjust this diaphragm, after the condenser is focused on the plane of the object, the eyepiece is removed and by looking into the tube the movement of the diaphragm can be seen in the back lens of the objective.

Instead of allowing the light from the light source to fall directly on the substage diaphragm, a short-focus condensing lens, about three inches in diameter, is used in front of the light. By adjusting the position of this condenser until an image of the lamp is formed at the plane of the substage diaphragm, the lamp condenser itself becomes the apparent light source and any unevenness present in the light source is eliminated, the field being evenly illuminated.

For very low-power objectives, however, it is necessary to remove the top lens of the substage condenser in order to form a larger image of the light and cover the field. The substage condenser must be focused in this case after the top lens has been removed.

It must be pointed out that when the microscope is employed in the vertical position and the mirror is required, the concave side of the mirror should never be used. Only the plane surface will reflect the light without distortion to form an image of the light source and give critical illumination.

Figure 5. *Transverse section of female Ascaris worm.* 15× *magnification.*

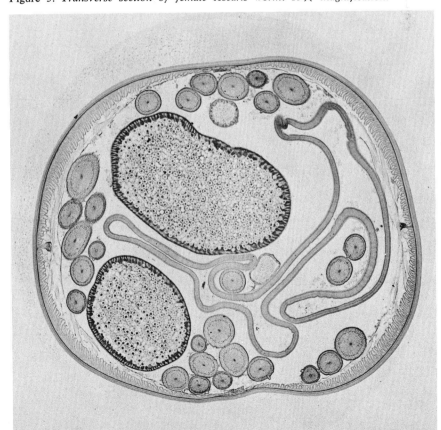

With the method of obtaining critical light described, it is desirable to have another iris diaphragm mounted in front of the lamp condenser, the function of which is to adjust the size of the field illuminated to the exact area being photographed. Cutting out superfluous light in this manner is very desirable. Because this diaphragm restricts the size of the field it is known as the *field diaphragm,* while that in the substage is the *aperture diaphragm.*

OPTICAL SECTIONING AND DEPTH OF FIELD

Just as in ordinary photography, depth of field plays an important role in photomicrography. Sometimes only those portions of an object lying in a single plane need be in focus. The less one sees of other planes, the better. Such a condition is termed *optical sectioning.* Then again a considerable depth of field may be essential.

The general optical laws controlling the depth of field present in microscopic work are similar to those of ordinary photography. In the latter increased depth of field is obtained by stopping down; in photomicrography it is achieved by the use of an objective of lower numerical aperture (which amounts to the same thing since means are not provided in ordinary microscopic objectives to change the aperture with an iris diaphragm). Thus we can state a general law to the effect

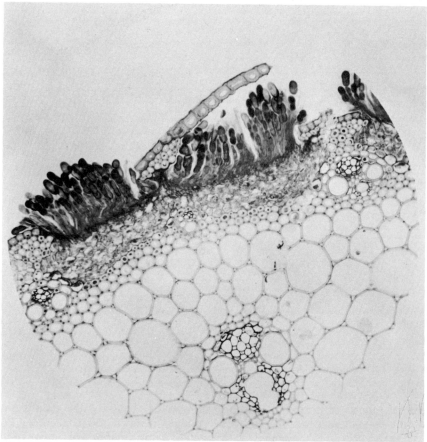

Figure 6. *Wheat rust, Puccinia graminis, Uredo spore stage. Shown on section of stem.*

that the greater the numerical aperture, the less the depth of field. Optical sectioning requires a high aperture; great depth of field requires a low aperture.

Figure 3 shows a transmitted-light view of bacteria at high magnification. As everything lies on the same plane, the highest possible aperture (an apochromatic oil-immersion 2mm objective with an N.A. of 1.40) could be used to give the highest possible resolution.

If the minute organisms are suspended (unstained) in fluid, it is desirable to show a considerable portion of the filaments in focus so that their nature may be properly interpreted, but at the same time a reasonable amount of plasticity should be apparent, to suggest a three-dimensional condition. Thus an objective with an intermediate aperture provides the best picture of this object.

ACCENTUATING AND SUPPRESSING CONTRAST

It has already been pointed out that practically all objects intended for study under the microscope by means of transmitted light require suitable mounting for the purpose. A large variety of techniques must

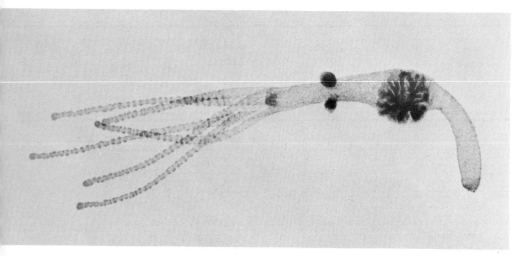

Figure 7. *Hydra in sexual development, showing an amoeboid ovum and two spermaries. 20× magnification.*

Figure 9. *Diatoms, Navicula (Pinnularia) nobilis. Accentuating contrast by use of the diffraction pattern. 250× magnification.*

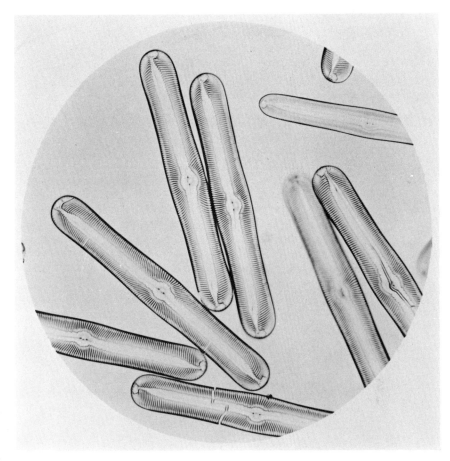

be employed in the preparation and mounting of various objects. Some are minute and can be mounted without sectioning. Some, though colorless and very transparent, cannot be stained; some require no staining because of inherent color; others must be stained to differentiate structures. All large objects must be sectioned and usually stained. The mounting must be such as to preserve objects indefinitely and support parts in their relative positions. This latter requirement involves the use of mounting media, the majority of which have refractive indices not greatly different from those of most tissues.

All of this implies that the photomicrographer is confronted with innumerable problems in photographing mounted transparent objects to get the exact range of monotone, needed for a proper rendition of structures in the black-and-white print. As in ordinary photography, the ideal condition is one where the complete scale of tone from pure white to jet black can be utilized if necessary. This may involve either accentuating or suppressing contrasts, depending upon the nature of the object.

Staining. Massive tissues of all kinds, animal and botanical, are prepared by sectioning methods so that thin slices, only a few microns thick, are made from the desired region. These are differentially stained with various dyes to bring out the microstructures present, for visual purposes. Figure 4 illustrates a section of this sort, a three-year-old stem of Basswood, and Figure 5 shows a section through an Ascaris worm, in the region of the uterus.

Filters. Frequently filters will make one constituent darker or lighter. The photomicrographer must therefore be provided with a complete series of color filters which, either alone or in combination, will give him a broad selection of spectral bands which can be used. The Eastman Kodak Company provides a set of nine filters, known as the *M set* for this purpose. The filters are placed in the light path so that the light used to illuminate the object is of the predetermined color. It is also possible to obtain glass filters corresponding to the

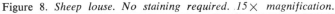

Figure 8. *Sheep louse. No staining required. 15× magnification.*

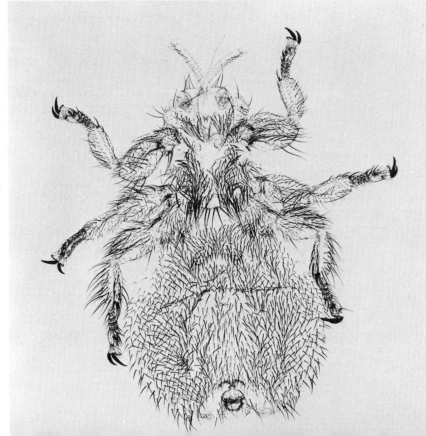

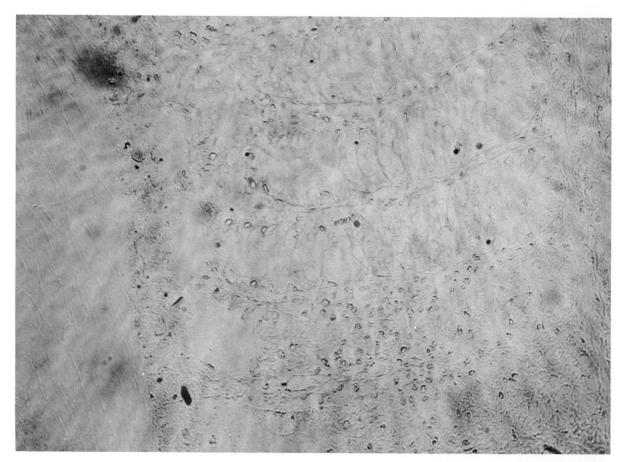

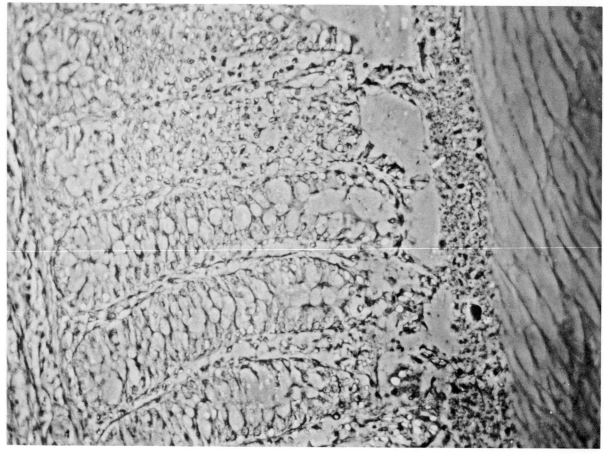

dyed-gelatin type. These are permanent in color and not affected by heat.

To accentuate contrast by making a certain color appear darker, the filter must be complementary to the color to be darkened. To suppress contrast, the filter must be a supplementary (or similar) color.

Occasionally some portion of an object will possess considerable color of its own even when not stained. An example of this is shown in Figure 6, where the dark red-brown Uredo spores of Wheat Rust are seen in a section of the stem, as they break through the cuticle. As a rule such objects should always be photographed so that the naturally colored portions will appear dark. In some cases it may be necessary to use a filter to lighten them to some extent; otherwise they may appear jet black and structureless.

Small organisms, both animal and vegetable, are usually mounted whole. Some require staining; others do not. In Figure 7 we have a Hydra in sexual development which, being substantially colorless, requires staining to differentiate it when mounted in the common medium, Canada balsam. Since the most important thing in this particular subject is the presence of the amoeboid ovum and the two minute spermaries, it is desirable to accentuate these parts, as in the micrograph, by means of a suitable filter.

Figure 8 shows a sheep louse in which the natural color is so evident as to require no staining. Such an object can often be photographed without any filter, but many insects possess such darkly colored chitin in the exoskeleton, usually a deep red-brown, that a supplementary dark-red filter is necessary to suppress the contrast.

Diffraction Pattern. The siliceous frustules of diatoms, one of the

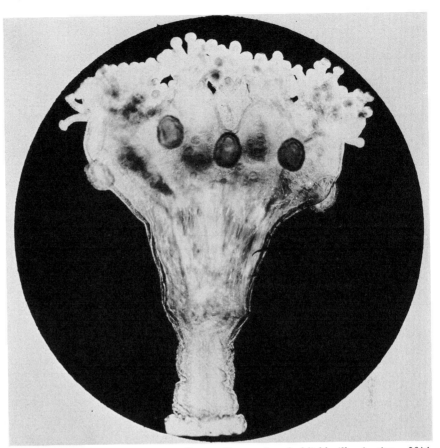

Lamp Polyp, Haliclystus Octoradiatus. Shown by darkfield illumination. 20 × magnification.

Top, left: *Figure 10. Bright-field illumination of mucous membrane of rat's stomach. 300 × magnification. See the same unstained specimen with phase contrast in Figure 11.* (Photo: Bausch & Lomb Inc.)

Bottom, left: *Figure 11. Phase contrast, mucous membrane of rat's stomach. 300 × magnification. See text for additional information.* (Photo: Bausch & Lomb Inc.)

favorite objects of microscopists, especially for test purposes on the resolving power of objectives, offer a problem of an entirely different nature. These cannot be stained, are colorless, and possess a refractive index not greatly different from the various mounting media employed; hence they are often almost invisible. Here the method of accentuating contrast involves the closing of the iris diaphragm of the substage condenser until the diffraction pattern produces a good image. Figure 9 illustrates the effect so obtained on one of the larger and more coarsely marked species, Navicula (Pinnularia) nobilis. For the resolution and photographing of some of the minute, finely-marked species, the light often requires decentering. Specialized types of illumination, such as darkfield and Rheinberg illumination, can at times be utilized to secure contrast or bring out an unusual feature in an object.

PHASE CONTRAST AND INTERFERENCE MICROSCOPY

One of the most important advances in microscopy in recent years, which has to do with accentuating contrast is phase contrast. The method of securing this in a practical manner was suggested by Zernike in 1935, and first put into practical use by Zeiss a few years later. In general the principles involved incorporate in part those of darkfield and Rheinberg illumination. Special condensers and objectives are required. These are equipped with ring diaphragms, the purpose of which is to either augment the illumination of the object and diminish that of the field on the one hand, or darken the object on a bright field on the other hand.

Phase contrast is of great value when it is necessary to examine unstained tissues in body fluids, or study colorless materials which cannot be stained.

A golgi silver-nitrate impregnation of the cerebellum at portion of the brain, showing the Purkinje cell. This very important nerve cell has charge of tremendous activities of the body, which are under the control of the sympathetic nervous system. 50× magnification.

Some manufacturers supply phase-contrast condensers and objectives which can be applied to standard biological, medical, or research microscopes. Others supply only the complete outfit, with optics, condensers and objectives.

Figures 10 and 11 illustrate what can be accomplished with phase microscopy on unstained biological material. A further modification for securing suitable contrast and in addition, making thickness measurements on objects, is known as interference microscopy. In this case use is made of polarized light. In this system complete microscopical equipment is a unit, and essentially a research tool. In both phase-contrast and interference microscopy visual and photographic work can be done.

PLATES AND FILMS

The expense involved in the use of glass plates, as well as other objections to them, has resulted in the general substitution of sheet film for photomicrographic use, as well as for ordinary photography. Eastman Kodak still supplies the Wratten M plate on special order, but it is no longer carried in stock by dealers.

The photomicrographer should plan to standardize on two or three types of film. For general use Panatomic-X is about the best. High-speed films are not recommended unless photographing of moving objects is involved. For 35 mm cameras, a slow panchromatic film should be used.

When photographing such objects as diatoms, however, where a maximum contrast is desired, color sensitivity is unnecessary in the plate and a slow, contrasty emulsion such as found in a process film is best. This type sensitive only in the violet and blue region, possesses another valuable characteristic where the utmost in resolution is required. Not only is resolution dependent upon the aperture of the objective, it also increases directly as the wavelength of the light used is decreased. Thus the use of blue light, with its shorter wavelength, gives an increase in resolution. Unless apochromatic objectives are employed, the use of the blue-violet (C) filter is recommended, since the focus may vary somewhat from that of the optical center of white light.

DETERMINING THE EXPOSURE TIME

The reciprocity law of exposure operates in photomicrography, just as in ordinary photography. The intensity of the light which finally reaches the plate is determined by several factors some of which are not present in camera work and all of which must be taken into account in determining the exposure time to be used.

To appreciate the effect of each factor, it should be assumed that all other factors are fixed. For instance, if the object is illuminated with a predetermined intensity of light, the first rule that can be stated is:

1. *The exposure time varies as the square of the magnification.* Doubling the magnification, quadruples the exposure; increasing the magnification three times means that nine times the exposure is required. This is true regardless of the objective, eyepiece, or bellows length employed to obtain the magnification.

2. Corresponding to the effect of the *f*-ratio in ordinary photography, *the exposure time is inversely proportional to the square of the numerical aperture of the objective, assuming critical light at full condenser opening is being used.* Substituting an objective of twice the numerical aperture and adjusting the condenser aperture to it with all other conditions as to magnification remaining the same results in cutting the exposure time to one-fourth.

3. *When the aperture of the condenser is reduced below the full critical-illumination value, the exposure is increased inversely as the square of the actual condenser aperture is to the square of the full critical illumination aperture.*

4. *The exposure varies with the filter factor,* just as in ordinary photography. While the filter variable is analogous to that applicable to ordinary camera filters, the factors themselves are often of a much higher value, in the case of some combinations amounting to several hundred times.

5. The nature and intensity of the light source is another factor in the exposure time. The plate speed and the density of the object are also obvious factors. The rule, "Always expose for the shadows and let the highlights take care of themselves" is equally applicable when photographing through the microscope.

Since only by chance could one hope to guess the proper exposure

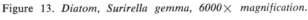

Figure 13. *Diatom, Surirella gemma, 6000× magnification.*

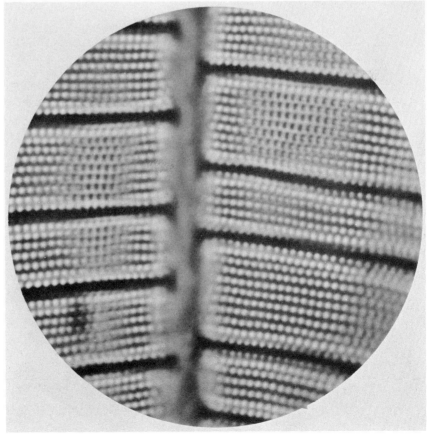

for a given set-up, the proper procedure at the start is to make a series of test exposures. Elaborate outfits are provided with special multiplicator backs for this purpose, but satisfactory test strips can be obtained by the use of the dark slide of the plate holder.

Assuming the object photographed to be of average density, the entire set-up magnification, objective, filter, light source, brand of plate, and so on, constitutes a basis for a standard-exposure condition from which any other combination can be figured on the basis of the effect which variations in conditions have upon the exposure time.

SPECIALIZED TYPES OF PHOTOMICROGRAPHY

The entire subject of photomicrography must of necessity include all microscopic work of specialized types. Most of these require special equipment and a knowledge of techniques peculiar to each subject. When such knowledge is a part of one's training and the required apparatus is available, it will be found that the general principles of ordinary photomicrography are fairly adequate to meet the requirements for these special fields also. The various fields that might be classified as specialized include darkfield microscopy, metallography, photography with polarized light, ultraviolet, infrared, and stereoscopic photography, color photography, and motion-picture photography through the microscope.

Darkfield Microscopy. Darkfield microscopic work is possible because the central cone of illumination corresponding to the full aperture of the objective can be blocked out so as not to enter the objective, while a hollow cone of illumination of greater aperture illuminates the object. By this means the object stands out brilliantly illuminated while the rest of the field is dark. It is largely used in high-power work on bacteria, colloids, and so on but can also be used on larger objects at low magnification. The main requirement when photograph-

ing darkfields is a brilliant light source. Where possible an arc lamp is preferable because of its strong illumination qualities.

Rheinberg Illumination. A modification of darkfield illumination, known as Rheinberg Illumination consists of using a two-color disc under the substage condenser, the center area, just large enough to fill the full aperture of the objective, being one color, for example, blue, and the remainder of the condenser aperture being a contrasting color, for example, red. The effect is to illuminate the object with the outside color and the field surrounding the object (which in the case of darkfield would be black) with the color of the central direct illumination. By using variously colored discs, beautiful effects can be secured which can be photographed in color.

Metallography. Metallography requires an entirely different arrangement of the illumination. It must be incident light, since only the surface of metals can be examined. But instead of falling on the surface at an oblique angle, the light is projected along the optical axis by means of a vertical illuminator. Because of this, the usual metallographic outfit is radically different in design from the conventional type. The specimen is placed upon the stage in an inverted position and the objective is located below the stage, pointing upwards. The specimens of metal must be suitably prepared for examination by polishing and etching. Magnifications up to the limit of resolution (several thousand diameters) are possible.

Special Illumination. Photomicrography by means of special illumination, such as polarized light, ultraviolet and infrared light, fluorescence effects, and so on, does not offer unusual problems of a photographic nature, providing one is proficient in the operation of the various special pieces of equipment involved and a technical background of experience is at command. Fail-

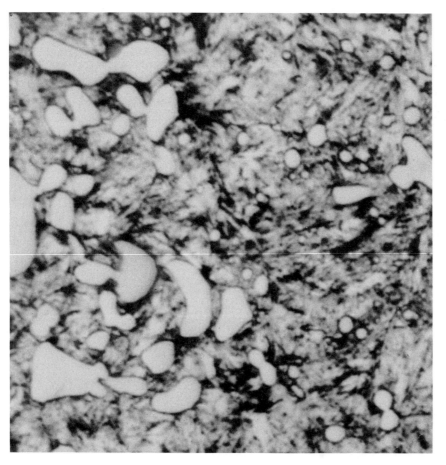

Figure 14. *High-speed tungsten steel, etched. 4500 × magnification.*

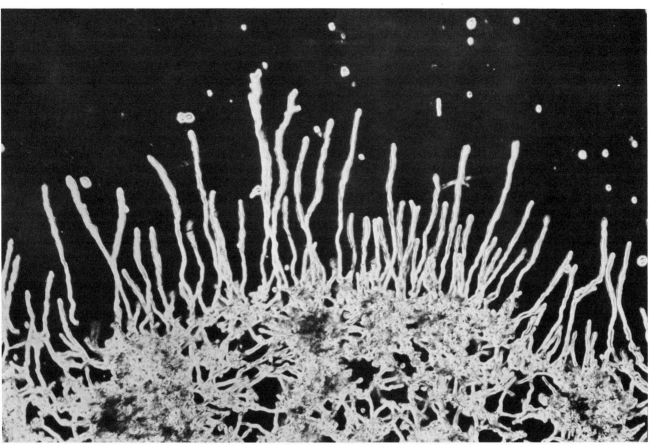

Living pencillium. This darkfield study shows the hairlike little projections of the growing mold arising out of the culture. 200× magnification.

ing in these qualifications, it is well not to attempt such work until after experience in visual microscopy along these lines is obtained (see *Polarizing Microscope Techniques with Color Photography*).

Motion Picture. Motion-picture photomicrography requires, in addition to the microscope and motion-picture camera, a special viewing eyepiece. The complete apparatus for the taking of motion pictures through the microscope is available from most manufacturers of microscopic equipment. In moving photomicrographs the photographer will often find a solution to problems which still photomicrographs cannot solve—and many phenomena are phenomena of motion (see *Micro- and Macrocinematography, Microscopic Movies*).

Stereoscopic work. Stereoscopic photographs through the microscope require the taking of two negatives which differ from each other in that they correspond to the views resulting from an angular displacement corresponding to the parallax of vision. This can be achieved by displacing the image on the ground-glass an amount equal to the interpupillary distance, or a special tilting stage can be employed. Commercial stereoscopic outfits for low magnifications are available from the various manufacturers of microscopic equipment.

The advent of the electron microscope stimulated a desire to determine what could be accomplished in higher magnifications with the light microscope. In the early days of the electron microscope when the range of magnification employed was from about 5000× to 20,000×, there was a tendency to show this big advance by featuring publicity for it with micrographs of mediocre quality in the range of 1500× to 2000×.

A determination on the part of the writer to show the true magnification limits of the light microscope brought forth micrographs of high quality far beyond the theoretical limits ascribed to them, which were about 1000 times the N.A. of the objective. Originally it was not real-ized that the theoretical limit with perfect optics and other perfect conditions, would stand several times enlargement without noticeable empty magnification, for normal viewing. Of course this must be accomplished photographically, since visual magnification must stop at the limit of objective magnification times eyepiece magnification, equivalent to photographic magnification at a projection distance of ten inches.

In recent years high magnifications with the light microscope are welcomed by all, while the electron microscope goes to magnifications of several hundreds of thousands. To illustrate what is possible in the way of direct high magnification, Figure 13 shows the resolution of a portion of the diatom, Surirella gemma, at 6000×. The row of dots on this specimen run 60,000 to the inch. Figure 14 shows the structure of high-speed tungsten steel at 4500×. These examples may stimulate others to see what they can do in this line.

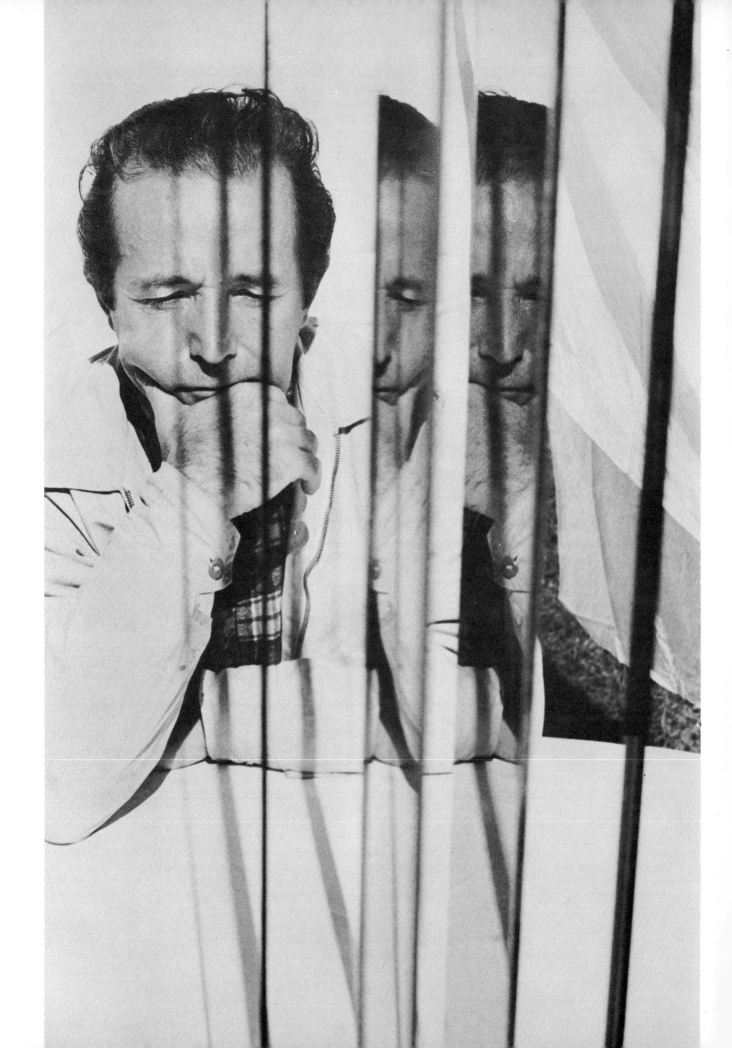

PHOTOMONTAGE

BARBARA MORGAN
Painter, Photographer, Designer
[The imaginative photographer will find the photomontage an exciting challenge, since it can and often does carry photography out of its straight and narrow path. The combined-picture image—weaving several photographs into one design unit—is described here from the esthetic and technical points of view.]
•*Also see: Abstraction in Photography; Dimensions in Photography; Enlarging Photographs; Esthetics of Photography; Juxtapositions in Photography; Surrealism and the Photographer.*

PHOTOMONTAGE MAY BE DEFINED as a photographic shorthand of the imagination; as units of straight photography fused for new meanings; as simultaneous images combined in one composition; as photography organized with drawing, constructions, or other supplemental media.

As his imagination prompts, the photographer-designer can bring together images from more than one negative to create an entirely new picture entity—a photomontage. He is not confined to what he sees at one time and one place in the objective world. By using straight photography as a starting point, he plucks out picture ingredients and reorganizes these realistic elements into unrealistic combinations to arouse the spectator to an experience which the single parts could not evoke.

ORIGIN

While photomontage is still experimental in the sense that one can

Multiphased portrait. Most photographers would have made a one-shot interpretation of the artist, Nassos Daphnis, concentrating behind the reflecting surfaces of his transparent plastic structure. But the photographer, Marvin Lazarus, has entered empathically into the transparency-reflection world that Daphnis is creating, and has given us a three-phase portrait, which suggest the artist's thinking rhythm as he ponders his creative problems. (Courtesy Castelli Gallery, N.Y.)

always do new things with it, the basic techniques are widely understood, at least in theory. It is not generally known, however, that from the beginnings of photography there has always been an off-beat stream of imaginative photographers, whose experiments have paved the way for the present extension of the medium.

Two important pioneers in the field were Rejlander (1813-75) and Robinson (1830-1901) in England, who made combination prints by laboriously piecing together picture parts from many negatives. "The Two Paths of Life" (1857) by Rejlander used 30 negatives. Rejlander also invented other multiple-image processes—his "Dream" (1860) is dramatized with somnambulistic manikins clambering through the "coils of dream" (the "coils" were lady's skirt hoops of the period). Today he would probably do it by shooting separate negatives. (*Negative 1:* Dreamer, *Negative 2:* Manikins on Hoop)— and then superimpose them in printing to express the simultaneity of Dream and Dreamer.

This and many other examples were precursors of surrealistic photomontage. But as we discuss it here, photomontage sprang more immediately from the same World War I ferment that also gave birth to experimental cinema, modern architecture, abstract painting, surrealism, psychoanalysis, and stream-of-consciousness literature. Certainly Eisenstein, Pudovkin, and Dovshenko in their nonrealistic cinema montage added momentum to the then avant-garde photomontage.

Maholy Nagy at the Bauhaus, Man Ray in Paris, Rodchenko in Russia and others, explored photogram, solarization, and many facets of photomontage. Compositions in which painting or constructivist techniques dominated the photographic parts, were usually called collage.

Meanwhile, Atget (1856-1927), during his prolonged documentation of Paris, made many photographic compositions of shop windows, in which he interwove, window reflections with manikins and objects displayed. This "natural

A feeling for speed and violence was wanted in a section of this motion-picture film, A Chairy Tale, by Norman McLaren. With long exposure, up to one second for each of these five frames, the actor was seen in the continuity as a blur for heightened dramatic effect. In still-photography presentation, the photomontage would have been boiled down to one image with multiple phases.

photomontage" was a revelation to painters and photographers at the time, and helped to make them aware of the validity of the multiple image, both as technique and as poetic statement.

John Heartfield in Germany made a devastating series of caricatures of the Nazi regime prior to his forcible expulsion from the country. Originally a painter, he discovered the excoriating power of photomontage. No other method, straight painting or straight photography, could have given the same sardonic effect.

In America, McKnight Kauffer' Herbert Matter, Herbert Bayer, and many others, have enriched the tradition and expressive range of the medium.

Trained as a painter and designer, I began in 1935 to experiment with superimposed images, and multiple exposures. Time-flow and rhythm, always central to my compositions whether painting or photography, were mysteriously alive in the multiple images I re-scaled and overlapped in the darkroom. In my experience of many years' exploration, photomontage is not an imitation of painting but very much a genre all its own. Like science fiction, the co-existing themes, which become altered in form and meaning (while retaining their root in what we call reality) simply teem with creative possibilities.

USES OF PHOTOMONTAGE

The versatile medium of photomontage is effective in a great many fields, some of which are:

Free creative expression (visual metaphor, satire, symbolism, humorous comparison, united time phases)

Photomurals

Advertising and poster

Exhibition arrangement and displays

TV and movie title backgrounds and sequences

Book illustration

Theater backdrops and projected slide transparencies used as photographic scenery

Table-top work coordinated with backgrounds

"Pop Art"

FURTHER DEFINITION OF PHOTOMONTAGE

Photomontage includes so many types and borderline combinations that it is difficult to say it *is* this and *is not* that. Actually it is a melting pot of visual possibilities,

The Dream (1869) by Oscar G. Rejlander. This imaginative dramatization in photography is a precursor of surrealist photomontage. "The coils of dream" are a lady's skirt hoop with manikins. (Courtesy George Eastman House collection)

Rhythm and movement. The sense of organic wholeness of a composition comes largely through accented rhythm. Let us examine a two-phase dance continuity, captured by Herbert Matter on a single negative. In this slow-motion study of the India dancer, Pravina Vashi, the overlapping flow-forms show upswing, down swirl, and resolution, all anchored from the toe-point.

where the wit, satirist, and symbolist can pick, choose, and recombine. Commercial art makes constant use of photomontage for its shock appeal and nonverbal communication of complex ideas. Endless varieties of photomontage appear in TV and picture magazines in a wide gamut of quality from utter crudity to creative validity and inspiration.

Unlike reportage, which is a series of individual pictures developing a theme, photomontage unites its diverse elements into an organic design. Pictures juxtaposed in page layout as "shock neighbors" sometimes border on photomontage. But actual photomontage knits into

formal composition the component picture parts which page layout only confronts. The photomontage is a visual hybrid that yields a meaning and impact that the elements, seen singly, could never express.

MODERN LIFE-LIKE PHOTOMONTAGE

In all, photomontage is no stranger than life itself. City traffic, TV, aerial views, car-motion blur, all add their special visual stimuli from the outer world which constantly interplays with the emo-

tion-colored imagery of our mind-pictures. Like a photomontage print, our consciousness (as well as our subconsciousness) is literally jostling with interpenetrating visions. It is from this subjective area that the designer plucks his subject matter.

DESIGNING PHOTOMONTAGE

Designing photomontage is far more complex, esthetically and technically, than composing a realistic photograph. Each part has to be rebalanced for its partnership

Multiphased moment. Harry Callahan has extracted an introspective vision from an everyday situation—men standing on pavement looking at a car. His image shift is a kind of awareness replay, both shadowy and real, which might touch off very different responses from different viewers.

in the final picture-mix. Image differences in their mood and meaning, their tonal range, perspective, and scale are some of the design considerations that have to be recast in the new composition. When coalesced, the new image nullifies the realistic times and places of the parts from which it was derived and establishes its own timeless, subjective reality.

The first essential is unification of picture parts, which means establishing a dominant theme. But the whole point of photomontage is its counterplay of form and idea. Therefore, in relating the unlike elements, the designer retains their separate identity in some

degree, much as a composer of a musical fugue keeps the identity of the "voices" while weaving the musical structure.

The theme picture should be pivotal, and stimulating enough to anchor the composition and the subordinate passages. Sometimes the very shock of ideas and opposition of scale is itself the theme. Once the basic thematic pictures are mated and meshed, then transitional refinements and details through photography, painting, or construction can be balanced in.

PERSPECTIVE AND CAMERA ANGLE

Perspective and viewpoint are enormously important in photo-

montage. In straight photography, with perspective lines converging at one vanishing point, there is automatically some compositional coherence. But when two or more negatives are combined, each with its own perspective and camera angle, a tension is created. This might cause a spreading open of the composition as in Callahan's "Men Standing on Pavement," or a wedging together as in Weegee's "The Guggenheim Museum."

LIGHTING, TONALITY, MOOD

Lighting often keys the emotional atmosphere and the tonal range. When the composition is made up of separate picture parts, each having its own lighting scheme, the designer needs some over-all dominance to hold it together. But lighting differences and multiple moods may be shockingly dramatized intentionally, and not reconciled in their new unity.

Lighting and tone control are effective ways of focusing interest and can be reciprocally planned in the original negatives. If necessary in order to coordinate with other parts, the negatives can also be modified beyond their original tone range in the final co-printing. Sometimes an oblique light or shadow swept across an entire complex will tie things together.

SCALE

Playful shifts of natural scale are often the mainspring of a photomontage. Suppose the Sphinx sitting in the desert sun should become gnat-small, while a buzzing gnat should become Sphinx-tall. The Sphinx would no longer be a symbol of majestic mystery, while the enlarged gnat could outwhirl a flying saucer. Monumentality, in other words, is relative. Caricature thrives on scale distortions and their accompanying psychological shifts.

In designing a photomontage mural, the image scale is a first consideration. It must be considered in terms of the surrounding architecture, and the kinesthetic relationships of the viewers—their approach, their eye levels, and their movement range within viewing distances. Large-to-small scale in the total design, the dark-and-light balance, the rhythmical linkage of parts—all have to be abstractly plotted before the diverse pictures can be intermeshed. In general, it is refreshing to see passages that are free-scanning and simple in contrast to other episodes which pinpoint attention. This sets up a visual pulse across the entire mural surface. Scale gamut is at the heart of a well-proportioned mural.

GENERALIZATION, CARICATURE, SYMBOL

Complex visual ideas can often be expressed in some form of photomontage. Diagrams, symbols, and concepts can be interpreted by picture linkage. Herbert Matter's contrasted diagrams for two facing

Rhythm and scale. In the photomontage of Martha Graham and her group, the meaning derives from rhythm and scale. "To interpret the dance, Deaths and Entrances, *as if a brooding presence were recalling a drama in a distant dream, I superimposed the two negatives in counter rhythm and exaggerated subordination of scale."* (Photo: Barbara Morgan)

pages (Figure 1) make a comparison between the development of human life from the atom, as opposed to mechanical constructions and automation. Most of the rendering is with pen, ruler and brush, with only the machinery details shown in assembled bits of photography. Since there is more hand art involved than photography, this design might also be called collage.

Realistic appearances, and anatomy, are often reorganized as caricature requires. This is usually achieved through exaggeration or distortion, such as the grafting of human heads on animal bodies. Photography, the supposedly realistic medium, makes the satire doubly ludicrous.

HOW TO MAKE PHOTOMONTAGE

Variation in contemporary photomontage and the potential of future invention is seemingly endless. Here follow some of the basic techniques:

Photomontage Paste-up or Construction

Also called collage, photomontage paste-up is a rudimentary form, which requires design ability but not necessarily photographic mastery. Photographic parts are combined with other hand arts, such as drawing, painting, lettering, and construction. When reproduced, the pasted joints and differing textures are not so apparent. If intended for a permanent art form such as collage great care should be used in the paste-up complex.

A smoother approach is to project photographic units directly upon a large printing paper, carefully masking off the areas allotted for the subsequent hand work. In "Man & Automation" by Herbert Matter (Figure 1), the machinery parts were cut out, pasted down, and photographed. Then the linear drawing was done over it.

Photogram

Made without camera or neg-

Neurotic Man and Pure Energy 1940. Note symbolic contrast of the inner ease of the motion of light with the compulsive stress felt in the human hand. "The light-drawing negative was one of a series I made by building up the image from my moving flash light in the darkened studio, with open lens. A little later, I shot this whirling hand at strobe timing of 1/500 of a second to fit the space and idea." (Photo: Barbara Morgan)

ative, the photogram is usually bracketed with photomontage as experimental photography. With the photogram, the designer interposes opaque or translucent objects, or masking forms, between the exposing light beam and the sensitive printing paper. If the paper is flipped right into the developing tray, one can immediately see, and subsequently control, the range of the grey scale and the design arrangement of the composition. In this simplest of all forms of photography, students and designers can do exercises right in the darkroom, without even understanding conventional photography with camera and film. Much of the work of Man Ray and Maholy

Figure 1. *Man and automation.* (Photomontage: [or collage] diagram: Herbert Matter, courtesy *Arts and Architecture* magazine)

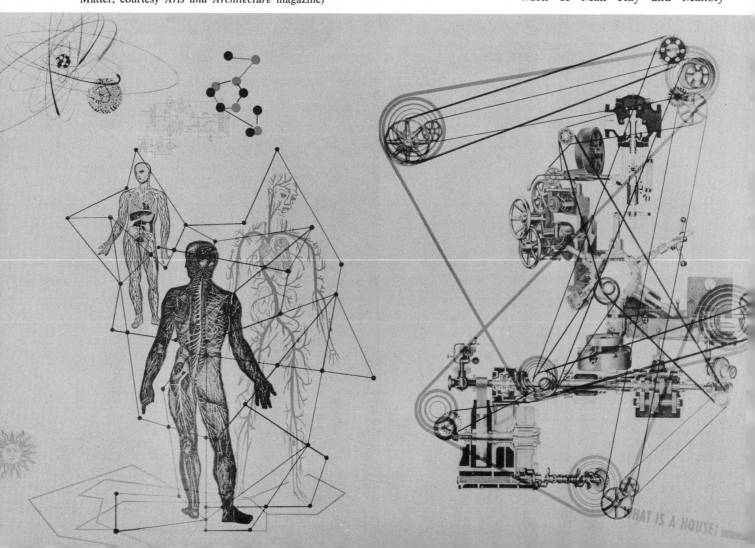

Nagy is based on the photogram.
Combination Photograph and Photogram

Many exciting effects can be produced by injecting photographic images from the negative into the photogram in various reciprocal densities. This may involve masking off parts of either of the component images of the mix. Hand art can also be used after the print is dried flat.
X-Ray Plates

X-ray plates give mysterious picture qualities when combined with normal photographic passages. X-ray transparencies are effective with illumination boxes and in conjunction with mechanically moving constructions.
Making Multiple Exposures on Single Negative

In making multiple exposures, it is a great advantage to have a master negative containing the image combination, since it can be printed directly without any fuss or manipulation. There are many ways of producing such a master multiple negative—for many cameras, in many situations, for many ideas.

A few basic tips follow.

1) For a design involving two or three negative portions, establish relative position, scale, and overlaps for the respective images. Transfer these individual images in proper space relation, scale, and density on three separate negatives of the same format (such as 4×5 or 5×7). Bind them together to insure correct registry for printing the simultaneously projected images.

2) If the objects of the design are to be used against a black background, there is an easy way to superimpose, providing the objects are available at one time. Using a view camera on tripod, draw the preconceived plan on the

Left *Lorelei. Two-negative, superimposed print.* (Photo: Andre de Dienes)

Below: *The bomb in man's mind.* (Photomontage: Herbert Matter, courtesy *Arts and Architecture* magazine)

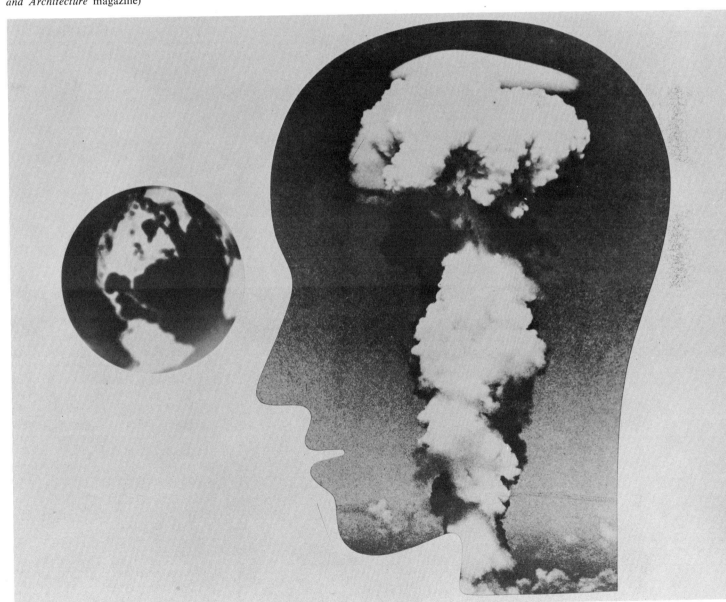

groundglass with grease pencil, showing scale, position, and overlap for each part. Then in succession shoot objects A, B, C, (or more) against the black background with their proper relative exposures and lighting. To achieve the desired scale, it may be necessary to move the tripod forward or back according to the groundglass plan. The black background in each exposure (since it does not reflect light) remains clear in the negative and thus allows continuing image-exposure overlaps to build up.

3) Action Superimposition. In both color and black-and-white, there are many ways of creating a sense of simultaneous action. With a slow shutter one may pan with the moving object and/or pause, getting various degrees of blur and partial image overlap. Such blur action can then be superimposed in printing with, let us say, a large-scale, nonmoving form to give contrast to the blur movement.

In studying dance motion, I have sometimes selected two phases from a dance which together sum up a theme. To the dominant motion I give the dominant scale. The secondary gesture might be used as an atmospheric overtone. These two motions are shot in sequence on the same negative with the dancer performing at different distances from the camera (refocused each time) to give interest to the contrast in scale.

4) A real object (transparent or opaque) may be set up before another enlargement, mural, or projection, and the ensemble photographed on a single negative with lighting emphasis. Such combinations are often used in fashion photomontage.

Superimposing in Printing

Multiple printing from ordinary enlargers is a laborious makeshift operation, requiring endless hours, patience, and too many sheets of test paper thrown into the wastebasket. The movie industry has animation equipment for making their time-sequence multiple images, which is, of course, extremely costly. It would spark more experiment and better-quality photomontage, if there were enlarger-accessory equipment of reasonable cost by which one could control superimposed-image projection. Until that time, multiple printing is a real workout.

Multiple printing is often done as follows: Assemble the two or more negatives and play them up and down in the enlarger, one after the other, until you discover the exact relative position, scale, and overlap that you feel will express your idea. One way to find this relationship of the participating negative images is to make a number of single prints from the different negatives. Then lay them together over a glass table, or against a window, to see their meshed position. Another way is to use architects' tracing paper for scale position and overlaps.

After finding the exact design relationship and making registry sheets for each negative's image, the next step is to find the proper exposure for each negative. Each negative used has to have the appropriate interrelation of exposure so that when the print is developed for, let us say 2½ minutes, each image will have the desired tonal weight in the ensemble.

This may mean that Negative A needs 20 seconds of exposure with a little dodging; Negative B, which is to act as an overtone, needs only eight seconds but with masking; and Negative C,, which is very dense, will require 45 seconds with both masking and dodging. To make these preliminary tests, the enlarger has to be racked up and down, as necessary, for each negative scale.

When finally the relative negative-exposure, timing, and aperture settings are mutually workable,

In his playful "The Guggenheim Museum," Weegee has tossed Frank Lloyd Wright's spiral building plus moving cars into a double-whirl design, making a compacted, dynamic exaggeration of this controversial building.

A 6×12-foot photomural lends atmosphere to the decor in a modern reception area. Mural has been illuminated with indirect fluorescent light at both top and bottom.

the combined photomontage print can be made. Lay the registry sheet down to find the position for each successive negative projection before shooting the exposure. Consult your timing sheet so that you can control your final results and, if necessary, correct them. Expose the correctly timed, correctly scaled negatives, one after the other, on the same sheet of sensitive paper on the enlarging easel. (While changing negatives, the paper will have to be put in a light-tight box or drawer to avoid fogging.) Usually it takes considerable refining of the correlations to get what you are after.

In a darkroom with several enlargers of the right size, one can set up the different negatives in their respective enlargers and carry the printing easel from one enlarger to another for the sequential exposures after having first established the reciprocal settings.

PHOTOMURALS

WILLIAM R. MELOY

President, W. R. Meloy, Inc., Shelbyville, Indiana

[The making of photomurals involves basic techniques that must be thoroughly understood for successful results. These techniques are explained in simple terms, with information given on suitable subject matter, uses of photomurals, projection equipment, exposure, processing methods, and mounting.]

• *Also see: Enlarging Photographs, Photographic Printing Papers.*

THE MAKING OF PHOTOMURALS does not necessarily require genius, but it most certainly demands the ultimate in careful planning and accurate procedure. Since there are numerous unsuspected factors which lead even the most experienced photographers into temporary disillusionment, the beginning darkroom worker should hold back the urge to make photomurals until his knowledge of the basic principles has been firmly grounded.

The true photomural must stand on its own creatively and not rely for its effect on sheer size alone. If the final product does not compel attention or evoke a mood of appreciation in the viewer, the basic purpose is lost and the worker may pride himself only in printing a wallpaper effect photographically, with much time and expense involved.

CHOOSING THE SUBJECT

The subject matter for the photomural should be chosen very

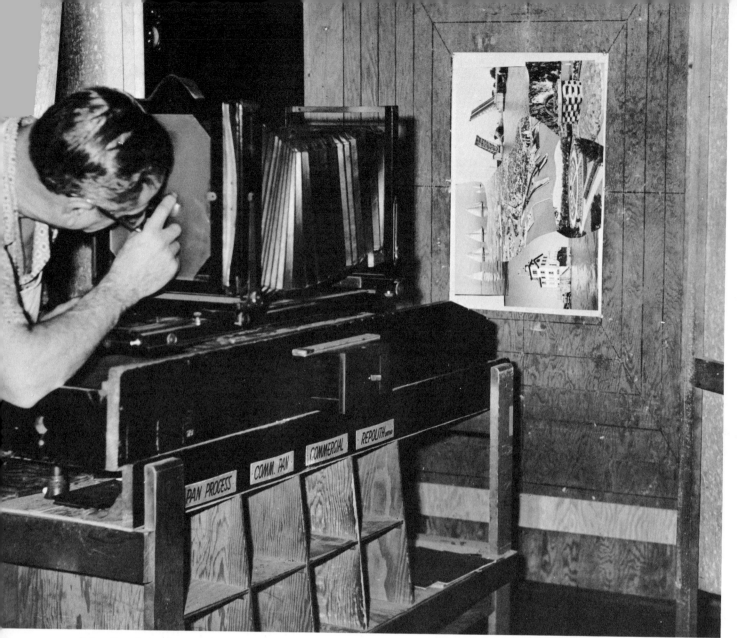

It is often desirable to make a copy negative from an original print. This procedure will allow more control over negative density and contrast when the negative is to be enlarged to extreme diameters.

carefully. The mural must not only appeal to you, your associates, and friends; it must also have enough appeal to hold their attention for some time to come. The subject selected must fit the environment where it is placed. For a business office or reception room, scenes relating to that business are appropriate, for example, a restaurant specializing in seafood and steaks might effectively choose seascape murals and some Western cattle scenes.

Many businesses even go so far as to change their murals seasonally. A store might well feature a cooling snow scene in the heat of summer and substitute a warm Florida-beach scene in the dead of winter.

In the home, the living room or den may be decorated with a restful scene from a memorable vacation trip; the dining room or breakfast room may have a beautiful garden scene framed to simulate a picture window; the family recreation room may display scenes of a more personal nature, such as sports, hobby, action, vacation and travel, or giant-sized informal portraits of a daughter with her first puppy or Junior when he has a front tooth knocked out playing ball.

MAKING THE NEGATIVE

Making the negative requires the utmost care in handling, for the quality of the negative basically determines the outcome of the finished photomural. The negative should be as thin as possible without loss of shadow detail. A $2\frac{1}{2} \times 2\frac{1}{2}$-inch negative that might print well to 8×10 with an exposure of $f/11$ in 60 to 80 seconds, might not be at all adaptable when enlarged to a mural size of 6×6 feet. A heavy or dense negative will also emphasize grain. If the negative can be read through a newspaper against an ordinary room light with all shadow detail present, it should be adequate for enlargement to extreme proportions.

In working with negatives that are too dense, yet print well on No. 2- or 3-grade paper, the experienced worker can produce a mural from a perfectly balanced copy negative. Should you run into a situation like this, make an 8×10 glossy print, properly dodged and burned, then rephotograph this on a slow-speed, fine-grained film, using fine-grain developer. You can control your copy negative to the extent that you will achieve a negative of the proper density for maximum projection.

It would be well for the inexperienced worker to make several copy negatives of various densities and then run a test to determine which will print best to maximum dimensions. Extreme care must be taken to see that no dust or foreign matter comes in contact with either the original or copy negative, as a fleck of household dust imbedded in a 35 mm negative could become as large as a thumbprint on a 4×6-foot mural.

EQUIPMENT

In considering equipment, let us first think about the enlarger. A condenser type is recommended, as cold- or diffusion-type enlargers tend to soften the detail required in a photomural. The enlarger should be of precise construction and be affixed to a firm chassis to eliminate vibration. The lens used should be of the highest quality; it is as important to have a good enlarging lens as it is to have a precision lens in the camera.

The finest negative will give considerably less than its best results if it is printed through an enlarger that is not capable of handling the job. Before printing a sizable enlargement, first be sure to check the age and condition of your enlarging bulb. If you realize that the bulb is nearing the end of its

Preliminary preparation of a photomontage. Once the finished size has been determined and the appropriate photos are selected, glossy prints in varying dimensions are pasted together in layout form and in direct proportion to the finished mural size. The center of interest in each print must be retained and skillfully blended with the accompanying photos to tell a graphic story.

useful life, replace it before exposing the print.

Most conventional enlargers are constructed to project the negative image from a vertical position, but in speaking of giant-size prints we must naturally assume that the image is projected on a horizontal plane. Many of the newer enlargers will convert for a horizontal projection; it is quite easy to remove the baseboard and, if necessary, attach it in a cradled position on a makeshift rigid table or a carpenter's sawhorse. Wooden blocks can be temporarily nailed to sawhorses to hold the enlarger in a rigid position. The slightest movement or jiggle in the enlarger would, of course, result in an unsharp reproduction.

The negative holder and lensboard must be carefully aligned or one part of the projected image will be out of focus. Several enlarger-equipment manufacturers have available a so-called focusing grid which is quite handy in ensuring that the enlarger is in true parallel alignment and properly focused. If such a grid negative is not available, the careful workman can make his own by drawing a geometrically true rectangle with diagonal lines from corner to corner, and then photographing it with a contrasty negative. If the projected negative or grid is sharp in the center and all corners, he will then have a reliable focusing-grid negative.

THE PROJECTION SURFACE

We have mentioned that the enlarger should be placed on a horizontal plane and projected on a flat wall area. The wall should be perfectly smooth and in a parallel plane to the enlarger. There should be no waves, depressions, or high spots in the wall, as irregular surfaces tend to reduce the sharpness of the projected image. A very

Darkroom technician is shown developing a 4×6-foot mural. Note that the paper has been folded in half for ease in handling.

After the mural has been developed and adequately fixed, it should be inspected for proper tones and sharpness of detail. This is essential when the print is made in several sections.

helpful addition to the projection area is a series of cross lines, vertically or horizontally marked at intervals of six to 12 inches, with diagonal lines running from corner to corner. Centering, measuring, and aligning of the projector and hanging the paper will be greatly simplified.

Before making the print make sure that your enlarger lens has been thoroughly cleaned and dusted. We then insert the negative or the focusing-grid negative and adjust the enlarger to the ultimate proportions and mural size desired, making sure that the center and all four corners focus sharply. The

lens should, or course, be at its widest aperture. When this is done, it should then be reset to the smallest aperture compatible with sharp definition.

Before taking a chance on ruining a considerable amount of paper, be sure that your darkroom or safelight will be safe during an extended exposure. If you anticipate an exposure of 15 to 20 minutes, first lay a sample of the paper you are going to expose directly under this safelight for the above-mentioned period of time. Develop it out, and if it shows signs of fogging, you will know that your safelight must be better shielded or

the illumination subdued.

PHOTOMURAL PAPERS

Photographic paper for murals is available in a variety of widths, lengths, emulsions, grades, and weights. We recommend a 40-inch width on semi-matte or rough-textured paper. One paper manufacturer produces a width of 62 inches, but we would not suggest that the beginner try to handle this much material at first.

The paper in rolled form must be carefully unrolled from the box, with the desired dimensions marked off to allow enough extra paper for trimming-out purposes. Be sure that the emulsion is in no way abraded. It should be mentioned here that the paper should be at the same

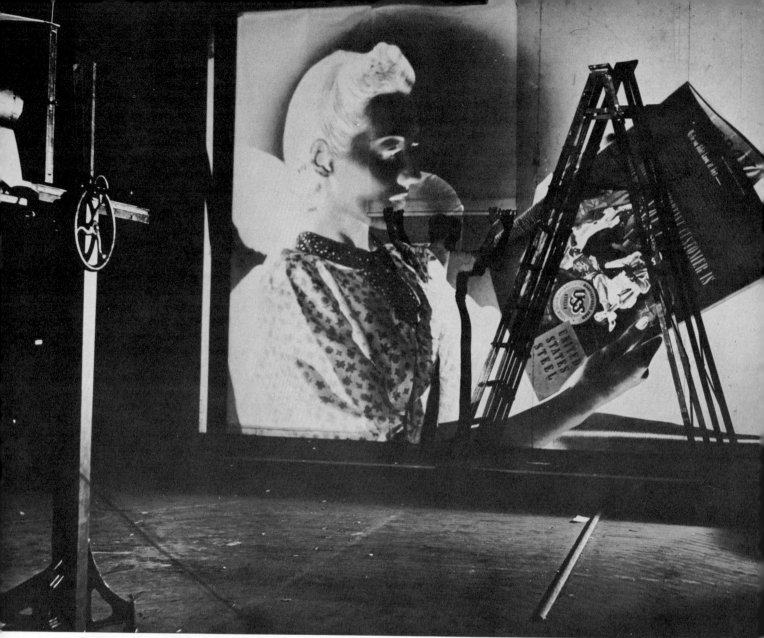

Projecting the image. Note technician in center rolling down the 60-inch-wide photomural paper sheets. Wall area must be perfectly flat and parallel with projector. Compare the size of man with that of the projected image from a 5×7 negative.

temperature as the room to which it is to be exposed, or it may tend to contract or buckle when it is hung on the projection wall. It is further recommended that the paper be subjected to this same room temperature for at least 48 hours and prehung on the wall three to five minutes before the actual projection is started.

When photo paper is wet it stretches in width about 2½ percent, or 1 inch in every 40 inches of width. The exact amount of stretch varies from roll to roll, so it is quite important that a mural made in multiple sections be cut from the same roll. On a large roll of mural paper it is quite possible that the emulsion will not be the same near the ends of the roll. Therefore, it is advisable to trim off the "salvage" from the ends of the roll, particularly when making a mural in continuous strips.

EXPOSURE

Again we must warn against the possibility of vibration during exposure—the slightest movement of the projector or a slight "crawl" of the negative, should it become overheated, will certainly spoil the outcome. In addition the slightest vibration, from someone walking over the floor or the wind vibrat-ing your ceiling or the projection wall, will create a distortion of focus. Remember now that we are speaking of an exposure in terms of minutes rather than seconds.

Since we are ultimately going to expose a large piece of paper we shall first test the various areas to be exposed. For the test at least five segments of paper (approximately 8×10) are hung in the four corners and the center of the exposure area. (It may also help to hang additional strips through the projected image, particularly in spots where the image shows definite highlights and shadows.) Expose and develop these test strips. The first test may fail miserably, but it will give a basis on which to judge the next test.

When we have completed our test strips, we hang the rolled mural paper on the wall. Cut to the desired size, it can be pinned to the wall area with aluminum push pins spaced six to eight inches apart along the edges. If the mural is large enough to require a splice, the additional strip or strips should overlap the preceding strip by approximately ½ inch. The spliced strips should be pinned to the wall with straight pins, pointed directly out from the paper towards the lens. These will leave minute white specks on the processed enlargement, which can later be spotted with pencil or dye.

The dodging or burning in of the enlargement should be handled basically as with smaller prints, although considerably larger dodging sticks or cards are needed. Be sure

Mural being mounted with the two sections of paper spliced or overlapped.

that you do not step in front of the projector during the exposure and remember to keep your dodging equipment in motion at all times. After the exposure is completed, remove the pins very carefully and roll the paper from the wall, emulsion side in. Do not let moist hands or fingers come in contact with the emulsion.

DEVELOPMENT

For development three tanks will be needed, one each for the developing solution, short stop, and hypo. Should you not wish to go to too great an expense and are interested only in a temporary, economical set of trays, we will not suggest the acid-resistant specially fabricated stainless-steel units such as those used by the professional mural firms. You can get by very well with the flat-type trays or tanks, constructed with four-inch sides, preferably cypress, redwood, or marine exterior plywood. The bottoms of the tanks can be made of ¼-inch tempered Masonite or marine plywood and sealed with plastic caulking. In lieu of this, sheets of vinyl plastic can be purchased inexpensively at your local hardware store and will serve the purpose well for a considerable period of time.

If the developing and short-stop trays are made 36×48×4 inches and the hypo tray 36×48×6 inches, they will accommodate large folded sections of the 40-inch paper. Approximately four gallons of solution will cover the bottom of the developer and short-stop trays to an adequate depth of ½ inch. The hypo solution should be filled to an approximate 3-inch depth, as it is essential that the developed print be covered with hypo at all times during the fixing which requires 12 to 15 minutes with intermittent turning of the print.

Let us say we start with a 30×40 inch piece of paper. Fold, but do not crease, the paper in half the long way. Grasp the two open edges, emulsion side out, and quickly immerse the paper in the developer with the open edges coming into contact with the developer first. Quickly carry the one side of the paper through the developer —then flip it to the other side. Agitate the paper constantly, gently

Mural being wet-mounted directly to wallboard panel. Mounter is smoothing out paste lumps with flannel covered wood block.

smoothing it through the developer with one hand. Be sure not to put too much pressure on the rolled or folded half.

When the print has reached full development, usually 1½ to two minutes, hold the paper up and let it drain. Then quickly transfer to the shortstop bath, turning the print frequently to insure that the development action has been curtailed. This should take only five to ten seconds. Then transfer to the hypo tank. Turn the print several times in the hypo and agitate it carefully with the hands for approximately two minutes before turning on the white light. We can then make a quick inspection of the print to make sure that it meets our expectations in all respects. Fixing can be accomplished in 12 to 15 minutes, with intermittent turning or agitation.

A fourth or final wash tank with constant circulating water should be available for the washing process. A bathtub can be used providing the print is turned often, and washed through three to five changes of water for one to 1½ hours.

After final washing the print is ready to dry. The print should suspend from a wire cable or clothesline with clothespins of the clip type and stretched taut. Since the print will still retain a good bit of water which will make it heavy, make sure that the clips are securely fastened to the salvage edge, nine to 12 inches apart. If the mural is made in several sections, it must be exposed from the same roll for the same amount of time, and developed, washed, and fixed for exactly the same amount of time, with the same amount of agitation. The slightest variation will result in paper strips that do not match in tone or density.

MOUNTING

Photomurals may be mounted directly to smooth plaster walls in much the same fashion as wallpaper is hung. A good grade of wallpaper paste should first be strained through cheesecloth to eliminate lumps. The print must be resoaked and applied to the wall wet. (If the mural is applied over

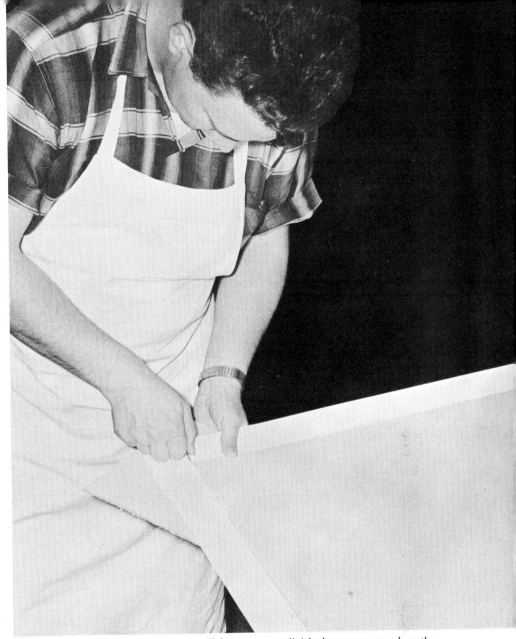

Lapped or turned edges. The mural will have a more finished appearance when the paper is carried around the edge of the mount and sealed to the back. Here the operator is trimming a corner to facilitate lapping of the edges.

new or "green" plaster, the wall should first be sized to seal in any chemically active lime remaining.) Paste should be generously applied to the wall, and the mural then placed in position. A damp sponge can be used to smooth out the mural and to remove any paste that might adhere to the surface of the print. Final trimming should be done while the mural is still wet, using a single-edge razor blade.

If a plaster wall is not available, the print can be mounted on either Masonite, wallboard, plywood or Homasote panels. Some of these

sheets are available in sizes up to 8 × 20 feet. The same procedure is followed in mounting, with the necessary addition of pasting sheets of 80- to 90-pound kraft wrapping paper to the back side of the mount in order to counteract warpage that would otherwise occur when the mural paper starts to dry and contract. If the paste seems uneven while the mural is still wet, do not be too concerned; it will usually smooth out upon drying. On particularly large murals, it is well to smooth out the paste with a wood block covered with several thicknesses of cotton flannel.

A mural that must be mounted in several sections must have the splices overlapping, the same as in the printing process. We have previously mentioned that the mural sections overlap approximately ½ inch to facilitate hanging the paper in the darkroom. The overlap can be cut down in the mounting procedure to approximately ¼ inch by trimming off ¼ inch of the underside of the paper which shows no image. The images on the two sections of paper should match perfectly in the mounting, but since they will contract somewhat in drying they should overlap approximately $1/32$ of an inch. Should the print come loose on a seam or a corner, you can redampen slightly with a sponge and apply more paste underneath.

Allow the print to dry overnight on a pair of sawhorses. It is important that the print dry evenly, with air reaching both sides during the drying process to further eliminate possible warpage. If the mural dries in a warped position the mounted enlargement will normally curl towards the face side of the print. This condition can be counteracted by dampening the kraft backing with a sponge and placing the print, face down, on a flat surface under evenly distri-

Murals with matte-surface paper may be hand-colored. Here an artist is spraying on water colors with an air brush. This may also be done with premixed transparent photo-oil colors, although it is a slower process.

buted weights for drying for four to six hours.

No mural is considered complete until it has been carefully inspected and retouched to remove spotting. White spots can be removed with drawing pencils. There are also a number of spotting dyes on the market that can be used equally well to obtain any tone desired; the dyes are best applied with a fine sable brush. Build the tone up with a weakened solution of these dyes; a concentrated dye applied with too heavy a color is hard to reduce.

Black spots can be eliminated by fine etching with a single-edge razor blade. This must, however, be handled very carefully, as too strong pressure on the blade may cut into the paper emulsion. The less experienced worker will probably obtain better results in removing black spots with a slow-acting bleach, such as Spotoff, and then filling in the light areas with pencil or Spotone dyes.

Most mural-paper surfaces have sufficient "tooth" to lend themselves well to hand coloring. Professional mural firms, dealing in gigantic-size prints, have trained artists who do the coloring with transparent water colors or dyes, deftly sprayed on the surface with delicate air brushes. This type of coloring is an art in itself and should not be attempted by those who have not had considerable

Giant enlargements can be produced from smaller film negatives that have been properly exposed and fine-grain developed. Here a portion of a 2¼ × 2¼ contact print is held up for comparison to the 8 × 14-foot mural made directly from the negative.

prior training. For the beginner there are many premixed, transparent oil colors. If a color mistake is made the color is readily removed with a solution supplied by the manufacturer.

To preserve the finished mural in either a black-and-white, toned, or hand-colored finish, a preservative coating should be applied. A mural mounted on waterproof board and coated with some of the newer sprayed-plastic finishes can withstand outdoor use for years.

A sheet of circuits printed with one exposure and ready for etching.

PHOTOSENSITIVE RESISTS

All photomechanical processes are based on the formation of a *resist image,* that is, an image that can protect the underlying surface from the action of an acid or other etching agent.

One of the earliest photographic processes was based on the fact that a type of asphaltum, known as Bitumen of Judea, was both sensitive to light and, after exposure, insoluble in the usual solvents. Thus, an image formed in this pitch would remain on the surface of a plate, after it had been exposed to light under a negative. The pitch was sufficiently acid-resistent to permit etching of the unexposed parts of the metal, while protecting the exposed sections. Its sensitivity was however, very low, and better methods were required for commercial photoengraving.

One particularly popular method, still used to a great extent in the making of zinc line etchings, is to sensitize the surface of the plate with a coating of albumin, containing ammonium dichromate. This coating is sensitive to light. After exposure under a line negative to the light of an arc lamp, the unexposed albumin can be washed away in water, learning the lines of the image covered with the exposed and now insoluble albumin layer.

The exposed albumin, though, is not a protection from acid, and the albumin image is turned into a resist by two subsequent stages. First, the image is dusted, while still wet, with a powdered resin known to the trade as *dragon's blood;* the powder adheres to the albumin image but not to the bare metal plate. The whole plate is then heated over a gas flame until the dragon's blood melts and is fused into a smooth, hard layer which is impervious to acid. The plate is then ready for etching.

In finer halftone work, the dragon's blood image is considered too crude, and a different type of sensitive coating is used, known (because no heating is required) as *cold-top enamel.* This is essentially a solution of shellac sensitized with dichromate; since shellac is insoluble in water, the exposed image is washed with alcohol to remove the unexposed areas. The hardened image remaining is basically shellac and is in itself a good resist to acid, although it is sometimes given a heat treatment to increase its acid resistance.

In recent years, the uses of metal etching have gone far beyond the early concentration on photomechanical reproduction of pictures or drawings. Currently, a good deal of electronic equipment is being made by the so-called *printed-circuit* or, more correctly, *etched-circuit,* method in which a board of insulating material has a thin sheet of copper laminated to it. At first, lines, corresponding to the desired circuit wiring, were drawn on the copper in an acid-resisting paint, with the copper etched away in an acid bath.

Naturally, this hand method was suitable only for small production. In manufacture, a photographic method was preferable, and in early experiments, the copper-clad laminate was sensitized with ordinary engravers' cold-top enamel, just as a plate to be etched for an image. The desired circuit diagram was then printed on these plates from previously prepared negatives, and etching done as before.

Nonetheless, this method was slow and inefficient, and, more recently, improved resists, based on proprietary sensitizers not using dichromates, have been introduced. One of these, the Kodak Photo Resist or KPR, can be applied to a plate by a simple flowing process, by dipping, or by spraying. It dries very rapidly, and is developed by simple immersion in a solvent or by solvent vapors in an industrial *vapor degreaser.* The image formed by this material is not very visible; however, the material can be dyed where a visible as well as an acid-

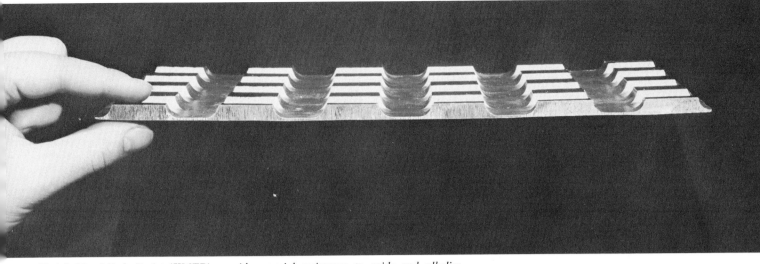

Kodak Metal-Etch Resist (KMER) provides special resistance to acids and alkalies and permits very deep etching of metals.

resisting image is required.

The exact method of handling this material varies according to the type of metal involved, and the use of the image. It can be used not only as a resist, but also to form an ink-receptive image on offset plates. However, its principal use is the making of etched nameplates, circuit boards, and photoengravings, and for similar purposes where its acid-resisting properties are particularly valuable.

New industrial applications are being found for metal-etching techniques. In space techniques, rocketry, and so on, metals are being used (such as titanium and others) that are exceedingly difficult to cut with ordinary tools. Here acid-etching methods are very useful. However, unlike earlier techniques, these often involve etching to very great depths, using only the most powerful of acids. (The usual etch for titanium is hydrofluoric acid, which is so powerful

Chemical milling or etching can be done from both sides of the plate.

it will dissolve a glass bottle.)

For extended treatment in very powerful acids, a more resistant and thicker image coating is required, and for this, another version of the Kodak Photo Resist is available. This version is known as Kodak Metal-Etch Resist, and is intended almost exclusively for industrial applications. The systems used include ordinary chemical etching, *selective plating,* and the so-called *chemical milling* in which etching is done from both sides of the plate right through its complete thickness. With selective plating, the resist image is applied and the material then placed in an electroplating tank. But instead of the unexposed metal being etched away, it is built up by the application of the same or a different metal from the plating bath.

KMER's ability to adhere to a variety of metals, as well as to reproduce detail, makes it suitable for manufacturing parts of many sizes, shapes, and design.

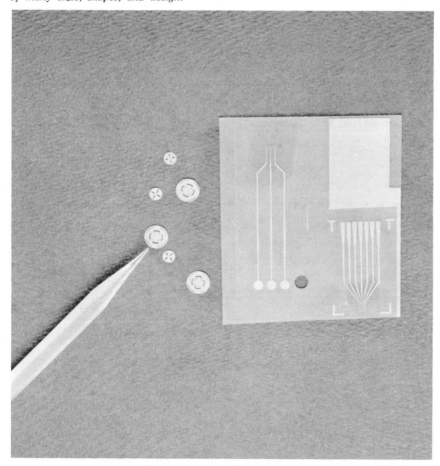

PHOTOTYPESETTING

With the growing popularity of offset lithography as a means of printing all kinds of material, various photographic systems for setting type have been developed.

In offset lithography, the original copy is first prepared by pasting up the various elements, body type, headlines, drawings, etc., and then making a large negative with a process camera. From this negative, the printing plate is prepared and put on an offset press for printing.

The original method of preparing material for this process involves first setting all material in type. After correcting the type forms, reproduction proofs (called *repros*) are taken, and pasted up into the necessary forms for photographing. Since the cost of the typesetting and the expense and labor of doing the paste-up, photographing it, and making a press-plate is excessive, it soon became obvious that some means of eliminating the type form was needed. One method

that was applied quite early was to use special typewriters such as the Varityper and the Justowriter, which could produce lines of even length at both ends. In addition, the Varityper had changeable types, for roman, italic, bold face, etc.

An even more efficient system, however, involves the use of a machine that produces a photographic negative directly, thereby eliminating the paste-up and photographing stage. A number of these machines are now available. In all of them, type negatives are arranged in the proper order and photographed onto film which is then developed and used to prepare the litho plate.

However, the paste-up system is still used for display work, since it enables the printer to combine type, illustrative material, and photographs all in one step. For producing large type copy for paste-up, several photographic typesetting machines are available. Some are essentially contact printers; a negative of the desired type face and in the desired size is inserted in the machine, and the letters exposed in contact on paper rolls. Others are optical printing devices and provide a wide range of sizes from a single-alphabet negative. In the latter, it is even possible to insert modification lenses which can widen or narrow an alphabet, or tilt it into an italic or backslant form.

A partial list of current machines, together with a short description of each, follows.

TEXT-COMPOSING MACHINES

ATF Typesetter, Model B. A simplified keyboard unit punches a paper tape, which controls the photographing unit. The photographing unit has several alphabets in negative form on a transparent disk, and controlled by the punched tape, produces composition on film or paper from 5 to 14 point, in lines up to 7 3/8 inches wide at ten lines per minute.

Intertype Fotosetter. Here, the entire operation is done in one machine, which operates much like a hot-metal linotype. However, the brass matrices have a film-negative

The Filmotype photolettering and typesetting machine is a desk-size unit designed to produce display headings. Headings are produced on either paper or film from many different styles available in sizes from 12 to 144 point.

inset, and after a line of matrices has been set from the keyboard, the machine automatically photographs them in sequence on film or paper. The machine has a 14-lens turret, and produces a wide range of sizes from a single font of matrix negatives.

Mergenthaler Linofilm. A very advanced three-unit system for text composition; can handle display as well. The three units are the keyboard, the photographic unit, and the Linofilm Composer. The keyboard punches paper tape to control as many as 18 different type fonts in one job in sizes from 6 to 36 point. The photographic unit is fed by the tape and produces 15 lines per minute of right-reading positive (black on white) type on either film or paper. The Linofilm Composer is an assembly device which is used to make up the material composed on the Linofilm into pages or layouts.

Monophoto. A two-unit machine. A keyboard unit punches a wide paper tape with hole combinations. This keyboard is identical with the one used with the hot-metal Monotype; in fact, the same keyboard can be used to control either machine. In the Monophoto, the matrix case contains a set of negatives of the various alphabetic characters. By changing lenses, the same font of negatives can be used to produce any size of type

from 6 to 24 points.

Photon. Another tape-operated machine. The printing unit is exceedingly fast and can handle the output of several keyboard units. Type fonts are in the form of negative disks, which rotate continuously in the machine. Exposure is made by the flashing of an electronic flashlamp at the instant the correct character is in position. The machine prints ten characters a second, can handle type sizes from 4 to 72 points, and can mix any or all types in one line. An electronic calculator makes all lines end evenly.

DISPLAY-TYPE SETTERS

Filmotype. An ingenious contact-printing device; uses negative alphabets in strip form in sizes from 12 to 144 point. Letters are exposed onto paper or film, one at a time, by a simple manual operation. Development of paper then produces sharp letters on white, perfectly spaced.

Friden Typro. A contact-printing machine, working like Filmotype.

Hadego. Letters are printed in white on blocks of black material, and are set up and spaced just like printer's type, by hand. The line of set "matrices" is then photographed on film or paper in a machine resembling a Photostat. Enlargement or reduction is possible in the photographic stage.

Headliner. (Varityper Corporation) Composes display and headlines types up to 72 point, on film or paper, either strip or sheets. Vertical- and horizontal-line spacing is adjustable; type can be set to match layout.

Morisawa Photo Typesetter. Produces display type from 12 to 72 point from a single-alphabet negative, by means of a set of 13 prefocused lenses. Automatically spaces as desired. Modification lenses are available for expanding, contracting, or slanting type faces.

Photo Typositor. An enlarger-type machine, using film negatives in strips; can use fonts from other

The Photo Typositor uses film negatives in two-inch strips and can print various sizes from the one master font. The image develops as the machine is operated, thus giving the operator a wide choice in spacing and changing sizes.

Intertype Fotosetter photographic typesetting machine, with circulating matrix.

machines such as the Filmotype. Degree of enlargement is variable, and modification lenses can be used for stretch, squeeze, or slant effects. Paper develops automatically while it is being exposed, so that the operator sees exactly where each letter is as it appears, and can do visual spacing, interlocking of letters, etc.

Protype. Simple contact-printing device, using alphabets in film-strip form, and a hand lamp for expos-

ing. Over 25,000 type fonts available.

Strip Printer. Produces display type from 6 to 72 point from film-strip alphabets. Machine is entirely hand-operated, and letters are spaced visually.

□

PHYSICAL DEVELOPMENT

In physical development, the silver that is reduced to form the visible image is not derived from

the silver halide in the emulsion, but comes instead from silver salts in the developer. The silver halide in the emulsion provides only the tiny silver speck of the latent image on which the additional silver is deposited during development. Physical development is used only in rare instances, mainly for experimental work in studying the development process and investigating the nature of the latent image.

A physical developer contains a reducing agent (Metol, hydroquinone, or both) and a source of silver and may be either acid or alkaline. In the acid bath, the reducing agents work very weakly, and the silver source may be simply silver nitrate alone. In alkaline solution the reducing agents work much more strongly, tending to reduce the silver nitrate ever faster than the halide in the image. Thus the silver nitrate has to be "complexed" with sodium sulfite or sodium thiosulfate for protection. In either case, the developer is somewhat unstable, and will eventually deposit silver all over the tray as well as the negative being developed.

The deposition of silver is most rapid where there are already silver specks in existence, as in the case of the latent image. It has been stated that silver specks as small as four atoms of silver are sufficient to initiate development. Interestingly enough, it is the number of specks rather than their size which seems to be the controlling factor.

Physical development, as compared to ordinary chemical development, is highly inefficient. With slow films, almost five times as much exposure is required for a fully exposed negative with a physical developer than with normal development. There is evidence that for the faster films, an even greater increase in exposure is required. This seems to indicate that the high-speed films (which gain their sensitivity by dye treatment) have a different mechanism of development and that in normal chemical development at least the silver speck is not the determining factor. In physical development, however, the latent image is apparently only the metallic silver speck formed by exposure.

Although a negative can be developed in a physical developer *after fixation,* this does not mean that a physical developer can be used to salvage a negative that has been accidentally placed in a hypo bath before development. For one thing, physical development, as mentioned, requires five times greater exposure, at least. For another, the hypo bath required for post-fixation development has to be specially compounded and used so that it will not destroy the silver specks of the latent image at the same time as it is removing the unexposed halides. Even then, some of the image is lost during fixing, and the method remains a purely experimental one for investigation of certain aspects of image formation. It is certainly not a practical method for photographers.

Practical Physical Development

Physical development can be used in certain cases in 35 mm photography. For one thing, since the image is formed by depositing silver on the tiny image speck rather than by reducing the entire silver grain, the image is much less grainy. For another, the deposited silver is in a very thin layer; hence the resulting image has very high sharpness and acutance.

The acid type of physical developer is faster but less stable, and therefore the alkaline type is usually used. However, in the alkaline developer, hypo is added as a complexing agent. Hypo tends to attack the silver halide in the film, and also to stop the chemical development which is part of the process (some chemical development needs to take place in order to initiate the physical process). To prevent the attack of the emulsion by thiosulfate, a forebath is usually used, based on potassium iodide; this transforms the silver bromide to iodide which is less easily attacked by hypo.

Procedure

For those who like to experiment, the following formulas will be of interest.

Forebath

Sodium Sulfite (anhydrous)
365 grains (25 grams)
Potassium iodide
145 grains (10 grams)
Water to make
32 ounces (1 liter)

Developer-Solution A

Sodium Sulfite (anhydrous)
1 ounce 290 grains (50 grams)
Silver nitrate
1 ounce (30 grams)
Sodium thiosulfate (hypo)
5 ounces (150 grams)
Water to make
32 ounces (1 liter)

Developer-Solution B

Metol
30 grains (2 grams)
Sodium Sulfite (anhydrous)
145 grains (10 grams)
Hydroquinone
50 grains (3.4 grams)
Sodium hydroxide
50 grains (3.4 grams)
Distilled water to make
3¼ ounces 100 cc.

The film is first immersed in the forebath for 1½ minutes. It must then be thoroughly washed to prevent formation of silver iodide when transferred to the developer.

The working developer is made by mixing 10 parts of Solution A, 1 part of Solution B, and 40 parts of water. It must be made up immediately before use and thrown away afterward; the mixed solution does not keep.

Development takes from 25 to 30 minutes at 68 F.

After development, the film is fixed in a strong hypo bath with the usual acid hardener. The hypo content must be at least 30 percent, and even then fixing may take over an hour, as the silver iodide formed by the forebath dissolves very slowly in hypo. After fixing, the film must be washed for at least an hour, and dried in the usual way.

Even after complete fixation, the film may appear slightly milky, due to a fine deposit of silver over the entire surface. This can be removed by a very short treatment in a weak bichromate bleach (1/10 of one-percent bichromate, with a few drops of sulfuric acid added).

An underdeveloped negative, that is, one lacking in density but having ample shadow detail, can be strengthened even after fixing, by the use of the same developer as above, freshly mixed. In this case, it is acting simply as a silver intensifier. The forebath is not needed, of course.

The developer has a strong staining action on the skin, and rubber gloves should be worn. It will also stain the trays and other containers; this stain can be removed by a standard bichromate tray-cleaner solution, such as Kodak TC-1.

NEW ENGLAND HOUSE

EZRA STOLLER

The austerity of traditional colonial architecture is emphasized by this composition of angular building lines in a New England house. The squares of the door and window, the parallel horizontals of the walls and the diagonals of the roof lines all fit together to create a photograph as rigorously organized as a Mondrian painting. Only the bush in the lower left-hand corner, the stepping stones on the ground and the fleecy clouds in the sky act as relieving elements in a design in which everything else is sharp, clear and straight.

Notice the additional lines and angles provided by the open door and window, creating shadows of their own. Also note that the photograph was shot with the sun high in the sky to give definition to the clapboard siding of the house, an important part of the over-all compositional design.

PICTORIAL PHOTOGRAPHY

MINOR WHITE
Photographer, Writer, Professor of Photography, Author of "Zone System Manual" and "Canons of Camerawork"

[Down through the past century of photography, the term *pictorial* has had many supporting groups and just as many interpretations. The author explains what is meant by the **various** approaches and discusses the classic and romantic traditions in relation to present trends. Further valuable information is to be found in the background information supplied with the illustrations.]

• *Also see: Composition; Exhibitions of Photography; Landscape Photography.*

Figure 1. *Coming Boats, 1894.* (Photo: Henry Peach Robinson)

ANYTHING MADE BY GRAPHIC MEANS is a picture, and if it is made with a camera it is a photograph. Distinctions finer than this are required by relatively few people. Probably most photographers on location give little thought to the verbal distinctions, definitions, classifications, and other refinements appropriate to the study of finished photographs. But any distinctions that plague them after the fact have a bearing on their photography; because anything that is learned, even subconciously, is applied to the next photograph.

On the other hand, photographers make the term *pictorial* and its shifting meanings a part of their everyday critical vocabulary. They habitually compare photographs, or one photographer with another, or photographs with paintings, or visual photography as a medium with the other visual arts.

Pictorial, so far as it suggests the amateur salon photography of pictoria*lism,* is in bad repute these days, but the term is still the most descriptive name for a frank acknowledgement of the camera and film as a medium, and the reality of the photograph as a new fact in the world—that is, a picture.

Pictorial photography has had an active history, and has functioned under a variety of names. Before 1920, it was known as *Pictorialism,* later as *Camerawork* by Stieglitz. In the 30's the Bauhaus group gave it the name of *The New Vision,* while in the 50's Otto Steinert, J.A. Schmoll, and Franz Roh called it *Subjektive Fotographie.*

In the broad sense, pictorial photography keeps a balance between the recording and the transforming power of lens and film. The esthetic object may be recorded or the unesthetic transformed into a significant picture. In either case the audience response is esthetic. The *revealing moment* (Weston) or the *exact instant* (Cartier-Bresson) may be recorded; or, by the transforming power of the medium, the photograph is the exact instant when the man is revealed to himself (Chappell-Lyons).

FOUR WORKABLE CLASSES

For our purpose it seems advisable to look at the place occupied by pictorial photography in the gamut of visual photography. Four broad classes will serve: informational, reportage, pictorial, equivalence. A former student, Mathew Herron, epitomized the four:

Informational: This is it and this

Figure 2. *Angelica: Overturned Car, 1959.* (Photo: Nathan Lyons)

is the way the *camera* saw it.

Reportage: This is it and this is the way *I* saw it.

Pictorial: This is what I saw and here is how *I feel* about it.

Equivalence: I have felt something and here is a *metaphor* of my feeling.

Informational.

Informational photographs predominate in fields where experts use the mechanical-recording characteristics of photography in the service of their own special purposes. Astronomical photographs are notorious examples of photo-

graphs considered beautiful by laymen who understand nothing of their scientific use.

Reportage.

Reportage embraces two approaches. The first of these is seen in the documentarians who come at the subject matter in a most neutral manner. (To name a few: Berenice Abbott, Dorothea Lange, Walker Evans, John Collier, Jr.) They make a great effort to leave their feelings out of their photography. They differ from the informational photographer because they bring a sense of time and man's condition in society to truth. While they claim not to be reformers, their work has often been used by propaganda groups on both sides of an issue.

The second approach is that of the photojournalist. For the photojournalist, time is a sense of history in the making and the newsworthy structuring of reality is a feature of their conscious responsibility to millions of readers. The names are familiar: Margaret Bourke-White, Alfred Eisenstadt, W. Eugene Smith, Henri Cartier-Bresson. For photographers of the reportage persuasion, their basic orientation to truth dictates reporting the object with its esthetic value left intact. So at times pictorial photojournalism is an exact classification of certain photographs.

A FUNDAMENTAL DISTINCTION

At least one working distinction between reportage and pictorial rests on the respective attitudes toward the photograph and its relation to the world of appearances. Both documentarian and photojournalist—and a few million readers—believe that the photograph brings the event, place, or person to the viewer, or conversely the viewer to the place, or person or event. The pictorial photographer for his part takes the stand that the photograph has significance in its own right. We should look at these two attitudes more closely, because the distinction is a basic one, separating responses into two modes and photographers into two groups which are usually reluctant to understand each other.

Figure 3. *Newsboys at Midnight, circa 1907.* (Photo: Lewis Hine)

When a spectator is looking at a photograph of the reportage school it is expected by photographer and viewer alike that the thing seen and the feeling aroused will be identical, or nearly so, to what the spectator would have seen and felt had he been standing beside the camera at the time of the exposure. The subject is allowed and encouraged to speak for itself with the photograph a kind of vehicle or bridge by which the event is brought to the man in the armchair. This is generally conceded to be communication.

Philosophers know that there is a nagging question in the matter of vision: do we see what we want to see, or believe what we see? Not so the rest of us; we are the willing victims of the documentary illusion. Without this pertinent question to guide us, we confuse the photographic shadow of the world with the world that the eye reports. Consequently the reportage photograph does function as if a report could equal the event.

SOURCE

Pictorial photographers treat the photographic rendering or report as an original event in its own right. They maintain a distinction between a record of a beautiful flower and the same flower related to its surroundings, which when photographed produces an esthetic picture. Pictorial photographs, then, are in some degree independent of the subject before the camera.

Krazena-Krausz, in the *Focal Encyclopedia of Photography* (1956) indicates that the pictorial photographers "are more or less interested in the subject for the picture it will yield." Since the subject is secondary, and the manner primary, the photographs may be said to be sources of experience in varying degree.

In contemporary times the concept of sources of experience is emphatically illustrated by those who exploit technical manipulation or the transforming power of camera and film. Had the viewer stood beside Nathan Lyons' camera (Figure 2) he might fail to see any connection between the original

subject—overturned car—and the photograph. The subject is no longer recognizable; hence the photograph becomes the source, the original trigger of response. If the viewer is to have a subject for it, he has to invent his own out of whatever associations the picture sets off. In this instance, he imaginatively enjoys whatever he brings to the photograph, or he gets along happily without a subject and responds to the photograph as if it were form for its own sake. Or he may enter into empathic relations with the photograph, in which case expressive form would be said to stimulate response.

SEEING IS FUNDAMENTAL TO PHOTOGRAPHY

The fundamental act of camera photography is the seeing relationship between man, medium, and object. Because of the nature of the medium, the art of seeing is common to both reportage and pictorial photographers. To the art of "seeing," the pictorial photographer adds the art of "seeing" composition and furthermore "seeing" in the terms of the unique characteristics of the medium.

The late Edward Weston said that "composition is the strongest way of seeing." He did not refer to an imposition on his subject

Figure 4. *Paris Street.* (Photo: Louis Jasques Mande Daguerre)

of that kind of composition which is appropriate to painting; he meant the composition generated, so to speak, by the subject and its environment by their own nature.

On the same point, Henri Cartier-Bresson writes in *The Decisive Moment:* "For me content cannot be separated from form. By form, I mean a rigorous organization of the interplay of surfaces, lines, and values. It is in this organization alone that our conceptions and emotions become concrete and communicable. In photography visual organization can stem only from a developed instinct."

Regarding medium, the pictorial photographer treats the print as the final product. To the reportage photographer the print is the step following the negative in a still longer process leading to a reproduction printed in ink, not in silver. To the pictorial photographer, reproduction in ink of a fine silver or platinum print, is the shadow of a precise reality.

THE CLASSIC AND ROMANTIC TRADITIONS IN PICTORIAL PHOTOGRAPHY

Within pictorial photography, two traditions prevail. They can be called classic and romantic simply on the approach to or use of the medium. "I use the camera faithfully," says the classicist. He means that he sticks to the unique characteristics of camera and light-sensitive emulsions. "Explore the potentials," cries the romanticist. With this manifesto he throws all restrictions to the winds.

The Classic Mode.

Classic uniqueness of medium, however, beleaguers definition. When the f/64 group in San Francisco defined pure, or straight, photography for themselves, they had as many reasons to include sandwiched negatives and multiple exposures, which they shunned, as sharpness fore and aft, which they stoutly defended. But then, all the definitions of visual photography over the years have been little more than fragile rearrangements of a wide variety of features. When "pure photography" or "experimental photography" or "creative photography" is not up to the demands of the wisdom of the psyche or the purpose of the moment, knowledgeable photographers will resort to any potential of the medium. Edward Weston once wrote that he would print on a doormat if by so doing he could evoke in others the precise emotional state he wanted them to have. Shackled by his own developed discipline, he never did.

We need now the names of a few men who have established the visual foundations of the classic tradition. We will name here the the conscious ones rather than the naive, and the writer-photographers because they have been able to be both verbal and visual about their aims. One is Peter Henry Emerson of the last century, whose work, according to historian Nancy Newhall, has that exact and exquisite balance between the lyrical and the accurate which is the hallmark of the pictorialist who uses the camera faithfully. A scene faithfully rendered is of the order of a translation of poetry from one language to another. An object faithfully rendered is more of a feel-alike than a look-alike. Alfred Stieglitz added scope and stature to the classic tradition without ever breaking the link to the world of appearances, while Edward Weston sometimes said that his pictures were a means of sharing a moment

Figure 5. *Abandoned Car, 1938.* (Photo: Edward Weston)

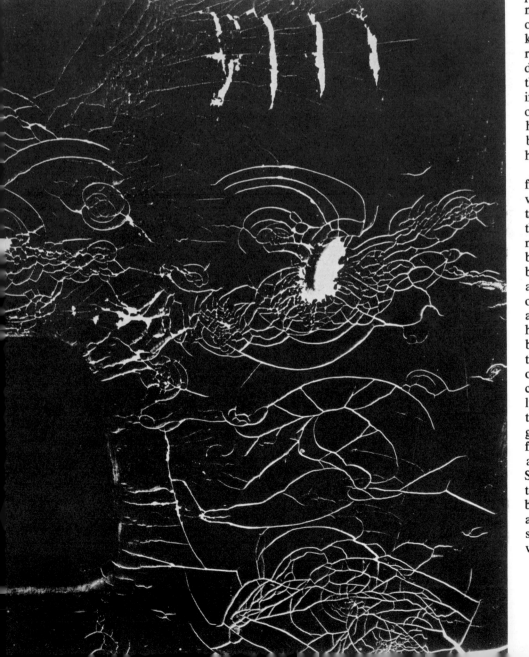

of beauty with other people who were unable to be there, or, if present, were, in effect, blind. Ansel Adams strenuously avoids the sentimental, the cozy, anything picturesque, and at the same time includes in his work some of the finest picture postcards of all. Those in the tradition of the classic use of the medium are willing to wait long hours, weeks, and years, if necessary, until nature or situation reveal themselves in such a way that the camera used for its own unique characteristics can render revelation.

The classic approach is also obvious in the work of the reportage photographers. What separates them from the classic pictorialists is the selection of subject matter. The esthetic subject is but a small part of their world. They seek to make the uncommon common, as Beaumont Newhall wrote in his article, "Photographing the Reality of the Abstract" (*New Directions,* 1956). Truth and disaster are preferred to beauty, but who ever found a brick wall between these two absolutes —at least in life?

The Romantic Mode.

Workers in the romantic vein of pictorial photography always seem to find themselves embroiled self-consciously with either art or Art. Since photography does not proliferate in a vacuum, it is fitting that such photographers should benefit by the ever-constant exchanges between photography and painting. They are involved with the maleability of the photographic image.

Hand-wrought alterations were the stock in trade of pictorialists before 1910. Typical photographic changes of the image after 1920 acquired the name of experimental. The term still sticks to this now 35-year-old tradition. In a general way, 1910 to 1920 were transition years. Prior to that time, the leaders sought to force pictorial photography to do what painting does—that is, to reshape nature for man's consumption, and especially for persons of cultivated taste. Since that time the transforming power of the medium itself has been explored, and occasionally

Figure 6. *Self-Portrait, 1902.* (Photo: Edward Steichen)

such exploration has been used to reshape, not nature, but man, so that he might understand nature and himself.

PHOTOGRAPHY AND ART

"Is photography art?" was the burning question before the transition period. By the efforts of the Photo-Secessionists under Alfred Stieglitz, Edward Steichen, and others, photography won its place in the fine arts 50 years ago. Since the transition, slowly and sporadically that question has changed. Now it reads something like this:

"What kind of art is photography?" ("Is photography art?" is still asked by newcomers to photography who, it seems, are really asking what art is. They question in all seriousness because they do not know. They think art is a kind of thing instead of a feeling state.)

Historians can see the many influences at work in the development of the kind of art photography can give us. The best of the romantics and classicists, as well as individual photographs of the documentarian are automatically included. Of equal importance to the art of photog-

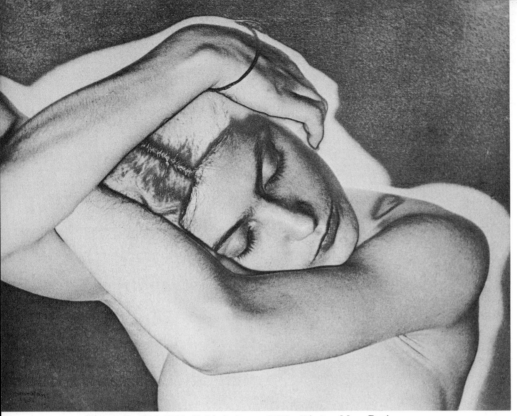

Figure 7. *Girl With Folded Arms, 1929.* (Photo: Man Ray)

raphy is the effect of self-expression extended to thousands of lesser talents.

The pictorial photography of the Photo-Secessionists was so successful by 1920 that a growing host of amateurs followed. Their efforts were poured into a pictorial concept aimed at emulating painting—not the vigorous and vital Cubism then current, but an older genre branded by sentimentality, pseudo-Impressionism, and diluted Whistler. A salon photograph came into fashion which was in keeping with the influx of amateurs with high faith in rules —so a style became reduced to a formula, and picture content to competition. Soon prizes were given for the best renditions of the formula. This still is pictorial*ism* today.

With the growth of the Photographic Society of America, photography "by the numbers" has been

Figure 8. *Cosmic Conversation, 1959.* (Photo: Walter Chappell)

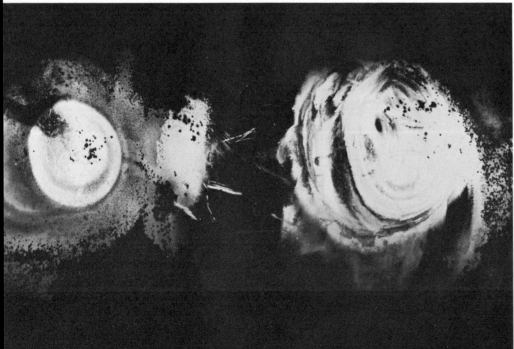

and still is the substitute for art experience, a substitute offered to thousands of serious amateurs and their audiences. Pictorialism will always be with us, changing its fashions behind the times, because it offers to a certain level of persons all they want of art, or can take. (We still do not know the effect of mass TV audiences on pictorial photography.)

Steichen's *Family of Man* exhibition and Ivan Dmitri's *Photography in the Fine Arts* are recent views of the kind of art photography can be, while the Newhall *Art of Photography* exhibition at the George Eastman House in Rochester, New York, holds classic photography up to the standards demanded by cultivated taste.

ABSTRACTION AND PHOTOGRAPHY

Moholy-Nagy and the members of the Bauhaus (1919-1929) are ordinarily credited with the introduction of the drive to explore all media and materials, including photography. Dadaist Man Ray in Paris invaded museums with cameraless photographs and solarizations. (It is noteworthy that he collected documentarian Atget's photographs for their surrealistic overtones.) In this country, Paul Strand, Francis Bruguiere, and Alvin Langdon Coburn had started to reveal the impact of cubism in their photography still earlier, and doubtless the prototypes of photographic abstraction had been emptied out of wastebaskets for years before that. Recently photographs have appeared that resemble nothing so much as copies of nonobjective paintings. So similar are they that they invite comparison on a basis of painting esthetic rather than unique camera rationale (Figure 8).

Beaumont Newhall has remarked in conversation that "all photographs are abstractions, or none are." It may be better to assume that no photograph is an abstraction, because the transforming power of the camera causes a somewhat different psychological process in the photographer than paint and brushes arouse in the painter. No matter how much the pictures resemble each other, the sources are different.

It takes a perceptive photographer to discover this through his own experience. George Schmidt and Robert Schenk edited a book, *Form in Art and Nature,* which pointed out the similarities between informational electron-microscopy photographs in color, and color reproductions of certain nonobjective paintings. The correspondences are sometimes so striking that it is a puzzle which is nature and which is the painting. Which one could have posed for the other?

The implication that nature was nonobjective or abstract before man is important to the considerations of pictorial photography. Nathan Lyons suggested in a review of the book that in one sense the comparisons are an affirmation that the figments of man's imagination already exist factually in the world before he ever thinks of them. If this is true, creative imagination is no more than a kind of intuition of what is already present. It is interesting to remember that painter Goya's drawings of bulls and their fighters were considered incorrect before high-speed photography proved the truth of his exceptionally fast eye.

The implications of the pictures published with this text are impor-tant because contemporary pictorial photographers are frequently accused of learning to "see" from contemporary painters, and their work labeled the *New Pictorialism.* Doubtless some photographers are always imitating an easy pseudo-art. Nevertheless the matter is not as simple as that, because photography always leads subjective man back to objective world, and, conversely, a developed talent for "seeing" misses little in the visual world.

To look at the world for what it is, as the classic pictorial photographer steels himself to do, repeatedly leads to rendering nature or situation at the moment of revelation—or to the imitation of nature. To look at the world for what else it is, as the romantic discovers, also leads to enlightenment—or to the imitation of painting. Meister Eckart forecast their manifesto a few centuries ago. "My looks are not my nature, they are the accidents of nature....To find nature herself likenesses have to be shattered and the further in the nearer to actual things."

PUBLICATIONS

Pictorial photography in the larger sense always has its special publications; so does pictoria*lism.* At the beginning of the century, *Camerawork* was in effect the official magazine of the Photo-Secessionists. Its editor, Alfred Stieglitz, wrote, "The only thing in Art that can not be imitated is Spirit." *American Photography,* under Frank R. Fraprie, served amateur pictorialism for years by tabulating the Point Winners. At midcentury, *Aperture* avoids group affiliation without difficulty. Editor, Minor White, wrote, "When the photograph is a mirror of the man, and the man is a mirror of the world, Spirit may take over."

EQUIVALENCE

The concept of *equivalence* is the most mature idea that has appeared in visual photography. Hence it affects the pictorial effort.

Recall the earlier epitomization: "I felt something; here is a metaphor of my feeling." Equivalence is not a style; there is no standard surface appearance. It is not a school. It is not necessarily poetic. Equivalence can originate in any class we have named—pictorial, informational, or reportage. It is reasonably defined by a person's response. To be equivalent, a photograph, both as thing and image, must function as a catalyst. Actually equivalence is not a photograph at all, but a kind of

Figure 9. *Three Images: a. Logotype, b. Ashby Starr, c. Walter Chappell.*

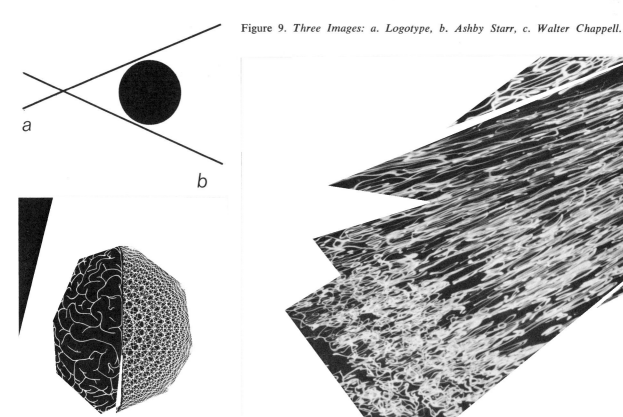

response, a *function*.

Alfred Stieglitz used the word *equivalent* first as a title for certain photographs he made early in the 1920's. Clouds had been in front of his camera at the time; even so it was the response which made the equivalence. This special response is described as an image taken into a person and retained because it is wanted. Once in mind and body, he turns it into his own private image. He may not understand his new private image, though it is one that will cross his mind when he is doing something else. It can be said that he remembers the image because he wants to, but in some instances it is equally accurate to say that he remembers the image because of a compulsion. From fear or love, from annoyance, anger, trust, euphoria, secrets, from negative storms or positive upwellings, he holds the image close to something in him, close in; it therefore changes him in some way.

To see something that is equivalent to an inner facet is to see that facet in a new light—hence change is imminent if the viewer is ready, and sometimes takes place. The facet may stem from some aspect of emotional "logic" or kinesthetic "thinking," as well as in intellectual habits. Stieglitz in his own lifetime extended the theory of equivalence to include all art, including the art of living.

In a random way, as differing from a conscious way, any photograph may act as an equivalent for someone—that is, any photograph might happen to effect someone in a profound and compulsive manner. When he first begins to learn about equivalence, the photographer himself may respond to a few of his own photographs as if he had never seen them before. If a photographer enlarges his awareness of the world and grows in consciousness of his medium, he may acquire the craftsmanship by which he can produce equivalence, not at random, but to his own purpose. With practice he may learn to predict the equivalent effect of his existing photograph on other persons. Still later he may be able to evoke known inner states in other people with the known equivalence of his own photographs.

The predictable use of equivalence can never be subjected to mass audiences until those audiences acquire more visual sophistication than they are ever likely to have. Equivalence will probably never be explored except by a handful of photographers in any generation, and in company with friends. Only a few will ever be able to bring about inner change of their own being with their own pictures; and still fewer will be able to effect a change of being in others with photographs in a conscious way. Equivalence at random—that we already have.

PHOTOGRAPHIC DATA FOR THE ILLUSTRATIONS

1. *Coming Boats, 1894.* Henry Peach Robinson (1830-1901)

One of the characteristics of the pictorial photograph is evidence of some degree of independence from the original subject. This is achieved in several different ways. In his very influential book, *Pictorial Effect in Photography* (1869), Robinson explained his technique of combining several negatives to make one photograph. Consequently, had the audience stood beside his camera they would have seen but one fraction at a time of *Coming Boats.*

Robinson's very vocal opponent in matters pictorial, Peter Henry Emerson, combined in his own photographs, not negatives, but lyricism and factualness. While his photographs amply show the kind of psychological selectivity that separated the art of photography from the art of painting, his writings seem to indi-

Figure 10. *Minor White, 1962.*

Figure 11. *Minor White, 1962.*

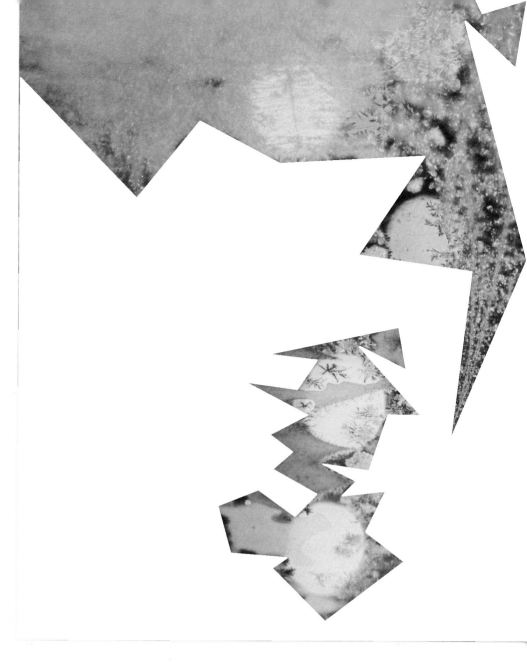

cate that he did not understand this difference between the two media. This is particularly evident in his *Death of Naturalistic Photography*.

Combination printing was widely practiced by pictorial photographers in the last half of the 19th century. The reasoning in part stemmed from painting practice—the artist gathered many sketched or remembered details onto a single canvas, and it seemed as if the photographer could do the same with his medium. The failures were not technical ones, but lapses of taste. Oscar Rejlander is still historically burdened with his critical failure and technical tour de force in *The Two Paths of Life* (1857), in which 30 negatives were combined. His *Two Gentleman Taking Wine* (circa 1860) is magnificent.

2. *Angelica: Overturned Car, 1959*. Nathan Lyons

The pictorial effect in this photograph by Lyons suggests something Oriental, either in scene or technique. The effect was achieved by a totally different method. Instead of combination printing, the camera was moved in so close that the familiar became unfamiliar—the photograph is in some degree independent of the original subject. In such instances the viewer either rejects the photograph because he cannot identify the original subject, or willingly engages the photograph because it is an event in its own right—a picture.

Coming Boats and *Overturned Car* are worlds apart. If Robinson appears to have been poorly represented in this comparison, we must remember that Robinson was popular in a Victorian setting and that Lyons makes his appeal to visual sophisticates in the atomic age.

3. *Newsboys at Midnight, circa 1907*, Lewis Hine (1874-1940)

Contrary to pictorial photographs, which are considered as events in themselves, documentary photographs are widely considered as a means for bringing the event to the man in the armchair. Lewis Hine used a 5 × 7 view camera and flash powder; today's documentarians use miniature cameras, high-speed film, and wide apertures. Beaumont Newhall wrote in the introduction to the catalog of the Eastman House exhibition, *Photography at Midcentury* (1959), "The photo-journalist, [has] essentially a desire to communicate, to tell about people, to record without intrusion the moment that has been called by Henri Cartier-Bresson 'decisive'...."

Pictorial photography presents a somewhat different purpose. Whether or not the subject is human pictorial photography is for people as well as about them. While making landscapes, for example, the photographer may remember that it is a person who will bring something of himself to the photograph.

Pictorialism periodically redetermines what will be considered appropriate subject matter, so it is always behind the times. Pictorial photography treats the world as something to be intently observed, and those manifestations of spirit which are visible to the camera, trapped. Thus the whole visual world is subject matter for the pictorial photographers—stone, water, air, light, wind, man's buildings, machines, art, man himself. Essentially this was the guiding concept behind the books and exhibitions edited by Dr. Otto Steinert in Germany from 1950 to 1958, entitled *Subjektive*

Figure 12. *Interior, 1958.* (Photo: Ansel Adams)

In the classic tradition the link to the "reality out there" may be stretched unmercifully (as Weston has done here) but never broken. In this case the faint trace of the square window encourages the viewer's identification of the original object. Only a wavering line separates the recognizable and the unreconizable objects in a photograph, yet to the esthetician, once the identification to the "reality out there" is broken, he is in the presence of the romanticist.

6. *Self Portrait, 1902.* Edward Steichen (1879-   )

Still another way to make stylistic alterations of the photographic image is by hand drawing on plate, negative, or print. The technique was thoroughly explored for decades. The Photo-Secessionists summed up this stylistic exploration in their exhibition in 1910 at the art museum in Buffalo, New York. The leaders, after this show, went on to other investigations of the nature of the medium. Not so the followers— soft focus, ink instead of silver images, diffusion, hand work, and so on blossomed into amateur salon photography, the traces of which are still seen in competition pictorialism. In this self-portrait, two sides of Edward Steichen, painter and photographer, combine in one picture.

7. *Girl with Folded Arms, 1929.* Man Ray (1890-   )

When handwork alterations of the photographic image went out of fashion, strictly photographic means were introduced and explored. All possible derivations of the medium have been tried out: solarization, negative prints, odd angles, melted emulsions, multiple printing, and so on. The present picture is an example of partial solarization. Man Ray was but one of many leaders in Europe during the 1920's who threw academic conservatism aside with Dadaist abandon in all media, including photography. Derivations from straight photography have become a tradition, generally called experimental photography.

In 1929 another landmark exhibition occured at Stuttgart, Germany, comparable to the 1910 Photo-Secession exhibition at Buffalo.

Fotographie. For some reason he lost sight of the central idea of spirit and went on to other concepts.

4. *Paris Street.* Louis Jacques Mandé Daguerre (1787-1851)

This is a modern enlargement of one of the earliest of the daguerreotypes. According to Beaumont Newhall in *The Daguerreotype in America* (1961), the characteristics of classical photography were established in the 20-year life span of this technique: window on the world, clarity of image, mass medium, recording ability in the service of science, newsworthy violence.

We see here a man having his shoes shined. Only the foot remained still long enough to register on the slow plate. In the technological progress of photography only speed and color have been added to the basic characteristics. In the minds of today's photographers the decisive moment is a split second. Actually, spirit stands still long enough to be recorded by the photographer it has chosen.

5. *Abandoned Car, 1938-39.* Edward Weston (1886-1958)

Film and Foto was organized in order to show what kind of an art photography is, or could be by a display of all its unique characteristics. Art critics of the time allocated various photography to all of the art trends of the period.

8. *Cosmic Conversation, 1959.* Walter Chappell (1925-   )

When straight, or classic, photography is used to produce a photograph resembling a nonobjective painting, as here, the esthetician balks because his lines of distinction are snarled. The photographer who is free of that trap does not have to say anything. He can let the image do its own work.

9. *Three images :* a. *Logotype of Aperture,* b. *Brain Geometric Illustration.* Ashby Staar, c. *Ten-Mile River* (Polaroid), Walter Chappell

Today it seems possible to prepare visual editorials for a visually literate readership. The three images shown may be "translated" somewhat as Chinese ideographs are converted into words. The words grouped below make no pretense at precision; they are simply the center of a cluster of similar implications:
A. Eye—Lens.
B. Brain—Geometric—Objectivity.
C. Reversible exploration by instrument.
D. The three together pertain to the lack of difference between inward and outward, objectivity and subjectivity.

10. *No Title 1962* (From the sequence: *Steely Barb of Infinity*) Minor White (1908-   )

Esthetic decision can be exercised in many ways in photography: hand manipulation as exemplified by the *Self Portrait,* combination printing according to Henry Robinson, photograms and other derivations of the medium as shown here by Moholy-Nagy, assembling various objects from scattered sources as Frederick Sommer practices. Sequencing photographs, or Layout, is another form and typical of the work of Minor White. This untitled photograph is but one unit of a sequence and so is analogous to a single frame from a cinema. The visual editorial is another example of the appearance of communicative and esthetic decision.

11. *No Title 1962* (From the sequence *Beginnings*) Minor White (1908-   )

This photographer has worked with the idea of the equivalent ever since his meeting with Alfred Stieglitz in 1945. At present he questions this approach thusly, "Must the moment always remain secret when the photograph becomes a mirror that can be walked into?" And answers the question, "When the photograph is a mirror of the man, and the man is a mirror of the world, then possibily Spirit might take over."

12. *Interior, Rochester, New York, Home, 1958.* Ansel Adams (1902-   )

Pictures on the spot have been next to impossible in photography ever since the daguerreotype was superseded by the various negative-positive processes introduced since the 1850's The Polaroid-Land process restored this remarkable charac-

teristic some 15 years ago. The effect on pictorial photography is not particularly noticeable in the appearance of the images. The major effect remains well within the experience of the individual— that is, whatever happens to the psyche while seeing the picture in the presence of the scene. The strongest experience of what pictures in a minute means to picture-making takes place between sitter and photographer during the process of informal or experimental portraiture.

Polaroid as a medium is automatically classic, because in this process, control is limited to overall value changes by exposure, and slight changes at that. Therefore selective seeing alone determines whether the photograph is documentary, informational, or pictorial.

13. *Leaf Pattern, circa 1925.* Imogen Cunningham.

In the caption for the Ansel Adams photograph, and for the rest,

Figure 13. *Leaf Pattern, circa 1925.* (Photo: Imogen Cunningham)

Figure 14. *Rock Wall No. 2, 1960.* (Photo: Paul Caponigro)

work more or less with the idea of the equivalent. Caponigro takes as a stated objective: to share beauty with others that stems from a known quality within the photographer. While the nature of the medium makes it necessary to find such pictures at random, Caponigro demands that the quality come from a known source within himself.

15. *Spring Onion, 1962* Herbert Hamilton (1936-   ).

Hamilton has taken full advantage of the educational complex in Rochester, New York. He imposes on himself the conscious task of photographing from a known inner state and of making photographs that deliberately arouse or evoke the same known inner state in the sympathetic viewer. Instead of reacting to the visual world, he attempts to use the visual world plus the transforming power of the camera to cause predetermined reactions for anyone who is willing to look with open eyes and open hearts. In this manner, the photographer acts, rather than reacts. In this way the response, not the photograph, reaches equivalence.

we have talked around the content of the photograph, and will continue the practice. There is a reason for so doing. The reason is to illustrate a doctrine of pictorial photography. The dearly held canon is this: the ultimate function of a pictorial photograph occurs during a private, visual, nonverbal "conversation" between viewer and photograph.

The Imogen Cunningham photograph was one of the American entries in the 1929 Stuttgart exhibition, *Film and Foto,* organized by the Deutsche Werkbund. Over 1000 photographs were gathered from all over the world to define the limits of photography as an art form, by showing its unique characteristics.

14. *Rock Wall #2 1960* Paul Caponigro (1932-   )

The generation of photographers now in their twenties include men trained or influenced by the philosophies prevalent in such schools as the Photo Department of the Rochester Institute of Technology; Institute of Design, Chicago; San Francisco Art Institute; Ohio University; Indiana University; and many others. Generally they acknowledge that vision is autobiographical, that photographs are self-revealing, and that anyone looking at a photograph sees himself first.

Tutor- and self-taught Paul Caponigro is one of many of the younger generation of photographers who

Figure 15. *Spring Onion, 1962.* (Photo: Herbert Hamilton)

Harald O. Berting